WARRIORS AND STRANGERS

'An extraordinary book. Mr Hanley gets under the skin of black Africa as no other English writer has done since his hero, Sir Richard Burton, went to see the King of Dahomey.'

Sunday Telegraph

During the war Gerald Hanley was posted in Africa, in an environment of 'swirling sandstorms, heat, and billions and billions of flies'. Isolated in a wilderness of burning winds and hot rock, the threat of madness was constantly with him. In 1962 Hanley sailed past the long yellow coastline of Somalia and was inspired to write about his time there and in Kenya. The result is a fascinating tale of black Africa and the white officers there: the madness and the suicides, the patience and the endurance.

11
22
23
24
25
26

WARRIORS
AND
STRANGERS

BY

GERALD HANLEY

A HAMISH HAMILTON PAPERBACK
London

First published in Great Britain 1971
by Hamish Hamilton Ltd
First published in this edition 1987
by Hamish Hamilton Ltd
27 Wrights Lane, London W8 5TZ

Copyright © 1971 by Gerald Hanley

ISBN 0-241-12357-7

Printed and bound in Finland
by Werner Söderström Oy

To all my friends
— black, brown and white

Part One

CHAPTER ONE

TRUE solitude is when the most restless part of a human being, his longing to forget where he is, born on earth in order to die, comes to rest and listens in a kind of agreed peace. In solitude, once the taste has settled, a man can think upon death with as much pleasure as upon life, and it is in solitude that one can best understand that there is no solution, except to try and do as little harm as possible while we are here, that there is no losing and no winning, no real end to greed or lust, because the human appetite for novelty can only be fully satisfied by death.

Thousands of days and nights spent in wildernesses taught me that a person can never truly know another, or be known by another, and that the pleasure of life is in the trying. A man can never convey fully what it is that so strangely disturbs him, the uneasy unrest in him that nothing material can properly satisfy. It is a fear of accepting this which makes a man fear what he thinks to be loneliness, a being alone, without other people. Acceptance of enforced solitude gradually dissolves this illusion. After long solitude when you sit and talk with others you realize that most of what we say to each other means very little at all. Perhaps that is why a Zen monk will give a silent sermon to a multitude, laughing without trace because he knows there is nothing to say which does not require emotional undertones to give it the appearance of credibility. Even so, one likes to go on talking rubbish with friends, while listening to oneself doing it. At least solitude teaches one to listen to oneself talking this rubbish, whereas before one thought one's every word was golden with value. In the early months of isolation in a wilderness, particularly when burdened with responsibilities which may suddenly turn dangerous, among actively violent and savage people, a sort of hysteria develops in the character. Ferocity will be replied to ferociously, out of fear, and fear is hatred. One's first sight of ferocity arouses hatred for the ferocious, and one is liable to respond with savagery. It is hard to describe the hatred and contempt one can feel for tribesmen who

3

have slain the women of their enemies, or caused them to die of thirst. Later, when hysteria has been replaced by acceptance of isolation—the fact that one is hundreds of miles out of reach of 'rescue' should anything go wrong, one feels merely contempt for savagery. You do not hate the active savage anymore. You realize instead the size of the pitiful value he places on the need to kill, the need for revenge, the desire to humiliate his enemy (which includes you), especially when thousands of helpless people were being slain by bombs in European cities every night. One knew then that one was one with the savage, while not being so innocently honest about one's savagery as the desert savage. Then despair tries to set in.

There is nothing like isolation in an atmosphere of electric violence for bringing before one's mind the understanding that the varnish of two thousand years is so thin as to be transparent. It is living in civilization that keeps us civilized. It is very surprising, and alarming at first, how swiftly it vanishes when one is threatened by other men, men of almost mindless resolve. They know if you are frightened of them. They know too if you will kill as readily as they.

But the fear does slowly seep in, if you are isolated for long enough among warriors who hate what you represent, a threat to their joyous wars.

I once told a chief that I would kill him myself if he let his warriors go killing again (something he was planning to do). He liked that. He smiled, after studying my face. After all he could understand that far more easily than the kind of government he thought I represented. Yet he knew I meant it because I had come to hate him, as much as he hated me. Even so he started laughing, and I laughed with him at the absurdity of our situation in that wilderness.

'What if I cannot stop the warriors?' he said.

'Do you *want* to stop them?' I asked him. He laughed. 'I will be honest,' he said. 'I do want them to kill their enemies. But I will try and stop them. You are not allowed by the government to kill me, are you?' he asked me, serious and calm.

'I'm not allowed to, but I will,' I assured him. 'All you have to do is to see that your warriors do no more killing.'

That threat to the chief was a sign of fellow savagery, though I did not know it until years later. It was a sign of fear, fear of what might come if tribal killing started again. If one could kill the real cause of the blood feuds, this chief, then the cause of the trouble

4

would be gone. It seemed simple, and the chief understood its simplicity.

I had no desire to civilize these wild nomads, and told them so quite often. They could kill again after I had gone, but while I was there among them I wanted peace. This seemed very unreasonable and selfish, to the chiefs with whom I discussed it.

'Then you do not care what happens to us?' one of the chiefs said, with that ready playful wit one appreciated so much among the nomads.

'If you chiefs could vanish,' I told them, 'your young men would have a chance to forget the feuds of the past. You are out of date now.'

And that was true, and tragic too: the story of all the tribal cultures which have seen the cement mixers and the schoolmasters on the horizon, and feared them.

The nomads were just as maddened by that huge glaring sun above as were we few white men thrown by chance among them.

Yet it was the isolation more than anything which was hardest to bear, at first. Eventually one grew to love it, and those who knew long isolation in those Somali wastes and survived it, will miss it forever. It was the most valuable time of one's life.

One had years of wilderness in which to brood on the reasons why men kill each other, in wilderness in which killing a man was only an act of pleasure, though disguised as a tribal duty. One had years to discover that one's longing for mail, newspapers, radio, could slowly diminish. After Somalia nowhere would ever be lonely, or isolated, again. The silence of wilderness eventually seeps in and makes an area which will always long for that kind of silence again.

To wake up at first light, a flea on a prairie of rock and sand, each morning, is to realize that one's own importance is something one highly overrates. It also teaches one to love life, and to try and not kick too hard when death slips in and it is time to go.

One was mad, all right, after a year of it. One sees that now, looking back.

CHAPTER TWO

PASSING down the long coastline of Somalia in an Italian ship the other week I saw again the scorched, burned, dried-out rock and hot sand on which I used to sit with Hashim at night and talk. I have never forgotten one particular thing he said to me.

'When all your machines, and ships, and aircraft, and all those things you make, when they are all finished, our Arab dhows will still be sailing the seas, and we Arabs will hold together the world that we made, from India and farther East too, to here and to Europe. We are not finished yet, even though we are beggars now.'

Even if he had not confided that thought to me one could never forget Hashim; his gentleness, his fine presence, his dignity, his quiet, sardonic humour, and most important of all I can never forget how he helped Chas and myself to keep mutinous troops (and they had a right to be mutinous) from shooting us out of hand.

Kalanka. Hordio. Those two names for me will always summon up memories of swirling sandstorms, heat, and billions and billions of flies, and a threat of coming madness, and of Hashim, the merchant, the calm, knowing, patient, friendly Arab who was isolated with us in that wilderness of burning winds and hot rock.

Staring at the Somali coast, five miles off, I wondered if Hashim was still there, back in the trade which the war had destroyed for him, or if he had gone to Hadramaut or Yemen.

He used to wear a striped turban, a loose jacket of white cotton, and a long *lungi* reaching to his sandals. He had a face like an Andalusian Spaniard; long, sallow, grave, a handsome face with calm, watchful black eyes. He was about forty.

'I have nothing left to give you,' Hashim said to me the first time I sent for him. It was the end of 1941 and I had been a few months in that wilderness, a thousand miles or so from base.

'What have you ever given me?' I asked him. 'I've never even met you before.'

'I mean your army,' he said. 'I have lost my trade and my money because of this war, and when your army arrived here they took my camera and my pistol.' He smiled. 'I have nothing left to hand over to you. I am not dangerous any more.' He spoke good Italian, and good Swahili.

'I want to borrow some money from you,' I told him.

'Ah!' He eyed me sardonically. 'Money? The army wishes to borrow money from Hashim? Why? And what money? I haven't any money.'

'But you have more money than I have,' I told him. 'I have nothing. And I must find something to pay the troops with.'

'I have loaned what I could afford to the other officer,' Hashim told me. 'A few hundred lire.'

'You know the state of things here, Hashim,' I said. 'We are cut off, an enormous distance from base. No trucks come. We have no news. We are isolated here. We have had no money to pay our troops. I want you to help again.' He laughed, and I laughed with him. Then Chas came in and he was laughing too, two conquerors trying to borrow money from an impoverished Arab so as to pay the troops, who were all recruited from ex-Italian askaris.

'It is an interesting situation,' Hashim said.

The pay department never did solve the mess that it made of the pay situation up in that wilderness.

Chas and I used to have conversations that went something like this: 'Tension's mounting among the askaris again. They've been sulking all morning.'

'How long is it now since they were last paid?'

'Five and a half months, except for that six hundred *lire* I borrowed from Hashim and gave them. But what's the bloody use of that, about ninepence halfpenny. I don't know why they don't shoot us.'

'How many times have they mutinied now?'

'Three.'

'They can't get hold of any ammo, can they?'

'No. But those bayonets look a bit longer than usual today.'

'It's certainly marvellous how they put up with it. But they know *we're* living like pigs too, that we've had no mail for months, no pay, no booze, and anyway if I see any goatmeat again on my plate I'll kill the cook. I told him so last night too.'

'Again?'

'Yes. Again.'

We gave an order that in future the askaris could only mutiny on Fridays. They took it seriously, the sergeant explaining to me later that the troops could not understand why the conquerors had

7

no money, sent no trucks up here, still had the troops using Italian weapons and equipment. Where was the conquest?

'We're still fighting in Abyssinia,' we told the sergeant. 'Every truck is needed. And even if we had trucks to spare they probably couldn't be spared to come a thousand miles up here, yet. Patience.'

Alone Chas and I cursed the transport people and the pay department, wanting the transport officers, who were drinking gin in Mogadishu, marooned in a stifling wilderness, as we were, so as to learn, etcetera . . .

As if to dominate the troops, as if to show iron will, we drilled and trained them in the hot sand each day, and then drilled the raw N.C.O.'s, breaking them all from their Italian drill, and they began to respond, even forgetting their legitimate grievances for an hour or two. They were beginning to feel the approach of that mass surrender in drill on the square, when a unit begins to feel as one person in the steady, unragged crash of perfected arms drill. I used to watch their faces, their eyes.

Sometimes during these drill sessions, which were held on the hard open sand arena in front of the sun-dried barrack huts, Hashim would come and watch from the shade. I used to wonder what he thought of the sharp, savage cries of command and the intense crashing responses of hands, rifles and feet from the troops. Did he, I wondered, begin to understand that it was this machinery of drill and discipline which had torn his world, and other worlds like his, to pieces? His expressionless, handsome face, his steady stare as the drill progressed, his folded arms, his whole patient and perhaps contemptuous gravity as he watched the stamping, wheeling soldiers who came from so many tribes, noble and base, caused me for the first time in my life to see that what is most stirring and martial in our civilization is also often the most ridiculous, if stared at long enough. One simply could not imagine Hashim ever allowing himself to be in the position in which he would have to cavort like these soldiers, a rifle on his shoulder, listening tensely for yells of command from someone like myself, for pay and rations.

The troops were getting no pay, and their rations were deteriorating as time went on and our isolation lengthened. Bully beef was finished, and now they had biscuits and dates and a cigarette issue, while we slew a ghostly, scraggy camel or a few famished goats for all of us as often as we could. We signed chits for these animals and handed them to the owners. One day everyone was going to be paid. I used to swear it to them, and they said they believed me, though

8

I knew that a general rage and anxiety was growing on all sides. Hysteria came at times and we would compose long, bitter, sarcastic letters to command headquarters, which might have been on Venus or Mars, for we had no way of sending these cries of anger.

There was a signal station, an old Italian military relic, the equipment in it so dangerous, due to electrical shortings, that the Italian soldier who looked after it used to pray before he used it. We had sent many pleading signals to headquarters a thousand miles away, until finally warned to stop. We had been told for the last time that help was on the way. So we were silent after that, and waited.

How strange it was in 1962 to be sailing past that blazing yellow coast on which one had thirsted and yearned, and dreamed of onions and salad and bread and beer, and even of drinkable, *living* water. One would be going down to lunch soon, to the air-conditioned dining room, to every kind of food, and with a bottle of wine to go with it.

One remembered the bully beef and the problem of *halal*, discovered by the Mohammedan troops only when reminded of it by a holy man who had stormed at them. They had eaten that bully beef gladly until the holy men came and told them that this imprisoned beef in the small cans had never been killed according to Islamic rite, was *haran*—unclean, and not *halal*, fit for eating after the beast had had its throat cut by a sheikh. And yet it disappeared if one left it around.

One remembered those nights at Gardo when one sat up and watched the fast-moving shadows of askaris moving across the sand to pick up the cans of bully beef one had thrown there in daylight, making sure in that daylight that one was seen throwing it away. It was good beef, and if even you wanted to commit suicide after months of it for every meal, it was still good beef, and very eatable, and they ate it, in darkness. Then the authorities, the Staff intellectuals, thousands of miles away, got a sheikh to kill some cattle, and after that a label appeared on the cans of beef saying in Arabic, Swahili and English that this beef was *halal* and had been killed by a saint, and was fit for all Mohammedans to eat. And one respected the holy men for making this struggle, even though one could have killed them in that wilderness, tortured as one was by a thousand insoluble problems, the biggest of which was oneself, while nodding understandingly as one saw those askaris gliding in darkness like hyenas to snatch up so silently the unclean, eatable bully beef.

9

How fast our date supply went once we had discovered how to make liquor with it, and what was the name of that brilliant, ragged, haggard Italian prisoner who had made the liquor for us? It was better than arrack, and then he had made *liquore di datteri*, a sticky oily date liquor. The three of us had got drunk on it at two o'clock in the morning and then went for a swim in the ocean.

When the date problem became acute there was only one man to turn to, Hashim. He brought a dhow full of dates in to Kalanka six weeks later, how, we never discovered. He had his contacts. We doubled the date ration to the askaris, and drank more date liquor ourselves. And then one day, when the atmosphere among the troops was at its most delicate and worrying worst, a message came through on the dangerous sputtering radio to say that a convoy had left base and would reach us in about eleven days. There was money aboard, silver money. We rushed out and called the troops on parade, and I can remember that my voice was trembling with excitement as I told them that the long promised money was on its way. Carried away, Chas and I gave them an extra ration of the musty cigarettes, and the rest of the day off. Then we went back and started a date-liquor party. A few days after this Chas went down with dysentery again, and this time he nearly died. And thinking of Chas and that third attack of dysentery made me think of Carlo, the brilliant, lovable doctor of the Italian army who became our companion and friend as Chas sank under the ravage of that dysentery. How Carlo had fought to save him, with no drugs, and had saved him, and how he was repaid by the Base Wallahs two thousand miles away when they got their hands on him at Mombasa.

CHAPTER THREE

YOU always woke up in the morning at Kalanka covered with slow-moving exhausted flies dragging their way through your sweat, and the nausea soon lessened so that you learned to lie there and let the flies stay on you. It was only when they tried to get into your mouth that the anxiety mania fell upon you again and you sprang from the stale, sweat-soaked sheets. The flies liked to cluster on the edge of a cup of tea, and if you left a cup standing for five minutes there would be a struggling crust of flies drowning in it. At times during the height of the fly season you became hysterical and I once saw a friend of mine screaming at some flies, his face showing grief and hate, his left hand pressed tight over the mug of tea he was holding in his right hand. Millions and millions of flies swarmed on to us as the heat increased, and Chas lay sick under the mosquito net we had rigged up for him. Carlo was worried when he came one night and I told him that Chas had had thirty-seven bowel movements that day, and was weak and delirious, though still making his usual jokes.

'Can't they fly a plane up here for an officer as sick as this?' Carlo asked me, his large, black eyes flashing with anger.

'A plane?' I said, 'A plane? Why they won't even send a truck with the rations.' Even Chas laughed when I told him about 'the plane'.

At about two o'clock in the morning Carlo would come in softly in his rubber shoes and stand over Chas's bed and study him, watching how he slept. He found some old Italian army drugs and used these on Chas, and fed him goat meat soup, and camel milk. There was nothing else anyway. Chas, tall and strong, with thick, dark, curly hair, seemed to be fading into a pallid, thin ghost, and what he longed for most was a few bottles of cold beer, or an onion, or a slice of bread covered with real butter. We used to talk about lettuce and beetroot and fresh eggs in increasingly burning and passionate words, while Carlo listened and then said, 'If you go on like this you'll get dyspepsia. You're over-eating, both of you.'

There was nothing left to read in that place, and I was driven to reading the stack of military pamphlets I had used as an N.C.O., the grenade, the bayonet, the Bren, the Small Arms Manual, the two inch mortar, and that laughable answer to the Panzer Division, the .55 Boyes anti-tank rifle.

I must have been going 'sand-happy' at that time, for it was a few years before I realized the enormity of the act I committed when a convoy of camels at last brought the box of money to our piece of wilderness, along with rations, mail and the booze supply.

'The money's in a big wooden chest, Effendi,' the excited Somali sergeant came to tell me. There had been a very sullen and angry conference with the troops that morning, about money and justice and loyalty and patience, and money.

I went down into the armoury, seized a pick-axe and ran through the sand to where the mounds of stores were being unloaded from the camels into the sand by the askaris. I forgot everything except the money for the askaris.

The chest of cash was a splendid thing, about six feet long, a foot high and a foot wide, of solid, heavy, smooth wood, and I noticed the red seal of wax in a counter-sunk pit in the wood That red seal ought to have slowed me up, for even now, whenever I think of it, I know I must have been as sand-happy as I was relieved and excited. I ought to have realized that this chest was addressed to the political officer, who lived across the sand dunes, and whom we hardly ever saw, and who was farther round the bend than Chas and I, at that time. He was to commit suicide in about a year's time, finally eaten away by wilderness and loneliness and outpost duty, but at that time, as I raised the heavy pick-axe over my head, he was still in possession of a good many of his faculties, and as desperate as I to see that long awaited money. I think it must have been the sheer anxiety to show the askaris the actual, shining, heavy money, on the spot, after these months of promising, lying, borrowing from Hashim, lectures about discipline and patience, and fear of a real mutiny, that caused me to shatter that perfectly carpentered chest of specie, which I had no official right to do. Heavy white canvas bags of Indian rupees glittered in the harsh sunlight as I tore away the splintered wood. A cheer went up from the askaris, and I think we were all a little insane together at that moment. They danced round the money, cheering.

'It's the money,' I said. 'It's here. It's actually arrived. I'm going to pay you at once.' To the sergeant I said, 'Get them on parade. It's a pay parade.' The troops, all of them stripped to the waist, rushed off to dress for the parade. I told the sergeant to put a guard on the dump of rations. I sent a runner to tell Chas that the money had arrived, and the runner came back with a note saying, 'To hell with the money, what about the MAIL, and the BOOZE?' Chas was getting better.

Chas, weak and pale, and as happy as I, got up for the pay parade which we held in the office. We wore polished Sam Browne belts, pressed khaki bush shirts and shorts, long puttees and our infantry side caps of navy blue trimmed with red cord. The askaris came in, saluted, held out their trembling hands for the heaps of silver coins as we entered up their paybooks, saluted, and rushed off into the poverty-stricken village of straw huts to buy themselves a dose of clap. When it was all finished I sent the remaining canvas bags of cash in the shattered wooden chest to the political officer, not forgetting to send with it an excited, happy note telling of the pay parade, and actually expecting an equally excited reply from the political officer saying something like, 'I'm delighted for you all. This is wonderful. I'm paying my fellows too. What a day. Coming over tonight for drinks.'

He came over rather earlier than I expected him, and not for drinks. He was shaking with rage when he came running into the fly-infested room in which Chas and I were toasting the world in mugs of whisky, the table covered with opened letters and bottles of beer, gin and whisky. I had only met this political officer once before. He was the first mental casualty of Somalia's fastnesses, for me, though I did not know what was the matter then.

'You're just in time for a snifter,' I said gaily, and still gay, determined to stay gay even though I could now see that his blue eyes were glaring threateningly from Chas to me, and from me to Chas, went on, 'Gin or whisky? The beer's still boiling, I'm afraid, after the trip on the camels, so gin or whisky?'

'Who did it?' he whispered, clenching his hands. 'Who did it? It's a bloody court martial offence, I'm telling you. Who did it?'

'Did what?' Chas had told me that this fellow was 'sand-happy'.

CHAPTER FOUR

EVEN now, twenty years after, as I think over that wild scene with the pick-axe under that sunglare, the askaris laughing, their thin Somali faces alight with expectation, their cries of acclamation when the pick-axe tore the wood away and revealed the snow-white canvas bags of money, even now I cannot understand how I forgot that the political officer was the one who should conduct the slow, steady, careful ritual of the reception of money, its checking, its handing out, and its meticulous recording in various books. There is no doubt about it but that it was the beginning of the intense individuality, on occasions merging into madness, which that strange landscape and its fierce peoples brought out in all of us who wandered its wastes for years. One never knew when one was acting strangely. It was only the other fellow with you, whom you noticed was acting strangely, and he noticed your erosion too, but you never mentioned it to each other.

'The askaris have been over five months without pay,' I told the infuriated political officer. 'What's the difference? It's money, there are the askaris, and they've been paid.' It seemed as simple as that. I know now that the long and steady struggle to keep the askaris happy had affected my judgement. The punishments one had handed out which ordinarily would have been accepted as military routine over breaches of discipline, had seemed bigger and more ruthless than they actually were, to soldiers who were soldiering without pay, and the sight of that huge chest of money had united the askaris and myself in a delirious moment of long promised justice. But I still could not explain to the political officer, how I, a junior officer well drilled and disciplined through the ranks, wearing the badge of a famous regiment, had hacked down a whole traditional area of governmental procedure—which in out-stations is government itself. But he must have seen that the two junior officers with long, thick curling hair (there were no barbers), drinks in their hands, were marooned like himself in this lunar wilderness, and, like himself, were not quite in their right minds. So, after a long and neurotic lecture on procedure, he accepted a drink. But he never really forgave me.

Jaysee, our company commander, came back from a routine inspection of our wilderness shortly after that, and I told him about 'the scene' with the political officer. But even he, a soldier of much more experience than Chas and I, was too thrilled by the paying of the troops to see it as the mortal sin which had appalled the political officer.

We got out the drinks and wound up the sandy, rusty Italian gramophone and put on our three records. We had played them hundreds of times and they were now worn out, fine dusted sand in their grooves, but they helped to produce that careless, wild background to our drink and talk. One record was by Edmundo Ros and his rumba band called, 'Blen Blen Blen,' another was a strange, quavering, queer male voice against a background of drums and trumpets imploring a woman to walk the hills and heather with him, together, forever, and we used to sing this with him while the drink lasted. It says something for merciful time that I have completely forgotten the third record.

Jaysee came and saw the troops on parade, and approved. We sent for Hashim and paid him for the loans and the dates. There was still nothing to read and it was about that time that an askari brought me the skeleton of an Italian machine gun he had found in the sand dunes. That machine gun, and its companion, kept me sane for the rest of my stay in that God forgotten place. We were short of automatic weapons and I told Jaysee that I thought I could remedy this shortage if I could only find the rest of the weapons where the retreating Italians had thrown them. There was plenty of the particular ammunition in the armoury and I knew that the machine gun parts must be lying in the sands of the dunes. The askaris became as obsessed as myself in the search. None of us had ever seen this type of machine gun before. It was a medium of nine millimetre calibre, a Schwarzlose from the Austrian Waffen Fabrik Steyr, part of the material captured by the Italians during the First World War. All I had to begin with was the barrel and the body casing with its traversing handles and trigger, and wandering in those rolling dunes one heard cries of triumph as askaris found parts of the gun, and one day two of them came staggering in with the heavy tripod itself. In the evenings we sat for hours in the armoury with the growing set of parts, learning by experiment how they fitted into the gun. The sergeant, now as obsessed as myself, used to haunt the dunes in his spare time, searching for a piece of steel we knew must fit into a long, curiously shaped groove which ran along the right side of the body casing. I knew it must be the piece that forced the oil-spray on to the working parts.

The sergeant was of a tribe considered inferior, by the askaris, to the noble tribes to which they themselves belonged, and Chas and I had opposed all their efforts to have him transferred, to have him disgraced, to cause him to appear a thief, a despot, an upstart, a mistake made in the chain of command; for them, command was dependent on nobility, which depended on tribe, and the sergeant was from one of the tribes of the Juba river in the far south. He was stronger, more intelligent and firmer in character than all of the askaris who so resented his command. And, worse, for they loved good looks, he was handsome.

They tried everything they could think of to bring him down, until one day I told them on parade, while the sergeant was absent, that even if the vendetta went on for a hundred years they were going to lose it, and that if ever the sergeant was transferred it would be to become a sergeant-major over other noble tribes. The sergeant himself had come to us one day, tired and dispirited that particular day, and asked us if we thought it was really worth all the trouble that he should stay sergeant over these tribal fanatics. 'That depends on you,' I told him. 'There's no tribal gradation in the particular kind of infantry we're evolving in this country now. It's all a matter of military talent, nothing else. You've got it. Use it. Dominate them. Don't let them cow you back into what is supposed to be your inferiority of status. A soft touch here, a heavy hand there. Don't give up. You've got the makings of a sergeant-major in you.' The hysterical aristocrats among the askaris, brainless, brave, never gave up their scheming to destroy their sergeant. It was their hobby.

Remembering that quietly bitter struggle with tribal mania, I looked now, twenty years later, at the glaring, sunbaked Somali coast and thought of all the other struggles with it we had had in the two hundred thousand square miles of its interior, which we had controlled and administered with useless weapons, battered and broken down trucks, spavined camels, and I recalled all the suicides and strange insanities which had broken so many of our friends in isolated parts of the great wilderness.

Just over there on the right, behind that jagged cliff of yellow hot rock was where Sergeant Elmi and I had nervously and excitedly set up the completed machine gun, the askaris assembled thirty

16

yards behind us to watch the firing, or the explosion—none of us knew which it would be. You cannot tell how an unknown machine gun will work until ammunition passes through it. Sergeant Elmi was number two on the gun. I was number one. We were laughing as we stood ready for the drill, waiting for my command of 'Take Posts!'

I had cleaned and oiled every part of the gun after many doubtful assemblings of the parts sieved out of the sands during those obsessed months. I had put a gauze through the barrel—a gauze should only be used through a barrel as a last resort, and on the order of an officer—and it was pleasant being an officer and using one's own gauze at one's own will. I had selected the best of the coiled machine gun belts in the armoury, and had even learned to work the Steyr-model belt-loading machine which we had found lying in a heap of old rifle parts. 'Take Posts!'

Would the oil-spray work properly? Would the cooling system in the water jacket function if I fired a lot of ammunition, if the gun did not explode?

'Ready, Effendi,' Sergeant Elmi said from where he lay beside the tripod. I pressed my thumbs against the thick red trigger, the traversing handles so different in shape and function from the Vickers machine gun which the fanatical and patient Sergeant Major Breen had taught me night after night in those cold, dank gun pits in Britain after Dunkirk.

'Cracks like a bloody whip. Fires all day,' he used to shout when he sat down to instruct me. 'Hold up an army for ten years.'

I narrowed my eyes as if expecting a blast of metal into my face and pressed home the trigger for a burst of five rounds, and the gun obeyed. I could see the strike of the rounds in the sandhill three hundred yards to our front. A cheer went up from the askaris, for even though the low caste sergeant, and the white officer who so perversely supported him in power, were firing the gun, it was *our* gun, having been salvaged by all of us, and it worked—even when I held the trigger down and fired a burst of thirty rounds. I fired the whole belt and slabs of the hillside crumbled and collapsed under the blasts of fire.

Everyone volunteered to serve in the machine gun platoon, and those who were chosen served willingly under Sergeant Elmi. They never let him forget that they were superior to him in caste, ridiculous as always in their doing so, for he was far their superior in brain and character, and as a soldier within the unit in which their whole life was lived, he was their superior officer and they obeyed him.

One of them had come to me one night, passionate, rolling his eyes, thin Somali hand on heaving chest, to tell me that he would no longer serve under this sergeant from a slave tribe, and that he was going to run away unless I altered things.

'You want to run away?' I asked him.

'If I am to go on serving under this man from the Rahanwein (the river tribes of the south), yes, Effendi.'

'You can strip off your uniform right here and now,' I told him. 'Strip naked, and you can go.' I waved to the two hundred thousand square miles of desolation behind us. 'Go. I will burn your paybook. You can vanish. Take off your uniform and vanish.' He laughed with amazement, disbelief, until he understood that I was serious. Then he came to attention and said that he did not want to go, even if I *did* mean that I would turn him loose in the desert, naked except for his noble blood and his parasitical pedigree and his vanity. That vanity would be only of use in an action when its owner decided to show that he was braver than all the slaves from the river.

Now, the soothing bells were ringing for lunch as the ship lurched down past Cape Gardafui. Where were they all now, those quarrelsome, faithful, fanatical, patient askaris? Where was Chas? Where was Jaysee, and Carlo, and Sergeant Elmi? Did he ever become sergeant-major, or did one of the nobles plant a knife in him one day when all that soldiering time was over and the Somali wastes became their own again?

Drinking the pale Salaparuta from Sicily down in the ship's dining room I wondered how I would find Kenya, after seven years away from it, but Kenya could not get through the screen of flooding memories of the Somali country which the sight of that barren coast had evoked in me. I wondered if I could get permission to go ashore in Mogadishu, the old headquarters of the vast insane asylum we had been lost in. In that ocean of scrub and shale one had been like a flea on a blanket, an aching speck whose eye had turned more thoughtfully, fearfully, inwards, as month after burning month went by among those hostile wastes.

CHAPTER FIVE

IT does not follow that because all the suicides I knew were very serious, earnest men with little sense of humour, that only the humourless kill themselves when they are in good physical health and still young. We do not know the size and strength of our own manias until they fall upon us and drag us down, or the barrenness of our inner deserts until real loneliness, fear, bewilderment and sun-madness have cast us into them. There *is* something huge and dark in the African world which can chew through the defences of white men who have not been harnessed to that continent's almost mindless friendship with suffering and annihilation. Concrete buildings, clinics and city settlements can hide it, almost, but out in the wastes you never forget that the friendly hyena is there to clean you if you should die in the grey grass among the thorns. It is truly a mighty continent and you feel it when you lie down in darkness under the stars, your blanket around you, and you listen to its powerful silence, a silence made up of various small sounds become one steady background drone and clicking, of cicadas, insects of every kind, mosquitoes, all whirring and hissing in one silence peculiar to Africa.

Of all the desiccated, bitter, cruel, sunbeaten wildernesses which starve and thirst beyond the edges of Africa's luscious, jungled centre, there cannot be one more Christless than the one which begins at the northern foot of Mount Kenya and stretches to the foothills of Abyssinia, and from there to the dried-out glittering tip of Cape Gardafui where the hot *karif* winds blow in from where the long sharks race under the thin blue skin of the ocean. You can never think of those wildernesses without thinking of daggers and spears, rolling fierce eyes under mops of dusty black crinkly hair, of mad stubborn camels, rocks too hot to touch, and blood feuds whose origins cannot be remembered, only honoured in the stabbing. But of all the races of Africa there cannot be one better to live among than the most difficult, the proudest, the bravest, the vainest, the most merciless, the friendliest; the Somalis.

I knew an Italian priest who had spent over thirty years among the Somalis, and he made two converts, and it amazed me that he got even those two. The Prophet has no more fervent, and ignorant, followers, but it is not their fault that they are ignorant. Their natural intelligence is second to none and when the education factories start work among them they should surprise Africa, and themselves.

I never saw a Somali who showed any fear of death, which, impressive though it sounds, carries within it the chill of pitilessness and ferocity as well. If you have no fear of death you have none for anybody else's death either, but that fearlessness has always been essential to the Somalis who have had to try and survive hunger, disease and thirst while prepared to fight and die against their enemies, their fellow Somalis for pleasure in the blood feud, or the Ethiopians who would like to rule them, or the white men who got in the way for a while.

'Now, take your pistol out of your belt and shoot me,' a tall, lean, shining black Somali said to me after finishing his story. We were standing over the heap of hacked, slashed, bleeding meat which had been another Somali until this other one had dealt with him. That was the first time I had come up against this peculiar and terrific satisfaction in a killing well done and the readiness to die for it, having been caught.

'You want me to shoot you?' I asked him.

'Certainly,' he said. 'That's your law, isn't it? Well, I'm ready. I've done what I want, so you can get on with your law. You have your pistol in your belt. Shoot me.' His long, sharp, heavy dagger was on the sand at my feet. An Italian doctor was on his knees beside the meat with a hypodermic needle in the hope that something might still stir within the bloody mess. But no.

'*E' finito*,' the doctor said, lighting a cigarette. He was very tired of Somalis, this doctor, having spent years amidst their electric violence. 'Shoot him,' he said to me. 'It'll save a great deal of trouble.' The Somali really did want to die, totally satisfied with himself after waiting for this enemy for over a year. Instead of being about a camel, this death was about a woman, something of far less value than a camel. The woman was sliced up in a hut nearby, alive. She would survive, after a fashion. Every night at the same hour for ten days, the husband, the one who wanted me to shoot him, had gone to the hut and shouted a warning outside it, telling the interloper to go. They were both of a great and noble tribe, inland from Merca on the Southern coast.

'He would not go. He wanted to die, so I killed him,' the tall warrior said to me. 'I am happy.' He pushed the dead meat with his sandalled foot, thoughtful, sombre. 'He was stubborn,' he said. 'He could have gone, but he was stubborn, daring me to kill him. It was too much.' It was the stubbornness, not jealousy over the woman, which had caused the killing; the stubbornness and the insult contained in it.

'Take him away,' I told a corporal, and as he was being handled off the scene the Somali turned, shouting, 'You're not going to start all that court business, are you? What's the use of that? You've got your pistol. Shoot me and have done with it.' He was trembling with anger, with impatience when he thought of the cell in the far town, the dreary court scene, the statements, the tiresome rigmarole of the legal machine far from the desert where this simple, logical thing had been done with a knife.

Death by shooting used to be the method of execution in the early days of the occupation after the Italian collapse, Italian law followed to the letter. The Somalis died as they liked to die, contemptuously, throwing off the cloak-blanket and staring at the firing squad, sneering at the trembling rifles. They had had their fragment of living, their brief satisfaction, and they had prayed. Now die. *Hrun sheg! Wallahi!*

I never knew a Somali to commit suicide, though I have been told they do it sometimes.

The first European suicide I knew was an officer who took over a year of loneliness in an outpost to decide that he had been a failure as a soldier. He was actually a very fine and able officer, but he had given up the effort to eat at a table months before his suicide, leaving half empty cans of bully beef about his bedroom in the fort, had given up shaving (in him a terrible offence), and had come to believe that the loss of a pistol over a year before, during the campaign, was a piece of criminal negligence on his part. He wanted to be court-martialled for it, but nobody would take him seriously. Nobody bothered about a pistol in a savage territory in which the Italians had left thousands of rifles and machine guns which had come into the hands of the tribes.

It is almost impossible to describe the *malaise*, the very special weariness of spirit which isolation among fierce tribesmen brings, hundreds of miles from base, and which eats into one after the sixth month in the midst of the tension, and the hot silence. Fits of rage used to come over one after too many killings among the tribes, for one found oneself getting used to it and deciding to do nothing about it. Let them kill each other. They liked it. Yet one had to go on pretending that it mattered to one, while it did not matter to the Somalis. And there was the endless and ingenious intrigue among them, the only pleasure beside killing open to nomads in practically waterless country. At times you looked out across the silent glaring desert and began to wish you were dead, for a few minutes. With some it lasted longer than a few minutes, and they shot themselves, or went mad. I know of fifteen cases of madness in that wilderness. But the first suicide I knew did not shoot himself in his outpost. He waited until he was going on leave, and then shot himself after drawing his drink ration. None of us could find out what he was thinking of that last afternoon in Mogadishu.

It was a Sunday, I was told months later, that he chose for his death, a hot, silent Sunday afternoon. He drove about in his truck, looking for friends, but they were all asleep, or away swimming in the sea. Perhaps the English Sunday which follows the English everywhere, perhaps even into hell, fell upon him, the grey memory of it, maybe the longing for it, like a shadow in that sunglare, for he drove off into the bush and stopped his truck at a deserted and broken Italian fort. Here he unloaded his drink ration from the truck, lined it up like a set of soldiers, took a piece of charcoal from an old Somali cooking fire and wrote on the wall of the fort. 'This is the only way for a rat to die.' Then he shot himself. Nothing very much happened about it. It was soon forgotten. It was not until about four years later, after many suicides and cases of madness, that some staff branch down in lusher Africa sent a psychiatrist up to see what was the matter in the Somali wilderness. I have a copy of his report. He did not go far beyond the towns of British Somaliland, a fairly quiet little area, never entered the real desolation, but his report said that nearly every officer was slightly to violently unbalanced.

We were only as unbalanced as the Somalis about us. Nobody could remain sane in that arid world.

I ran into the beginning of the end of the next suicide when I was on the last lap of a mad, frantic drive down from Cape Gardafui to Mogadishu, heading for my first leave in over a year.

CHAPTER SIX

I HAD never had any real patience, no application, had never done any inner grazing into myself, until marooned for the first time, completely marooned among the thorn scrub in the sand and shale of the Somali country. I had known loneliness in Africa before the war, but not a loneliness that got inside and rang and echoed in one as in Somalia. In Africa before the war I had hunted, worked with beasts, ridden long and hard in a kinder clime, and the Africans were not like the Somalis, the Somalis who were restless, violent, romantic, vengeful and proud.

It was fourteen months after my arrival in Somalia before I got leave, and I can remember throwing my kit into the back of the borrowed, battered, unreliable Chev truck which had had its heart broken long ago on the trail to Addis Ababa. Askaris going on leave climbed into the back, one or two of them with the big-hipped, rolling eyed, nubile women they had picked up during their service in the Mijertein country we were now leaving. A hundred miles south of the Nogal I stopped and shot an oryx bull and we feasted on it round the fire that night. I had no liquor and I knew that I would get a drink at El Lagodei where there was a friend of mine administering that slice of purgatory. We drank thin, smoky, salty camel milk. I begrudged myself the sleeping out in the bush, the delay, and I was longing for a drink of beer, whisky, anything. I took a poll among the askaris. It was midnight, the moon huge above us on the desert. They were for moving on. We threw our kit back into the truck, dragged the snoring women out of their cover, filled the radiator, lit cigarettes, and went on, the truck bumping and rolling over the rocks, and again and again we had to get out and push the truck out of the thick sand in the *tugs*, the river beds which had not seen a river since long before the Prophet's death.

Drink never meant much to me, until I was marooned in Somalia, and has never meant as much since. I like drink, but not nearly as much as I liked it in Somalia. There were no hotels there, no pubs, no shops. You couldn't get a drink there when you had finished your drink ration, and when you got your drink ration you drank it up as soon as you could, and then craved for more.

Driving down to El Lagodei in that ruined Chev I was in a kind of ecstasy, a ragged second lieutenant, overdue for full lieutenant-hood and twenty-eight days leave, driving farther and farther away from that fly-infested hell-hole in which one had experienced for for the first time the steady, silent creep of hysteria approaching. That place in which one had learned to do one's first inner grazing, to gaze inwards, the thinking eye, driven inwards, perhaps by the harshness of the life outside, was disappearing now as one pressed the accelerator down and stared through the approaching dawnlight for the first signs of El Lagodei fort.

My khaki shirt, one of those early cellular well-cut shirts which vanished towards the end of the war as utility won the day, was ragged, torn, patched, and I had only one pip to wear, on my right shoulder. I had lost the other one and my left shoulder strap was buttonless anyway, hanging down in a flap. I had no stockings left and was bare-legged, wearing Somali sandals, and my shorts were ready for handing on to the company cook. I was badly in need of a haircut, and in the mood for one of those nervous-release drink parties that we in the field-force began to indulge in at that time, when we got the opportunity. During my leave I was going to buy a thousand books to take back with me to the next piece of wilderness, wherever that would be. I would order cases of gin, take drawing materials with me, steal a radio from some army dump in Mogadishu, arrange with some Italian or other to send me onions and fruit some-how on any convoy he could find going to my next piece of wilder-ness, and never again would I find myself without reading matter, or drink, or onions, but even then I knew, as we all did in that field-force, that after the third month in the wilderness we would be short of everything once more. And in Mogadishu I was going to seek out bread, and eat it until tired. Real bread. I could not eat another army biscuit, I thought then.

El Lagodei. I could see the faint grey squareness of the fort away on the horizon. I could hear the askaris in the back shouting, one of them thumping on the cab roof, shouting 'It is there. We see it. El Lagodei.' They began to sing in the back of the truck, the thin, yelling Somali singing on five sad, haunting notes. They too wanted a fresh scene, new people, gossip in the *makaya*, the coffee shop in the village, women, boasting.

I stopped the truck, paraded the askaris and let them adjust their equipment, button up their pockets, while I borrowed a safety pin from one of them and pinned up my left shoulder strap. I buckled on my web belt and pistol, hammered my sidecap on the truck until all the yellow dust of the Mijertein had gone from it, put the cap on, laughed when one of the askaris said to me, 'None of us can look smart in our rags, Effendi. But we must try.'

'Will they give us decent uniforms, soon, Effendi?' another askari asked. 'In the Italian army we dressed far better than this,' which was true, for the Italians had looked to the bright and dashing tastes of the Somalis in their army, going in for high fezzes with splendid badges, dashing grey cloaks, splendid bandoliers, stars and bright yellow, green and red tassels and pom-poms for the *Gruppo Banda* and the *Dubat*, those dashing irregulars who still spoke fondly of their major, Cimarutta, and proudly of Colonnello Bechis.

'In wartime you wear rags,' I said. 'Smart rags, properly laundered when you can. The nice uniforms are for the clerks and the storemen at base.' It was the only lie I could think of just then, having used most of the others up in the times of the sullen waiting for pay. They stood there listening to those lies, tall, black, lean, good-looking men who knew all about camels and the various tastes of the waters of widely scattered waterholes, their *modello* 91 rifles at the order, their grey square leather ammunition pouches which I had salvaged from dumps, starving for polish, their sandals broken and worn, a shower to look upon if I ever saw one, but a shower who could walk me off my feet in this wilderness anytime.

The officer at El Lagodei had no drink, and he too was aching, waiting for a convoy. He showed me his transport, a smashed Chev standing on four wooden boxes, and reminded me that the Chev I was driving was his, and when would I send it back? He had somehow stolen it, and I promised I would send it back, and did, with his drink ration in the back. As time went on we of the field-force were to look after each other more and more, stealing kit, scrounging materials of all kinds, sharing loot, united in a sort of military monkhood in our outpost cells.

I drove down through Garowei, that lonely fort in the brown barren hills of the northern Mudugh. Garowei was also drinkless, the officer there imploring me to shoot some of the staff officers for him when I got to base. He had been here six months and had had only one drink ration, and, heady and careless with joy, had drunk the lot in three nights with another officer in off patrol.

'You look pretty far gone, you know,' he said to me. 'I hear you're all round the bend up there at Gardafui.' He added, before I could say it for him, 'And I'm pretty far gone myself, I know it. I've begun to talk to myself. Do you ever do that?' He looked at me keenly.

'Often,' I told him.

'Do you know the Italians never let their officers do more than three months up here?'

'With a wine ration every month. Yes,' I said.

'Hundreds of bloody askaris to carry the wine ration when they went on patrol.'

'Green vegetables twice a month sent up by truck.'

'It's a bloody disgrace, that's what it is. Don't forget to go in and raise hell about my booze ration, and my mail. I've got to go on a camel patrol tomorrow. I hate camels. I really hate the bastards. Every tried to load one?'

'Ever eaten one? An old one? They tell me the young camel is like chicken.'

'Catch me eating a bloody camel, boy,' he said. Yet we ate plenty of camel together a year later east of that particular piece of wilderness, and we ate it young, freshly born if possible. New-born camel was the best meat I ever ate in Somalia.

On to Galkayu ('The place where me White Men ran away'—referring to a time when the Somalis repulsed an attack by European troops in the time of the Mad Mullah). It was at Galkayu that I saw the first tall cool bottles of beer in many months, proferred by a friend with a generous hand, and I sat down as I was, covered with dust, tired and sand-weary, and we began to graze each other in that special gladness of companionship known only to shagbags of that time and in that Godless place.

CHAPTER SEVEN

JOE was a tall, dark, sardonic fellow, very good and fast with a rifle, very widely read, cool and able with the excitable Somalis, an old Africa hand, a few years older than me.

'I've got a nutcase here on my hands,' he said quietly after the second bottle of cold beer. 'I want you to take him away for me before he opens fire on himself. He's only loading and aiming at present, but it could get serious. He's only been here a month but he took one look at The Shag and the Somalis and went into retirement. He's in there.' He pointed towards the green, paint-starved lattice work which ran round the half walls of the room we were sitting in. 'A good chap but more suited to the quartermaster's store, say, or a staff job somewhere nice. Kidding apart, though, I'm worried about him. So take him down with you to Mog. This is my last chance. There'll be no more transport to Mog for months. Be a chum, will you?'

'The Shag' was our name for all of endless Somalia.

'How far gone is he, really?'

'He's swinging his thirty-eight up like this. Need I say more?' Joe had an invisible pistol in his hand and swung it up to his temple, again and again. 'He does that sitting in there. I've watched it. Go and see him. He's quite a nice chap, but he's had his chips already. In a *month*, mind you. He's an expert. It takes me about two years before *I* start swinging my thirty-eight.' Joe, the old Africa hand who had come to terms with wilderness a long time ago.

'I've no room in the truck,' I said. 'It's packed with ration-eaters and kit.' Ration-eaters were askaris, like yourself, only interested in the next meal.

'Now don't start any of that, Gerry, there's a dear,' Joe said. 'You've got to take him or I'll find him splattered all over his room one morning, letter to mother on the floor, then courts of inquiry, and why didn't I evacuate this officer before things came to this stage? etcetera. What with? Seen the transport here, even if I had the petrol for it? It's special, Gerry, my transport—in pieces all over the sand. No, for Christ's sake, take this chum down with you. I'm serious.'

The second lieutenant sitting on his camp bed in the room I entered was far gone all right, no doubt about it. I could see that by the long, vacant stare he gave me as I introduced myself. Admittedly I looked strange in my rags, my long tangled hair, my bare sunburned legs and my rawhide sandals. In fact I was the living picture of what, it turned out, this officer feared he would become in this scorched and silent desert peopled by spear-carrying savages who were holding their Italian rifles in reserve, for now.

'What's the matter?' I asked him, sitting down on the floor. 'Are you feeling ill?'

He shook his head slowly, still staring at me.

'If you're ill I'll take you down with me to Mog,' I said. 'I'm pulling out in the morning.'

'Really?' he said. 'Where have you come from?'

'Cape Gardafui,' I told him.

'How long have you been up there?'

I told him. He put his head in his hands and murmured, 'I didn't join the army for this kind of thing. This isn't soldiering. It's impossible.' He looked at me. 'Do *you* call this soldiering?'

'I can't tell you what I call it,' I said. 'We're too young for that kind of language. But bullshit apart, you've had your chips here, haven't you?'

'Yes,' he whispered. 'I hate it. I hate it.'

'Come on, then, pack your bag and I'll give you a lift out of it. You don't look very well to me.' He was pale, drawn, and his hands trembled when he lit a cigarette. He refused to come and I knew why. It would look to authority as if he had run out.

I went back and told Joe. 'Let's open the whisky in that case,' he said. 'I'll send a signal to Mog and get *them* to remove him. I know he's going to knock himself off, this character, if he stays here.'

The officer was removed a fortnight later, a special truck being sent for him. He proved to be seriously ill with a deficiency disease. Two years later I heard he was a major in the Middle East, on the staff.

Three hundred miles to the tarmac from Galkayu, three hundred of the worst miles, over white rock and through foot-deep sand, but the tarmac to Mogadishu, which suddenly started at a non-existent place called Firfir, a mere place name, was always like a magnet to us on the last stage of the drive to Mog and salad and drink

and bread and friends at a real bar in the officers' club. I said
goodbye to Joe at dawn, promising to see Humphrey, that marvellous doctor who tried to do so much for us in our outposts, and to
tell him that the pistol-swinging officer was due for treatment in
Mog.

I drove all out that day, stopping only once to eat a tin of bully
beef and to drink some camel milk (the best anti-scorbutic in the
world), and, like the askaris, had to piss over the side of the lurching
truck as we moved, and made a game of it. Anything for speed out
of the desert. It was twenty minutes past midnight when I saw the
black gleam of the tarmac ahead in the moonlit sand and rock, and
the truck climbed up on to that smooth tarmac laid by the Italian
troops in 1935, as they advanced on Abyssinia. I was exhausted,
and happy. A sleep at Bulo and then down the tarmac at sixty miles
an hour to Mogadishu. I stopped the truck outside the headquarters at Bulo, a two storey house of white stucco with a verandah
running round it, climbed out of the cab and stumbled stiffly across
the sand, wondering who I would find in command here. A voice in
English said, 'Want a drink?'

'I want about twenty,' I said, 'but one would be a godsend right
now. Where are you?'

'Over here. Where've you come from?' I told him.

'Never heard of it. Come on. Over here.' I could now see the shape
of a mosquito net and a figure sitting on a camp chair beside it
about twenty yards away in the thick, warm darkness. He was an old
grizzled major stripped to the waist, tattooed on both arms, grinning
at me as he handed me a bottle of whisky. 'You're one of these
maniacs who live up there, I take it.' He jerked his thumb in the
direction of The Shag. 'Better you than me, anyway. Sit down.' He
pushed his ration-box towards me with his foot and I sat down,
poured some of his whisky into a tin cup and wished him well.

'I've just had the lousiest day in my life, son,' he said to me. 'And
the bird has flown anyway, but what a mess he's left.' He then told
me his story. It was about a transport officer who had fallen desper-
ately in love with an Italian prostitute who lived far down the tarmac,
in Mogadishu.

We did not know it as he talked, but the subject of his story had
already shot himself that day in Mogadishu.

He was an officer who had been sent by Command to check on
army transport coming down from the Abyssinian campaign, and
while in Mogadishu had fallen violently in love with an Italian

prostitute who had come down from Addis Ababa. He was stationed here at Bulo near the end of the tarmac and his trips to and from Mogadishu increased in frequency as the mania for her grew. She took all he had, and when he had finished all he had, he began to sell wheels, petrol, tools, trucks, used up the imprest account and started another, and went in for special book-keeping, until finally, when nodding Command suddenly sat up and took notice he knew that he was finished. But even then, alone at the end of the tarmac, thinking about the woman in Mogadishu, and knowing he was for court martial, he had to see her again. He must have passed my old grizzled major on the road as he drove down to Mogadishu, the major driving up to 'look into things', and to arrest him.

'Yes, he's flown,' the old major said. 'Have another whisky. The only thing he didn't sell here was the sand. He's flogged everything else. I wouldn't mind if the woman was worth it. Have you seen her ?' He named her. I said I hadn't seen her.

'An all-leather job,' the old man said. 'Solid rock heart and a born bitch, I'm telling you. I knew her in Addis. I wouldn't mind if he'd spent everything on a decent piece of crumpet, but this bag, it beats me. He's gone crazy about her, crazy. He'll get about five years for this little lot when they get him.'

I heard the rest of the story in Mogadishu the next night. The officer had gone around the town searching for his woman, but she, knowing that he was due for arrest, had retired into a convent in a hysterical state, begging for sanctuary, and he traced her to the convent. He ran up the steps of the convent in the glare of the midday, hammered on the door, calling her name. He had had a few desperate drinks by then. A nun appeared. He asked for the woman and the nun told him that she was very sorry but the woman could not be seen, would not be seen, and did not wish to see him again. The woman had already conveyed this to the officer, apparently, but he longed to see her and talk to her.

When he saw it was no use he drew his pistol and said, 'Tell her I love her,' and shot himself, rolling down into the sandy street in front of the Somalis. Died on Active Service. 'Poor sod,' everybody said. She was in action again some months later, a beautiful woman.

The club was crowded with officers drinking beer out of huge glass insulators which had been found in an Italian dump. Some of us from The Shag, officers come down on leave like myself, drank for twenty-four hours and talked, in our own Mess out on the Balad

30

road, about who was going round the bend 'up there' in The Shag, who had gone round it already, and about the chances of transfer out of this wilderness, to anywhere, anywhere at all.

'You can forget it,' a senior officer told us. 'You're staying right here, so get down to it. Drink while you've got it at hand, and forget words like Transfer and Posting to battalions.'

CHAPTER EIGHT

'Go ashore in Mogadishu?' the ship's officer said to me, his eyebrows raised. '*Perchè? E' il più brutto posto nel mondo*. You really want to go ashore there?'

The ship would only stay in Mogadishu for a few hours. There was no dock and the ship had to lie off. The only way to go ashore at Mogadishu was to be swung out in a canvas bag from a derrick and then be lowered into a boat which would take one to the jetty a couple of miles off. I said I knew this and had been swung off in a bag before, and could I be swung off in a bag again this time, and I would promise I would be back on the ship in three hours.

'*Bene, signore.*'

As the ship sailed towards Mogadishu in the warm darkness I could see lightning flashing over Somalia. Well inland, it would be over Eil and Sinadogo and Galkayu, the rare downpour which finished in hot steam, all sign of which vanished in a couple of days of the roasting sun. The *angarara* would come out of the earth for a while, the huge black centipede which appears with the almost unknown rain, and the camels would be worse tempered than usual, and the Somalis would run about naked, screaming with delight until the rain finished. That strange night with old Allen when we got caught in the rain on the way to taste the sweet water of Eil, a holiday from the wandering patrols in the bush. Eil has real water, water which is alive, fresh and sparkling, and you have to have drunk bitter, dead water from waterholes for months to know what real water can taste like.

All those who have had Wajir clap will know what good water tastes like after the desert waterholes. The ailment is called Wajir clap because it was coined at the wells of Wajir, but the ailment is the same from Wajir onwards, through El Wak, right across Ogaden to the rain pans in the *haud* on the borders of British Somaliland, on down into Somalia and south to the Juba river.

The first time I saw what it was we were drinking as water was when an Italian doctor opened a *filtro idro* we were using in a fort called Gardo. '*Guarda,*' he said smiling, '*il brodo.*' He showed me

32

what was at the bottom of the filter, a thick white glittering mass of mica and gypsum.

'*Ecco, la causa del* clap *di* Wajir,' he said laughing. Yes, there it was, that scintillating white mass of paste filtered out of the water we had to drink. This *filtro idro* was the only one I ever saw out in The Shag, and I never forgot it.

Clap, known to old sweats as 'pissing fish-hooks and razor blades', was very common among the troops of the field-force, one company reaching seventy-eight per cent after eight months on the borders of Southern Abyssinia. (Don't bother to mention 'prophylactics', please—we were in Somalia.) Wajir clap is a very good imitation of the real thing, a tough old British sergeant told me, when condoling with me because of the agony I was having in pissing at a place called Bogol Manyo, after a longish diet of one particular waterhole.

The tiny mica and gypsum crystals tore the lining of the urethra, and after that it would be agony. 'I feel like a bloody shotgun today,' one would tell one's companion, 'the rifling's torn out of me.'

Sweet tumbling glistening waters of Eil, how I remember steeping my burning face in your coolness, and drinking you up, while Corporal Ahamed Hussein watched and laughed, for we had praised you before we got to you, drunk you in our heads through days of journeying.

The Somalis have as sensitive and knowing a palate for the taste of water as have some Spaniards, and like them will sing in praise of good water.

When old Allen and I decided we would go to Eil, on the excuse of 'showing the rifle' there (there were two machine guns hidden down there, but we never got them), I told him of the wonderful water, and of the patch of sweet potatoes which an Arab grew there. Sweet potatoes? He was ready to go at once.

I can never forget old Allen, the delightful companionship and the laughter shared with him, the oldest who served with us up in The Shag, a man who would flout rules, who treated base wallahs and their pieces of paper with a special cynical disregard, who could 'carry a can' for you. I never liked British colonialism, but I could see what jewels it sometimes threw up when I got to know old Allen, who had spent most of his life in Africa, and knew how to feel Africa with all his instincts. He had been very badly wounded in the battle of the Somme in 1916, was not romantic about soldiering, having been hit too hard on the Somme, and was a real shagbag in every sense. Much older than us, he never intruded his age. One forgot he was thirty years older than most of us, and he was wise and good and honest, and I would have gone anywhere with him, anytime, anyhow.

Perhaps I can convey something of his special style if I describe his farewell to a force we called Clapforce, when I and my officers paraded with the troops in front of a fort one midday, the laden camels bawling and showing their bladdered tongues twenty yards off. Old Allen came out wearing his bush-hat side to front, so that it would look like Napoleon's hat, and with his right hand stuffed into his shirt, like Napoleon. He knew that two hundred and sixty-three men, women and children had been speared, stabbed, hacked to death and those of the women who escaped, left to die of thirst in the bush, by the tribe we were going to operate against.

'Officers and men,' he shouted, while I shook with the effort not to burst out laughing, (which was what he wanted), 'My message to you on this solemn day, at this critical moment in our history, is—' he paused, and cleared his throat, lifted his jaw Napoleonically, 'is—Shag them to the roots of their gonads! Do not rest. Press on regardless. Leave no stone unturned. Give your all. Shag them, I tell you. The booze ration, the mail, the fresh vegetables, all we hold dear, depends today on your endeavours. I am proud of you.' He saluted, and I saluted for all of us. I gave the command 'Fall out the officers,' so that we could get away and laugh for a few minutes far from the troops, who had been most moved by the whole performance. And then we wound off in a long, trudging file into The Shag in search of the marvellous tribe who had only chalked up one more score in a blood feud a thousand years old, and now must pay for that. And I knew how well old Allen, who had hidden his feelings under this charade on parade, wished that all this killing would end and that Somalia would become like the other Africas, fatter, quieter, nearer the kind God of the Christianity that had been brought to them, while knowing that Somalia could never be like that at all.

The more I listened to survivors of the front line fighting in the First World War, especially old Allen, who described it in detail for me, the less I could understand how and why they were able to go on doing it for four years. Millions of Germans, French, British standing in stinking, sodden trenches, flinging explosives as fast as they came from the enormous factories, and then rushing on to each other's machine guns, dying in swathes to capture a hundred yards of shellholes, until the counter-attack, when they threw explosives at each other all over again. When you look at the photographs of the faces of the owners of that world, the kings and lords and generals and politicians, you see a hardness, almost a ferocity in some of them which made that kind of holocaust inevitable, almost a necessity. Those tight, glistening riding boots on the Generals, those monocles, those splendid chargers on which they sometimes rode past the next supply of troops waiting to run on to the machine guns, the whole master and man relationship which had lasted so long. When you read the literature and listen to the tales of the survivors you see 'The Front' as a special closed-in world, cut off from France and Germany and England, in which the professional Generals could use men by the million and ammunition and equipment by the mountain, and in which the troops went on suffering and dying, until it suddenly stopped, and everybody went home to unemployment, except the Generals. I doubt if any owners of people, factories, colonies, ever had such freedom to fling people and their sweat about for four years, to tear a world to pieces as they did, but most amazing of all is to think of the millions of soldiers killed, and the even greater number of millions wounded, and how they went on killing and dying in those trenches for four years, and for the second rate people who commanded them all to do it.

'They used to shoot them then if they couldn't face it,' old Allen told me over a campfire on the safari to Eil. 'Stand them against a wall and shoot them. You had to do it, if necessary.' Perhaps the mutiny of the French army in 1916 was the only realistic gesture made during that insanity, unless it was the fraternization of the German and British soldiers between the trenches in 1914, so quickly stopped. 'They shot one in ten of the French troops who mutinied,' old Allen told me, 'and the machine started up again. It had to go on, to the finish.'

'The world's always been a bloody madhouse anyway,' he said as we began to nod over the ashes of the campfire. We had curried the meat we had shot, eaten it while watching the black clouds massing over the moon and felt the chill coming into the tensing electric air. The storm exploded over us while we were asleep. We always slept in the open, never using tents, and we were very tired that night, and I found I had struggled up on to my knees, my head on my arms, still asleep, with a river racing between my legs and the rain lashing on to my back, while old Allen was shaking his fist at the sky a few yards away, sitting in a sodden mess of blankets, and angrily shouting, 'Why didn't you warn us, you bastard?' The askaris were huddled under a thorn tree trying to light a fire. The fire lit and we all sat round it shivering, trying to smoke damp cigarettes.

'And one day we'll wish we were back here like this,' old Allen said. 'Curious, isn't it?'

It is curious, for now, twenty years later, staring out from the ship in the darkness towards Eil, I wished I could have written to old Allen and told him he was right that night. I wished right then I could be looking down on Eil from the hills again as we did the day after the storm, the bush around us steaming in the sun, Eil, three or four tiny white buildings below us surrounded by green patches of cultivation, and the blue Indian Ocean washing up to it. Actual *green*, *fresh*, glistening gardens in which we knew there would be melons and sweet potatoes, and nearby, most precious of all, that beautiful, refreshing living water from the sweet spring.

'Taste it,' I said to old Allen, handing him a mess tin full of the spring water, and he drank it down, saying, 'My God, that's good, son. That's really good.' Here was water you did not have to pour six times from cup to cup until a few tired bubbles formed in it, as Doctor Ammanato had taught me up beyond Wal-Wal. He used to pour the water from one cup to another, fast, until a tiny semblance of life came into the dead, cloudy liquid, but even then when you drank it there was no life in it. Old Allen and I drank the Eil water, and then tried it out in the whisky we had with us. Once, with Jack, that best companion for long marches and dreary bivouacs in rocks, we had drunk water so bitter, so astringent it might have been the juice of aloes, that the mouth puckered up inside and the guts refused to work calmly for a couple of weeks after we got out of that place to another waterhole. A hot wind was blowing one evening while Jack and I had smoked under our sheltering rocks and had discussed whether we should finish the last of our one bottle of gin we had saved during the march. We had nothing to go with it but that bitter, angry water from that hole nearby. When we poured the water into our gin the mixture turned navy blue.

'Some kind of chemical reaction,' Jack said. 'Still, there's a taste of gin at least.' I have never been able to discover what could have been in that water to produce a navy blue drink.

The sweet potatoes from the garden at Eil, dipped in the lumps of rock salt and eaten from the hand, and tea made with the spring water which had no treachery in it; unforgettable, and melons, and *Jeb* nuts given to us by an old Arab who tended the gardens there.

I never forgot Eil, its peace, its isolation from the blood feuds and the casual ferocity inland, and the sound of its friendly waters in the white stones so close to the ocean. Every traveller has one treasure, one place he has found in which he would like to spend one year, and mine is Eil; better than Gavai, better than Lamu, farther out of reach, in fact forgotten, Eil remains in the memory as a tiny oasis on the rim of that savage world of camels, waterholes and spearmen under a merciless sun.

The blue lightning was now quivering all over the dark coast, and the ship was gliding through the sea with only a faint throb of her diesels quivering in the deck under my feet. I could see one tiny speck of yellow light on that black coast, and I wondered if half a dozen Somalis were sitting round it, their nightfire, over which they talked genealogy and history and camels.

I was going to Kenya but now I wished it was to Somalia I was going instead, in search of Jibreel and Hassan and Hersi and Mohamed Saad, and Kadija, and other dispensers of *wus-wus* and to find out how they had fared, and to travel across those wildernesses again, unarmed this time, and to live with the Midgan hunters for a couple of months and collect all their lore before it vanishes forever.

CHAPTER NINE

MOGADISHU; Mogadoxo of the Portuguese, Hamar to the Somalis. I could see it faintly a couple of miles off in the blue-grey dawn mist which was slowly lifting from the ocean. The ocean rolls smoothly here, like heavy liquid glass, blue, purple, green, white marble streaks running in it and fluxing in sudden patches of hissing foam. Somali fishermen in their tiny canoes disappeared slowly in the deepening valleys of smooth water, and rose again just as slowly as the ocean swelled and flowed on past them. There was a fruffing sound as a school of tiny fish scuffed the glistening blue skin of the water, turning the surface of the sea into a glittering, blinding million fragments of a broken mirror as the first sunflare was caught in it. I could see the small white buildings of Mogadishu now, and strained my ears in the hope that I might hear the wild, passionate cry of the *muezzin* who used to wake me from the sweating tropical sleep with his holy anger. 'Get up! Get up and pray! Get up, all of you sleepers, and pray.' And the sleepers would rise, and stumble to prayer, '*Allahu Akhbar*, the Compassionate, the Merciful,' and, low voiced, take refuge in the Lord of the Worlds, and from the Slinking Whisperer, from the devil, and from men, for a time. And one then saw the red fiery anger of the sun beginning to fill the sky, and marvelled again at the devotion of Islam, its fixed never forgotten regular prayers which I had seen said by the sophisticated and the simple on rivers in Burma, among rocks in India, in the ancient gardens of Kashmir, and in the farthest corners of the deserts beyond Mogadishu. But I could not hear the *muezzin* as the ship moved nearer to the coast, only the thin cries of the fishermen in the little boats as they sighted the schools of fish.

Now I could smell Mogadishu in the growing heat, sharp, almost rank, salty, mingled with incense and woodsmoke, like the smell of fresh camel milk in a smoke-cleansed gourd.

I was anxious to see Somali faces again, those lean, serious faces with the large black eyes, the skin brown, or black, an expression of strain, tension, a certain curious readiness in every face, as if listening for a magic word, the eyes watching always as if to see the

38

unexpected. I wanted to feel again that strange almost electric energy they possess when in a crowd, when arguing, when laughing, when moving towards hysteria or quarrel, or decision after urgent discussion. And as the sun rose I could feel that sharp, stifling heat again. If the skin has a memory mine awoke then. It began to tingle as the sun struck it, as if suddenly startled by real heat again after years, and the sweat came as if by command. Once more one's eyes screwed up, narrowed as I stared across the glaring water at Mogadishu, at the three ancient tramp ships lying at anchor in the slow swell, the rumble of their rusty winches the only sound.

I began to wonder now if I did want to see Mogadishu again, if I did want to hear the harsh Somali language again, if it was any use to walk up those streets again after twenty years. It had assumed the power of a longed-for paradise, once, as the months went by up in the wilderness, and had seemed the greatest place on earth when one got there, ragged and slightly crazy, driving in the heavily laden truck straight to the club, knowing that that marvellous old Colonel of ours would forgive one brief appearance in dusty rags at the bar for that one longed-for drink, the first on leave.

'Here's another shagbag come back for a drink,' someone would shout at the crowded bar. 'I heard you'd shot yourself long ago. Come and have one.'

Were those circles of Italian bayonets of every kind, a pedigree of blades, still on the walls of the Duca d'Aosta's Club which we had used so well? The bar would be gone now, swept away in this new free Somalia where bars would be taboo, gone with the *Kafir*, the infidel. How one drank when one could get it at that time. How one would drink again like that if one had to live that life again.

'*Pronto, signore*,' the old Italian bosun said to me, smacking his frayed leather gloves together. '*Ecco il motoscafo.*' He pointed to the huge motor barge wallowing towards the ship, the same barge of twenty years ago, battered, ragged motor tyres hanging all round her as buffers, Somalis in bright checked *lungis* waving from the stern. The bosun pointed to the big green canvas bag on the deck, ropes leading from it up to the ready derrick. It could take about ten men.

'As soon as you've seen the police, *signore*, I'll sling you down to the barge,' the old bosun said. 'Here are the police now.'

These tall Somali policemen in their greenish khaki shorts and tunics were friendly and courteous as they dealt with my permit to go ashore. I went with them into the saloon and handed them my passport. I think it must have been the first Irish passport they had ever seen. The three of them bent over it to inspect the golden harp stamped in its cover.

'Ah,' one of them said. '*La Repubblica d'Irlanda.*' He smiled. 'Republic? Good.' He liked republics. And then one of the other policemen dashed off a written permit which allowed me to go free in Mogadishu for three hours.

Swinging high over the water in the canvas bag the fierce sun held me now and the sweat came out of me in a rush, soaking my thin shirt. A dozen lean Somali hands reached up and steadied the bag as it reached the deck of the barge. They were all laughing, greeting me, friendliness itself. The *nakuda* of the barge was fat and solid and black, a brightly coloured skull cap on his head.

'*Jambo,*' I said to the *nakuda*, guessing he would know Swahili with that shining blackness of his, a coast Swahili-Arab if ever I saw one. '*Uhali gani?*'

'*Jambo sana!*' he replied, offering me his big hand to shake. He said his news was good, his life untroubled.

'Cigarette?' I offered him the packet.

He smiled, telling me he was longing for a smoke, for he had come without any, having been working since two o'clock that morning. He sat down beside me in the stern of the barge and began to ask me questions about my voyage, the ship I had come in, my job, my plans.

'How many passengers are in that ship?' he asked me, pointing up to the towering white mass of the ship from which cases of wine were being lowered into our barge.

'Hundreds,' I told him.

'I always wonder how they feed so many people for so many days,' he said. 'I have never understood it. You're going to eat those. Do you like those?' He showed me sacks of blue-brown spiky restless lobsters which were waiting to go aboard the ship.

He spoke real *safi* Swahili, and it was wonderful to hear and speak that beautiful, mellifluous tongue again, here in the heat, smoking a cigarette with a descendant of the slavers who had worked this side of Africa almost as hard as the whites at the other side.

'My Swahili is rusty,' I said, yet it was coming faster now, the mysterious machinery of memory working for my nervous tongue, stirring the files where lay the vocabulary in the rust of eight years. But we never forget a language we have used, and enjoyed using.

'We are oiling it now,' the *nakuda* said, smiling. 'To talk is the best oil for the words. Describe the journey here, the places you saw. Were you in Italy? Egypt?'

He wanted to know the speed of the ship, how many days it took to come from Italy, shaking his head, saying, 'Everything is going faster the older I get.' What did I think of all the changes taking place in the world these days? Take his son, now. His son now read books in Italian and English and wanted to go to Europe and become a doctor. What with? How? He was laughing. 'The young men nowadays don't seem to worry about money. They write a letter to some foreign country and expect a shower of money for their education. Ashore then,' he pointed to Mogadishu, 'they'd go without food now for education. School, school, school, that is the word you hear every minute of the day. I suppose if I had been to a school I would be in an office now with a small boy bringing me cups of coffee every time I rang the bell. I have never seen anything like the madness about education that is going on in these times. They would *eat* a book if you gave it to them, some of the young men nowadays.' He got up and uttered an angry rush of Arabic curses at one of the crew who had fouled a rope leading from the cargo sling. 'That's another one driven mad with the books,' he said, nodding at the young Somali who had fouled the rope. 'He wants to sit in an office.'

'All is ready,' the Somalis shouted from the front of the barge. Four young Somali policemen were coming down in the bag now. They landed and came and sat down beside me, inspecting me, and then questioning me. The conversation with these young men for the next quarter of an hour confirmed everything the old *nakuda* had said about the passion for education among the Somalis today.

'Are you coming here to teach?' one of the policemen asked me.

'No,' I said. 'Only to look round the town for three hours. Why? Are you expecting a teacher?'

'More than anything we want teachers,' they told me, each butting in on the other as they talked in the way I remembered the Somalis talked when they were interested, hastily, urgently. 'More than anything we want teachers of English.' So far the conversation had been in Italian, none of them knowing Swahili. 'Could I speak English?' When I said yes, they beamed and began to try out their English, and as usual with the Somalis, without fear of hesitation, vying with each other for the longest sentences.

'We want many school here to teach English,' they told me. 'It is the language everybody in the world must know now. We want

41

teachers to come here, plenty of them.' Then they began to praise a certain Englishman who was now in Mogadishu teaching English. They could not praise this man highly enough, telling me that he even made jokes and imitated various ways in which English is spoken throughout the world. He was a wonderful teacher and they only wished they could find more like him to come to Mogadishu and help the Somalis get ready for the world of today. As the fever of their pleasure in this talk got hold of them they came and sat round me and I saw that particular and likeable Somali urgency again, that thrill in self expression, that longing for every kind of information which could keep the talk flowing fast and bright. They began to try out long words, eyebrows raised for my nod of assent and understanding of their pronunciation, then racing on with the sentence. Sometimes one of them would sit back and sigh, with pleasure in this success in experiment, meanwhile thinking of new sentences containing new and longer words. They were all from the Mijertein, and when I told them I knew the Mijertein they were delighted, and hurled questions. Did I know the Daror, the Nogal, Alula, the Haud? I did? Tell us all about your time in the Mijertein, they said.

The pride the Mijertein tribes take in being of the Mijertein, the most barren of all the Somali deserts, is as if that territory was the garden of Eden itself. They always speak of it as a place in which you can get anything and everything, in which a man wants for nothing, in which men know the meaning of plenty.

Down south, on the Juba where the trees drip bananas, lemons, pawpaw, where the thick soil pushes up every kind of vegetable, where the small, fat, black men can eat chicken, eggs, beef and have never been without a drink of water, I have heard Mijertein askaris sneering at all this, and telling the local 'slave people' that until they see the Mijertein they do not know what living is.

And in the Mijertein you would have to kneel down and pray to a single blade of grass to come up, and cry on it every day to help it live.

I could not help laughing as these young Mijertein tribesmen in police uniform spoke of their wilderness with exaltation, and yet I was touched again at this loyalty. What these Mijertein people meant was that up there you got the finest camel milk, and for the nomads there is no greater praise of a howling wilderness than that.

The policeman stood up and shook hands with me as I got ready

42

to land from the barge, all smiling. I asked them how they liked running their own country now.

'We are proud,' they told me. 'We have a lot to learn and a lot to do, but we will do it. We need help and friends. Tell everyone you meet outside our country that we want their help and friendship. Tell teachers to come and teach us.'

There cannot be anywhere in Africa such ready and hungry people, with such swift minds, waiting to read their way out of a thousand years of dependence on the camel, and the spears that had ensured its possession.

CHAPTER TEN

THE first thing I saw when I stepped on to the jetty from the barge was a camel, scrawny, evil tempered, stupid, faithful, a load on his back, being led by a small boy into the massing whirl of cars and motor cycle taxis beyond the wicker gate at the end of the dock. I tried to feel some kind of affection for the camel, to forgive them all through this one behind the small boy, but it was no use. I hated them still. I remembered how one of them had broken out of that long stumbling line in the heat one day, Jaysee's gramophone and records tied on its back (which I had promised so faithfully to transport up into The Shag for him from Mogadishu) and then how the camel had, in one of those mad furies which overtook them, rolled on its back until it had smashed all of that precious load. I had raced after it, the askaris streaming behind me, a pistol in my hand and an overpowering desire on me to murder it, to lecture it first, and then shoot it. Not quite as stupid as the horse, the camel is all right to work with once you have got into his rhythm, his sauntering stumble, but the hardest work I know is trying to walk at the same slow pace as the camels in thick sand, after the long, difficult ritual of the loading, the camels kneeling there and bawling while the grain is poured out for them on the sacks laid out reverently in front of them by the askaris. '*Toog, toog, wario*,' the askaris used to croon to them.

It was cheering to know, standing on that jetty, and smelling camels again, that one would never work with them anymore.

There was a Somali waiting for me on the jetty, and his anxiety to take me over, to guide me, made me feel that he must be a police agent, for I had never seen a Somali dragoman before in Mogadishu.

In build, face, colour, bearing, he was obviously from one of the warrior tribes north of Wal-Wal, but he told me he was a third generation in Mogadishu, and that he thought his ancestor had been 'a camel man'. He was wearing a clean, freshly ironed khaki drill jacket, white linen trousers, old battered sandals, and a blue and red cotton skull cap. I told him I had three hours and that I wanted to walk round Mogadishu, and would he take me to the Croce del Sud hotel first where we could have a drink of fresh lime

44

and water, if they still served it, and if he wanted one too. He said he would be pleased. He suggested he paid for everything and that we reckon up the score when we came back to the dock, and I agreed.

We drove to the Croce del Sud in one of the new motor cycle cabs, through streets swarming with Somalis in crowds I had never seen in the past. The guide, Ali, told me that more and more Somalis were pouring into Mogadishu. As we drove into a wide, sandy side street I recognised it, with an unexpected and painful memory of something tragic I had come upon here at two o'clock in the morning nearly twenty years ago. I told the taxi to stop, Ali to pay the driver, for I wanted us to walk from here. While Ali paid him I walked across the street and looked up and down it, evoking that horrible scene again which I had once come upon in the moonlight, as a duty officer.

That street reminded me of old Seymour, whom I had not thought of for years and years. He must surely be dead now, that tough old man, that mine of African lore who looked up at me as the telephone rang at nearly two o'clock in the morning and said, 'That sounds like trouble. Well, *I'm* sober. How about you two?'

'Sober,' we said. The old timer meant that whoever was going out on this call must be in control of all his faculties, and we had drunk a lot of whisky (and I was glad of this when I walked into that night's mess.) We were not even half shot, having been talking more than drinking. I was down in Mogadishu on temporary duty training two hundred ration-eaters in infantry tactics at a barracks called Wardiglei on the edge of the town.

At the other end of the telephone an Italian was speaking excitedly, telling me there had been a killing, and I must come at once. He named the street and said he would be waiting there.

'*E' un soldato inglese,*' the voice said. '*Lui è morto.*' He went on to say that the soldier had been stabbed and was lying in the street.

But the soldier, a heavily built, tough looking N.C.O., was alive, his false teeth lying in the sand, himself in a glistening pool of blood, his belly slashed open from side to side, his intestines beside him. He was unconscious. He was dressed in a khaki shirt, ripped across and bloody now, shorts, web belt, and his slouch hat was still on his head, the chin strap in place under his chin. He looked about thirty. Before he was put into the truck I searched him and found his paybook in his hip pocket, with thirty East African shillings in notes in the back of the A.B. 64 wallet of the paybook.

I felt certain he could not live with that frightful wound, and I noticed that the whole length of his left arm was slit open on the underside. I knew what had caused those wounds; the big razor sharp *bilau*, the dagger used by the Somalis. The nearest hospital was the Italian military hospital and I sent him there at once in a truck, went back to the station and reported the business to the police officer, who rushed out with a patrol to join the other which had fanned out in the area of the stabbing. Then I telephoned the Italian military hospital, and asked the duty officer if the casualty had arrived.

'*Si' E' arrivato*,' the duty officer told me.

'Operate,' I told him. 'Immediately.'

He said he did not think the man could live but that they were going to operate, adding, 'As soon as we have the permission of the senior British army medical officer in Mogadishu.'

'Why?'

'If he should die on the operating table the major here thinks we will be accused of killing the British soldier through negligence.'

I threatened to come right up and arrest him if his major did not at once start the operation, but he would not retreat from his position.

'You must understand, *signor capitano*,' he said, 'that we are in a delicate position here with a gravely wounded British soldier, and we *must* have the permission of the senior British medical officer to do this operation.' So, anxious and angry, I roused the British Colonel by telephone, who then telephoned the Italians and ordered them to go ahead with the operation at once.

Old Seymour told me to go up to the hospital and get a statement from the wounded man, if it was at all possible. I found the Italian duty officer in his white uniform and blue duty sash pacing the verandah of the hospital.

'*E' una cosa molto grave, Signor Capitano*,' he said, and then we argued the fine points of military bull about operating on enemy soldiers who were dying, and when he saw I was still angry he spread his hands.

'The major has had his difficulties before in matters like these,' he told me. 'You must know that in a tragedy like this one we would not try and be difficult, with a man's life in the balance, unless we had had awkward experiences before. I am sorry.'

I had a great admiration and liking for the Italians, knew them to be warm and kind, and they had shown enormous courage and dignity in their defeat and the poverty which followed it, and in the presence of the Somalis who could now insult them whenever they wished. They had conquered Somalia, and now they were conquered too, in front of their subject population, and in their humiliating position they showed the greatest stoicism and character.

'Do you think the N.C.O. will live?' I asked the duty officer.

'For a time, yes,' he said. 'But his guts have been badly damaged. He is healthy, but it is unlikely that he will live long.' We smoked cigarettes until it was dawn, when I was told I could see the N.C.O., who had regained consciousness. I made it as quick as possible.

Name, number, regiment, home address, length of service. What happened?

He was a good liar, fatalistic, and, as it turned out, as loyal as they come to his friends, companions, or acquaintances who had deserted him when he most needed them. But the statement he gave me was well thought out, and even when I told him I knew it was untrue, he smiled and said he was sticking to it, and he did.

He told me he was coming along that moonlit street of sand, smoking a cigarette, when a Somali came up to him and asked him for a match. He was just getting his matches out when the Somali drew a dagger. 'I raised my arm and he slashed me with it along my arm. Then he put it in my stomach, and when I fell he took my paybook. It had thirty shillings in it. Then he ran away and left me. I don't remember anything after that, sir.'

I wrote it all down and then read it back to him slowly. He watched me steadily with his small, cool blue eyes, an old sweat with over ten years service. I asked him if his statement was correct, and if he wanted to add anything. He shook his head. I then took his paybook out of my tunic pocket and showed it to him, with the thirty shillings still in it.

'There was no robbery,' I said. 'If you want to change this statement, change it now, and we'll get this fellow who stabbed you. Help us and we'll get him. What was the real score?'

'That's my story, sir,' he said, meeting my eyes and I thought he was going to wink at me. Then he looked away, his face with a bitter expression on it. 'My guts are hanging out,' he said. They were in a huge wet bandage of a kind I had never seen before. 'The bastards.' Then he closed his eyes and I left him. He lived for three days.

He had been stabbed near the Abyssinian and Somali brothels, and it did not take K. long to get the story, though the dying N.C.O.

refused to confirm it, even though it was plain to him that K., who went to see him, knew the truth, he stood by his original story.

What had happened was that the N.C.O. and two officers who were passing through Mogadishu, had gone to a brothel together, and when they came away there was an argument about the prices. The pimp had come after them with a knife and the N.C.O. stayed and took him on, while the others ran for it. Died on Active Service.

Ali and I walked to the Croce del Sud and gradually I began to remember the town again, the shape of the geography reforming in my memory as I saw this building and that one appearing.

Over there was where Chas was standing the night the Somalis came out with the rifles and grenades, a company of troops splitting into sections to surround the area, Chas with an N.C.O. beside him, and Chas, pistol in hand with bullets flying over him, turned a fraction to speak to his N.C.O., when the bullet meant for him went straight through the N.C.O.'s head, killing him instantly, while J., that relentless pursuer in action, stood waiting in the alley for a door to open, the rifle bullets smacking into the stones. He knew that door would open, and it opened and a Somali face looked out and J. put three rounds from his pistol through it, trapping the Somali's rifle with his foot as it fell before him. And at the other end of the shooting area was Johnny, huge and without much Swahili, and unfortunate to have Swahili speaking troops in the unit under his command. The Somalis were throwing their arms away and rushing past him, some of them being caught by the African askaris, one of them a *Haji*, a holy man with a red beard and green turban. Knocked to the ground by a rifle butt the holy man was set upon by a corporal with a *kurbash* he had found, a rhinoceros hide whip, and Johnny, anxious for peace, trying to remember some Swahili, was shouting, '*Piga sana, Piga sana,*' intending to mean 'Stop hitting him. Don't hit him,' but actually saying, 'Hit him harder, harder. Hit him hard,' and almost in tears as the African soldier gave him a quick stand to attention and said, '*N'dio, Bwana,* I'll hit him harder,' and went on flogging the screaming holy man, harder and harder.

'Eventually, I had to drag the bastard off the holy man myself,' and it was some time before he knew why the corporal was puzzled.

I wondered where Johnny was now. Johnny, who, isolated in The Shag for months, alone, was found by the officer who relieved him, to be sitting at a table with a large looking glass in front of him, in deep conversation with himself, and eating bully beef straight

48

out of the can (always a sign that you were ready for leave, or treatment). It was Johnny too, who, weary of the bloodshed between the two warring tribes near his fort, and who were using Italian rifles on each other, sent ammunition out to them and let them get on with it. Then, when they had come to a standstill, he arrested the chiefs and made the tribes ransom them with camels.

I could not recognize the Croce del Sud hotel. The white stucco had gone from it, crumbled and fallen away. It looked as if it had been hit by blast from a stick of bombs, and baulks of timber were holding the front of the building up. Ali told me it was being repaired, but the whole town looked like that, run down and tired. The open air café was packed with Somalis, every table with three or four of them deep in chat, most of them in the Somali town dress of *lungi*, sandals, light jacket and skull cap. It was the first ex-colony I had visited, a place where the subject population had taken over not only the government, but the places of amusement, the hotels, the once sacred to whites only cafés, and it was a relief to be the odd man out for a change. As all the dark eyes, hundreds of them, turned to watch Ali and his white companion walk through the sitting crowd to a table, I knew what it must be like to have tried this as a black man in a white hotel. Yet every eye I met was friendly. I never met any anti-white feeling of any kind in my three swift hours in Mogadishu, but was not expecting to anyway with Somalis, who had never smarted under any inferiority feeling. A Somali always felt himself to be twice as good as any white man, or any other kind of man at all, and still does, even when he is wrong. Islam does wonders for the self respect of non-white people and Christianity is right to worry about the spread of Islam in Africa, and must honestly face the question of why it has happened— there is nothing so depressing as hearing some unhappy bitch of an ex-suburban memsahib fretting at a hotel table because there is an African sitting at the next one, and watching the African listening to it in silence as he eats. I have never been able to find any colour bar in Islam, and, dreary though the ignorant and fanatical portion of Islam can be—as dreary as Victorian Imperial Christianity was— it does start off from a firm base about colour. It does not *try* to show it has no colour bar; it has none.

The Italians, unlike the British, did not hide their own peasants, labourers, artisans, from the Somalis and Abyssinians. The first thing I saw on the first day I entered Mogadishu in 1941 was an Italian blacksmith, stripped to the waist, burned dark brown by the sun, working at a forge with three Somali assistants. You would never have seen that in Kenya, and I got out of the truck to take the scene in properly. The Italian blacksmith had skill, and the Somalis knew it, and there was an accord there of a kind I had never seen before with a European and African. But the Italians did not allow Somalis into restaurants in Mogadishu, and an ex-sergeant major of the Italian army, a Somali, who had a deep affection for the Italians, told me that 'things became very difficult after fascism took over. But the genuine Italians ignored the Fascist outlook and we were friends.'

'How do you like freedom?' I asked Ali when a servant brought us two fresh lime drinks. 'Does life feel any different?'

'Now we have got it we have woken up,' he said. 'We see all the problems. We need help. We need friends. We have no money.'

Behind us, a couple of miles from where we were sitting, this jumble of white buildings ended, and then The Shag began, and there was nothing in The Shag anybody wanted except a few goatskins and some incense, unless the Japanese came and started a rock factory or found some use for sand as an export. Wandering in The Shag were Somalis with some of the sharpest intelligences in the continent, nomads who had been forced into being parasites of the camel, for centuries, and could anyone ever find a way of using all that courage and intelligence? This unique people, with their great vanity, and their touching bravery in the way in which they try and cope with their difficult life, have no palm oil, no cocoa, no coffee, gold, no diamonds to sell, only their camels.

Ali thought that God had handed the Somali race the most barren piece of Africa, and it was all I could do not to ask him if he had ever heard that the original fathers of the Somali race were cast out of Arabia into Africa because one of them had stolen The Prophet's slippers. I have never been able to trace the origin of this tale which so used to enrage the Somalis whenever anyone threw it at them during an argument. Ali was gloomy when he discussed Somalia's chances in a world dedicated to buying and selling, and while he talked I was looking across at the two grey towers of the Italian cathedral and recalling the stir in the crowded pews when, with another junior officer, I had walked up its aisle in the uniform of the enemy, to hear mass at a time when none of the conquerors were allowed to fraternize with the Italians.

When the priest came into the pulpit that hot morning to deliver his sermon I saw him look sharply at the two crisp khaki drill uniforms with their twinkling brass buttons and the glistening Sam Browne belts, and I thought our presence might alter the sermon, but I don't think it did. His sermon to his flock, conquered by an army with no Catholic affiliations, and surrounded by a fanatically Mohammedan population, told them to stand together, to have courage, to keep up their morale, and their religion; to rise above their misfortunes and to give an example. It reminded me of when I was a small boy at mass in the Irish quarter of dreary Liverpool, when the flock, addressed by Father Daly or Father Hanlon, were told to stand firm by the faith which Saint Patrick had brought to our pagan ancestors, and to have dignity when the Orange fanatics around us took anti-Catholic action (spitting on your shamrock on Saint Patrick's day, throwing stones at a priest who was on a sick call, or celebrating with grim passion and drums, with King Billy on a white horse leading the procession, the final defeat of the Catholic Irish at the end of the seventeenth century, the defeat which had sent them down into slavery and had finally cast them in rags into the far slums of Chicago, New York, Glasgow, Liverpool, perhaps the slums of Heaven, too.)

How hard I had had to think back, when, with the regiment, the pipers and drummers in their green cloaks and their saffron, had led us, the Irish Catholic soldiers, to mass one week, and led the Irish Protestant soldiers to their service the next.

I knew at mass that morning in Mogadishu how the Italians must be feeling as they sat and listened to that sermon, for, coming together like this as a community they must have felt their oneness, their group identity in a hostile area, so that their personal loneliness was diminished for an hour and they felt some kind of strength and courage, for they could not know how many years they must live in their difficulties in occupied Mogadishu. I came away from that mass convinced that nothing was ever going to put an end to our human idiocy about the loot available in this world to the strong, about war which seemed to be man's favourite pastime, and which had now condemned all these gentle women coming out of the cathedral to nobody knew how many years of poverty and danger in Somalia. Forty-eight of them were slain by the Somalis in one paroxysm a few years afterwards.

I could not see one Italian in the crowds passing where Ali and I were sitting opposite the cathedral.

'There are only a few Italians left here now,' Ali told me. 'The times have changed in many ways.'

CHAPTER ELEVEN

ONCE, at a place called Donkukok, I rose at dawn from the blanket laid on the sand and stared out at the oceans of desolation stretching on every side. Nearby, my patrol of askaris were moving about in preparation for another day's march. A dozen of them, some sitting hunched over the fire gone suddenly shabby and pallid as the yellow sunglare engulfed it in greater fire, others cleaning their rifles, their black leanness shining in the sun. And I wanted to get out of there, soon, and forever. I felt a disgust with all that vast pointlessness stretching about me, and a sick weariness with the sun which was rising for one more day of crushing heat, and in those wastes there is no shade which is not broken, which is not thinly thrown from thorn trees which have no real foliage. There is no escape from the sun until night, and that morning as the sun hit me again and burned through my khaki drill bush shirt I felt faint and exhausted. I wonder why we remember some moments of our lives more keenly than millions of others, moments which add up to very little except a more powerful few minutes of vision or realization, but from which come no particular lessons. But those few moments on that morning, when the flinching eye stared more sharply inward, while appearing to search outward, told me that 'adventure', as it is called, is a luxury and should never be daily life, for you get tired of it so quickly. The bought safari must be infinitely more rewarding as 'adventure' than the permanent safari which is daily life as lived in Africa. That morning I wanted a library, my own books, a room of my own to write in and read in, in a climate in which the eyes could range without being screwed up against incandescent light, and in which old men had happier memories to tell than those of the peculiar desert hell I was marooned in.

And yet I loved it, while hating it that morning. What did I own? All of it lay on the sand in front of me. A set of infantry web equipment, fraying now at the edges, unblancoed, thank God, for over two years. Its water bottle was Italian, my issue bottle cast away long ago to be replaced by this much better Italian one. Two blankets. A bedroll. A very accurate cut down 303 rifle. Two P.36

hand grenades. An Italian ammunition chest containing a dozen tins of meat and vegetable, bully beef, biscuits, a hurricane lamp, about five hundred Crown Bird cigarettes, some gin and whisky, matches, pepper, and the strange useless rock salt we had to use, and a few books, one of which was still unread, called 'Engineering Problems in Paraguay', and which I knew that one night, under some thorn tree, I would be forced to try and read. That was the lot.

I remember the chest from the Carnegie Library of America, which, by some slip made thousands of miles away in an army office, had been allowed to travel to Somalia. I stood around with other officers and dipped into this box of treasure, and we went at it in the same excited, ridiculous way as the infantry, who, when loot-ing among stuff in a captured ruined town, cannot carry the loot anyway, and must leave it for the rear troops who have the transport, flinging the stuff right and left just for the sheer thrill of knowing it is there to have. Book after book I hauled out and dropped. Some old woman with a blue rinse in America, good hearted, anxious to do her part in some scheme for the Allied soldiers across the oceans, had unloaded her grandfather's useless library and here was some of it after its thousands of miles of journey across oceans in convoy, and across deserts to this grey fort where we ransacked the chest with cries of laughter and disbelief. *The Bower of Poetry*, in blue leather, 1863, with grey pen drawings of long tressed girls languish-ing on window seats and gazing out at fallow deer above each sickening poem, *The Chronicles of Penelope Porchinghurst*, or *Nailed to the Masthead, 1881*, and in browned careful handwriting in the front, 'To Hester, lovingly from Mother', (that sudden gust of pity one feels for the vanished unknown dead who have left this fragment of handwriting), volume after volume, until *Engineering Problems in Paraguay* began to look like possible reading for the wilderness. I took *The Bower of Poetry*, sprinkled talcum powder throughout its pages, pressed sprigs of thorn tree among the glistening pages, and inscribed it in front, 'To Bobsy and all the chaps of Bogol Manyo, from Auntie Geraldine and all the girls at Galkayu Hall', and sent it off in a truck convoy to Bob who was desiccating on another frontier. He sent us back a large sack full of rocks and dried camel dung, a Christmas present from Bogol Manyo.

I never read *Engineering Problems in Paraguay*, though I tried many times.

53

Looking down at the small collection of kit that morning at Donkukok, and realizing that it was all I possessed, and had possessed for years, and would possess for what threatened to be years to come, I felt that powerful nausea which must come to all soldiers far from what were called amenities, stripped down to what you could carry on your back in the end. A desert within and a desert without, and miles to go. I hated the war and the desert and the army and the world in general, and then sat down and had breakfast, black tea and a cigarette as the sun rolled above and poured down on us. To hell with it all. Why move? Why walk? For what? To where? For how many times again and again?

I knew I had had all the 'adventure' I could ever want. I would be far happier in a prison cell with a few books and no useless responsibility. I had only one ambition, to write, and I could not write. It took all the will I had to stay interested in this military wandering of which I was now weary. I wrote book after book in my head while walking on that bitter sand, but the only actual creative writing I could do was arms and ammunition returns, official reports, because I had to. One day, though, when this treadmill stopped, I would write something—but it might be too late then, I used to fear. A first novel should be published at twenty-five, and I was twenty-seven, and time was racing away from me, etcetera. My God!

At Donkukok that morning, while the askaris waited, I wrote some more controlledly hysterical demands for transfer, to the Italian front, the Burma front, to the new special unit said to be forming in Egypt, to anywhere at all where there was what one thought of as action, but which really meant a nearness to regular drinking and eating, books, white women, fruit, and all that went with it far from Donkukok and its surroundings.

'Can we load the camels, Effendi?'

'Yes.'

It was no use sending these applications for transfer on the truck that would roll south next month to the headquarters in the gin belt. They would only anger the good and patient colonel who had had enough of all our applications. I knew it gave him pain to read them, for we were splendidly trapped here, officers he could not replace, and another set of applications would take him beyond pain into anger. For we were devoted to this elderly colonel who did all he could for us, and of all the commanders I served under during seven years I never was to find one whom I would serve so gladly and fully. His name was Patrick Mundy, and he knew all about soldiering and campaigning and isolation, and it was with a special and knowing eye he watched us all succeed, or fail, or commit suicide, or go mad, and he tried to get onions and cheese and drink for us, for our particular wilderness came last in a world of finely graded priorities. He could look at you with his experienced blue eyes and know how far you could go, and how far you were never going to get too. He read books and he was witty. He was an unforgettable person.

So that evening, a long way from Donkukok I tore up the applications and watched them blow across the shale and disappear among the rocks.

I had developed a neurosis about spirillum ticks at that time. Africa finds all your fearful areas eventually, and develops them to the full, as you slowly fray in the sun.

One day, slumping down under a thorn tree, I had told the askaris to pitch camp, and then I saw one of the forgotten spirillum ticks wriggling about on the hot red sand towards my sandalled, sockless foot. I turned it over and yes, there it was, the strange white violin shape on the underbody which marked this disease laden bloodsucker. I would not have recognized it for what it was had it not been for Hankson, an officer who had stayed with me to hunt lion before the war above Isiolo in Kenya. The lion were killing the cattle and Hankson had heard about them, and being on leave he came to join me in pursuit of them. He was still in the early blood-lust stage of East African shooting, which all newcomers go through, a kind of fever, like looting, caused by living in a world swarming with herds of game.

He told me he was scared of spirillum fever down in the frontier region where he was serving, and one day he showed me a spirillum tick. Months later I got the news that he had been bitten by a spirillum tick and had been invalided out with the resulting fever. The disease can kill you, or ruin your heart if you live.

When I saw that first spirillum tick under the thorn tree in Somalia, I remembered Hankson, and after that I always looked for spirillum ticks when camping at night, and always seemed to find them.

As always, one had to give this kind of thing up, or you would drift slowly into the fretful, querulous obsession peculiar to Africa. We all developed these manias after some months alone in the rocks and sand, a sort of hobby with which to fill the emptiness, but a dangerous hobby.

To live in isolation requires training and experience. It is astonishing, the first discovery that one is unable, or afraid, or so mentally unfurnished that isolation becomes loneliness and that one cannot live with oneself and learn to screw down the wings so anxiously beating for flight. It is a very different thing when one has decided to 'do a safari', for pleasure or study, because one has chosen to, and which will end at a certain time. But to not know how many years the unchosen safari will go on soon gnaws at the edges of the will, especially when it is young and anxious to do a million other exciting things. Learning to wait was the good thing we of that small scattered unit learned best, I think, though on the whole the years I spent on that silent burning moon did me more harm than good. Harm that is in relation to other people, for though I could live with myself I did not learn to live with other people for years, and even now find, to my regret, that I can live without other people if necessary. Always gregarious, one had become a gregarious solitary. If people were there, splendid. If they were not, it was just a pity, and that is not a good thing in the long run. One had learned to live alone within one's head; after much anguish it had had to be learned. I noticed this in my companions, especially those with the tendency to absorption into the bush life of the tribes among whom we were sunk. I say sunk because there is nothing fine or noble about savagery and illiteracy and superstition, no matter how splendid looking the warriors and the women. After a good long dose of savagery it is interesting how much one has learned to prefer the gentle and the sophisticated. Primitivism is a very much overrated way of life, and is merely pitiful in essence, no matter how fascinating the carvings and the masks and the quiet zoomorphic ravings on stone and wood, those endless circles in which the tribe has wandered and lost itself, waiting for the stranger to come with the message, even when it leads to the atom bomb. It doesn't matter how you kill your brother, with a wooden spear or an atom bomb, it is a bore and a waste, but you can't do very much with the energy behind a spear, at least. I suppose Hitler's willing druids with their runic stones and their collections of skulls, and their gas ovens, were proof enough that it is easy to be primitive again, even after any number of centuries.

After the enormous orgy of torture and massacre in Europe and Asia, I felt it was impossible for any white man to preach again, self-righteously, about goodness and peace, to any non-white man. And that shame may have been the reason, bigger than African and

56

Eastern restlessness, which caused the white man to pack his kit and go home after the second world war. We must have all felt something of that shame, I think, and acted upon it without really knowing why. That was why, in 1945, I stood at the back of an army cinema and watched with a sort of sly, ashamed fascination when African soldiers were watching the film of the liberation of Belsen, and the other film showing the bulldozed hills of corpses. I watched the African soldiers when the lights went up and I am certain that many of them were looking at us, the white men, with a strange, new kind of eye. They were as appalled as the rest of us by the scenes in Germany, but they had an extra reason for puzzlement, and perhaps they knew that until the white man could manage his own anthropoid passions he should stop feeling superior to blacks merely because he was a white man. There was no doubt that the African recognized, by 1945, that it had long been agreed that the white man was a very special and superior sort of person who had been sent into this world by a sort of guardsman-public school educated God to rescue the non-white world from its savagery and dirt. They agreed no longer with that. Mau Mau itself was a scream of anthropological rage, a puzzled and bloody turning upon the Christian varieties of religion which the white men themselves did not bother with. It was not enough for the Kikuyu that God should be a good chap with the right background, a gentleman who lived in a church reserved for white men.

Despite this I have never subscribed to the school of worship of the African primitive, or any other primitive, Nazi or Stalinist. The whole world, it seemed to me during those long nights on the sand under the thorn trees, was in need of rescue, as one world of people. I have never believed that any race of people is better than another race. They are all splendid when allowed to be, and brutes too when the chains break, and they need a government now, and in about a century or two they will have it, if they can resist the longing to smash it all up when boredom sets in. For men will be bored without war for some time to come, that oldest way out and pastime of all, an historic habit.

'What do you want most?' I once asked an old Somali.

'To be well governed, but to be left alone,' he told me.

I often thought of that and found that I agreed with it, but how to get it?

57

CHAPTER TWELVE

IT was very strange to be walking alongside Ali in the white glare of the sun, feeling the surge of memories certain places in the town aroused; memories of a time which seem bruised with all the violence and tragedy of the period, violence which had thinned in the memory in the years away from the scene. As usual the memory had held hard to the good and amusing things of that time, the friendships which had been so precious in those conditions, the comical happenings which had learned to overlay the horrific and the brutal. Here on the left was the spot in which an Italian, a Somali dagger locked in his bones, had bled to death so that his skin was snow white when he was found, and over there was the restaurant, its wooden latticework the same faded yellow, in which poor doomed H. had fallen face first into the enormous plate of piled spaghetti.

Of all the suicides H. was the most unlikely person, I thought, to take that lonely, despairing way out, though what was in character was the way he used an automatic weapon to do it, firing a burst into himself, for he was always thorough, painstaking in everything he did. Perhaps he was too painstaking, too thorough, too scrupulous. He was in a far off place when he killed himself and I often wondered if he ever wanted his body to be found, if he did not wish to vanish altogether so that nobody would ever know what had happened to him.

I looked into the restaurant after twenty years, and it had not changed, except that the customers were now all Somalis, and I could remember the manager being delighted when I used to ask him to play records of Carlo Buti singing those *troppo dolce, troppo triste* songs he specialized in. It was here that H. had got into his trouble, when, frayed after many months with us on operations up in The Shag, and well filled with whisky he had gone into this restaurant for the thing he had craved for during those months in the bush—a large plate of spaghetti *con sugo di pomodoro*. None of us in that group of officers which had just left for Mogadishu, were in our right minds, I feel, looking back now. Yet you do not know when you are near the end of your resilience, when your nervous structure is too tattered to last out, and H. had had a few months too long in hopeless places, and when he once found himself walking through a shower of poisoned arrows, while pursuing some raiders, he felt, as he told me back in the fort, that he was 'due for a change of scene, even a lousier scene than this one'. He was physically tough and could walk as far as his Somalis, but he was more bitter than most of us because he could not get a transfer out of our particular purgatory of frustration. After the operations I recommended him for a captaincy, which he got.

He was not able to cope with the *piatto abbondante* of spaghetti when it came, and weary after his long journey across The Shag to Mogadishu, battered inside his head by those miserable months behind him, and made sleepy by whisky, he feel face forward into the piled tomato-sauce covered spaghetti. Conduct Unbecoming and all that regimental, but it was a very long way from here back to the world of the whitewashed coal dumps, the Mess dinners, the glittering quarter guard, and the lively climate of the drilled battalion, a whole desert away. When he awoke to the Italian manager's gentle prodding he stared up at that fat, kindly Italian who knew a sand-happy officer when he saw one. H.'s face was covered with spaghetti and tomato sauce, and it hung from his big moustache in strings.

'It's a bad show, isn't it, signor,' H. said sadly. 'It looks as if you'll have to feed me with a spoon yourself. *I* can't manage it,' and then fell asleep again, until the Military police arrived. He lost his new captaincy.

Soon he found himself in another moon landscape among armed bands of savages again, alone, and when we heard of this reward, after his long dose of desert with us, we felt it might have been better had he been given a desk job for a few months instead, nearer to ice-boxes, a plentiful supply of cold beer, somewhere in Mogadishu where the going could be so good when you knew your way around. He must have thought it over one night among the rocks of his new parish and perhaps saw no end to this procession of days and nights in isolation, and, used up, he had fired half a submachine gun magazine into himself. Died longing for more Active Service, with a little more civilization to hand than had been obtainable during the past three years. I often think of him and wish that some accident by some headquarters clerk had sent him

59

mistakenly to a unit far from that country which had finally eaten him up.

As Ali and I strolled through Mogadishu he asked me about communism, looking searchingly into my eyes as he spoke, and I told him I had never heard of it, did not know what it was, which did not seem to satisfy him. Once, in a certain country during a time of tension, I had a police agent pounce on a radio I had in my station wagon. He was going to confiscate it as a transmitter, and ever since then I have hated police agents, out of a sort of boredom with their pipe dreams of reporting in to the boss with the big news about the spy. He asked me if I would like to see the Russian Embassy and I told him I had seen a couple of them in other places and that would satisfy me for a few years to come. I got him talking about the Arabs and as we walked I went on with my awakened memories of this place which seemed now so much less handsome, so much more shabby than it had appeared to us in The Shag when we looked to it as the fountainhead of drink, rations and mail.

My foot went through the crumbling sidewalk, up to the knee, and Ali helped to drag the leg out again, explaining that a recent fall of rain had loosened the old cement up, and there was so little money to do things with. This was outside the old Italian café where we used to sit over coffee when on leave, when the novelty of plentiful alcohol had worn off, where there had been a barber who used to shear the long hair we brought down to Mogadishu. It was now some kind of headquarters for a youth movement, but swarming with old men in skull caps who were talking excitedly about the chances of more rain to come. Nothing can be done for the poor old men of a finished culture when the new time comes among them like a denial of their very need to exist at all.

You come across these old men in all countries with long, unbroken race memories and tradition, some of them holding the remains of cultures in their illiterate heads, in those marvellous memories unimpaired by reading, knowledge which waited too long for the new popular interest in archaeology, folklore and anthropology to come and rescue it and give it the dignity which would make it respected by the youth who despise the old men. You can find these old men in Ireland, India, Africa, the remains of the ancient world which was defeated and cast aside for the worship of money and machinery during the time of the alien imperial power which had smashed their world so pitilessly. All their conquerors could do was consolidate and administer what they had

60

conquered, and despise the losers, often degrading them. It is interesting how a few generations after the conquest, the descendants of the conquerors start seeking for the bits of manuscript, the spoken traditions, the sad curios of the thing their forefathers trampled upon as not worth consideration. Germans, Poles, Swedes, Frenchmen, Englishmen trying to piece together remains of race memory in Ireland which might give them a clue to the kind of world that existed in Gaul before the Romans stamped it down into something which paid tribute and obeyed orders on time, and meanwhile, firing rockets in the first probes for the journeys which will carry them and their hungers into other worlds —where there might be new people to control, administer, order about, civilize. If there are people there they are bound to be inferior, that is to say, strange, different, due for instructions, overdue for conquest. The whole bloody journey of the powers had been, it seems, to create consumers for consumer goods, and one must hasten to admit how arduously one pursues those consumer goods, while trying to despise them, so that one's grief for the shattered civilizations is comical, and yet undeniable.

In a desert like this Somalia, cut off long ago from the culture of Islam, and left with a religion which became dried and narrow, fit for desert nomads who lived in fear of each other, the old men became only rejected, tired warriors who recalled times when the fighting was heavier, spoke of the Mad Mullah as the last hero, yet even so there is something pathetic in their wistful bewilderment with the new world which has fallen upon them in dark glasses and text books.

'He will die in a day or two, that old one, Effendi,' one of my Somali askaris said to me one morning. We were camped beside a waterhole in the northern Mudugh, watching a Somali camel train amble slowly away towards the flaring yellow glow on the horizon where the sun was about to rise. The thin chill of the desert night was dissolving in the rising heat and the askari was pointing to an old man who was stumbling along on the tail of the caravan, far behind the young warriors with their spears.

Nothing would be said one morning when that old man could no longer get up from his sleeping place as the camels were loaded. He would lie there and watch the *kariya* of his group move away without him, knowing it was done, this life-long wandering between waterholes, and he would be composed for his end. There would be no weeping, no cries of despair, no questioning. He would lie there, old and finished, and await his death, and a day or so later a couple of the young men of the *kariya* would come back to that place to find the corpse. There may be a *sheik* with them, one who knows the law and has the right to ritual. One of the young men will open up a hole in the parched sand while the others wrap the body of the dead elder in a piece of cloth. The *sura* for the dead, *Yassin*, will be recited. A circle of stones will be laid round the grave and the *sheik* will gravely go through the short ceremony, intoning in a mournful voice the farewell and the consignment to God. 'God made you from the dust,' the *sheik* tells the wilderness, 'He gave you life until this last day here, and now he has returned you to the dust. You are alone. If a stranger asks you who made you, answer "Allah made me. There is only one God, Allah, and Mahomet is his prophet".'

Then two angels come to the grave and stand invisible guard there. Swallowed up into eternity, the old man has vanished under the sand. The men who buried him hasten back to their *kariya*, to the camels, tearless, griefless, for how can a man weep at what is inevitable, as inevitable as birth?

Here was the old Savoia restaurant still closely latticed against the glare, and it was just here, I remembered, as I was about to report in to headquarters for details about my next place of exile, that I had heard a cry of surprise, turned round, saw that small, neat, laughing figure in white Italian uniform, and, to hell with non-fraternization, we embraced and slapped each other's backs, for it was Carlo. I had not seen him for well over a year, had not seen him since he had waded out into the surf, a thousand miles north at Gardafui, beside the sick officer lying on a stretcher carried by four Somalis to the rusty iron barge. The ship bound for Mombasa had been lying a mile off and Carlo had volunteered to accompany the sick British officer to Mombasa, for the ship had no doctor.

I had warned him to be careful before he went ashore in Mombasa as I had heard of other Italians, down in Kenya on a trip under our auspices from Somalia, being arrested and swept into the prisoner-of-war machine. Carlo would not believe that the military police would interfere with him, for after all he was part of our machinery in this wilderness, was a doctor, was on a journey of mercy and necessity.

They arrested him in Mombasa as soon as he had delivered the sick officer. They put him into a prisoner of war camp. It was a year before he saw Somalia again, and when I met him that day outside the Savoia he told me he felt bitter. I told him that he must know that all armies had this brainless, disciplined, and even vengeful machinery far back at base, and that that machine was there to arrest strangers in enemy uniform.

'*Una bibita*,' I had said to him, and we had gone into the Savoia, had a drink together, separated, and never saw each other again. He died in Italy in 1961. Since the war I had often tried to find him, had written to the Italian army authorities in Rome, but never was able to trace him, and it was in a strange way that I did come across his tracks, too late. I had corresponded on and off with a friend in Italy, and not knowing that she had known Carlo in Somalia, had described him, named him in a letter in 1961, and had said how I wished I could see him again and talk of Kalanka and our time there together twenty years ago. Back had come a letter to say that my friend had known him well in Italy, and that he had just died. My friend had telephoned Carlo's wife immediately after getting my letter from Ireland, and his wife had said that it was very strange, for Carlo too had often wondered where I was and had wished we could meet again. So, as I stood outside the Savoia restaurant in 1962, where we had last met, the fact of his death and of how very near I had been to meeting him again, had I only mentioned his name in one of my letters to this friend in Italy during the past years, became real for the first time.

It was all I could do to keep up the conversation with Ali about the possible discovery of oil by Americans in Somalia. Here were all the white buildings, the same though shabbier, and inside the Savoia was the table at which we had sat and had that last drink together while he made his usual, glittering, sharp jokes and gave me advice about how to stay healthy in the sick piece of country to which I thought I was about to be transferred. For a moment I could see why the desert Somalis, close all the time to death, never complained about it, never sought to deny it, accepted it as the end of the long and mysterious series of accidents which animate the forty thousand-odd days between birth and death. It was Hashim who had said to me once, 'You go that way, to some town, and your life is changed completely. But had you gone to another town instead it would have changed just as completely, but it would have been another kind of life altogether. It is no use trying to be exactly right. We have no control of the future, only of what we have let happen to us.'

63

Ali and I turned down a side-street into the alleys where the houses were low, and I could smell incense burning again. I asked Ali if he ever saw any people from the tribe called Malablei from the Webi Shabeli river who used to dance here during their ceremonies, and he said he had seen them in Mogadishu but thought little of them.

'All those river people are very strange,' I told him. 'They know many curious things.'

CHAPTER THIRTEEN

THE first time I saw the Malablei dancers in the narrow streets behind Mogadishu's façade they were wearing their goat masks, real goat skulls cut so that they covered the dancers' faces, and the long horns twisted upwards from them. There was something very sinister about the slow, jogging, turning of these dancers as they obeyed the thudding drums carried by the solemn men who so slowly turned and jogged with them. The tall Somalis of nomad blood stood back and made way for these black negroid looking bodies with goat masks on top, men who had forgotten all around them.

These Malablei who were here on a visit from the big river a few miles south, who had been in this country long before their taller invaders, the Somalis, seemed now as if they owned it again. There was a dark denial of all non-pagan religion in their pagan masks, so dedicated to the goat-power, and there was a kind of threat in their sensuous, sidling, circling movements, so that their conquerors, those tall, religious Somalis who despised them, kept well back and let them slowly pass through the streets with their cunning-handed drummers. They represented the real Africa, the Africa which has invented a thousand more new religions since the several hundred versions of Christianity began to puzzle them, the continent of the enormous brown rivers and of packed trees and alligator men, leopard and lion men, rainmakers and cursers and poisoners, and these haunting yet menacing drums were the pulse of it, brought out into the temporary streets, as if to show that not very much had happened to Africa yet.

As always, those drums had stirred me. They give you a feeling of the immensity and the age of Africa, these drums, and they beat their way right into you, right down into the invisible and forgotten areas of the soul, which open for their sound. Two of us had once danced to them, up on the Juba river, near Dolo, with about five hundred tribesmen and women who had welcomed us in our two dusty armoured cars.

'*Captanka Armati wai,*' they had chanted in Somali and Italian

65

gibberish, dancing round us, clapping their hands to the long booming drums on the flat red sand by that wide river. Swept into them, into their rhythm and into that mindless happiness, caught by the pounding drums around us, we had danced with them, clapping our hands with theirs, celebrating our being there in their raided wilderness with these machine guns in the armoured cars, while we waited for their chief to come and meet us. We were in sweaty shirts and shorts, bare legged, sandals on our feet, hatless, and we danced faster as the drummers worked up their tempo, all those white teeth; bony, black handsome faces spinning in the thin red dust which we sent up until it hung in the trees. Then the feast of camel milk and meat as the moon came up.

That evening in Mogadishu when I had watched the goat-masked Malablei dancers has always stayed in my memory as an unexpected manifestation among the buildings, of an Africa which may never completely disappear, which lived on through centuries while to the north Greece and Rome rose and fell. They never came down here, those conquerors in helmets. They went to cold Gaul and Britain instead. Those Malablei and their brother tribes along the hot river were still part of the forest, of its spirit, and they looked it as they danced through the Somalis who knew nothing of their secrets, their magic, their black mystery. It was K. who was to be privileged to see what these river people could bring out of darkness with their drums and chants.

I was stationed for a while on the southern Webi Shabeli river, at a time when it was very disturbed following the collapse of the Italian army and its retreat. When the thin cement of European police and order is torn off, a cement which has frozen the normal processes of an occupied country's life, history begins again, usually violently. The only way a country is truly conquered by another is when all the original inhabitants are slain, wiped out completely, unless they are mumbling themselves away into their own kind of cultural death, like the aborigines of Australia. But it is the police, with the threat of soldiers farther behind, who lay on the thin cement of alien peace in conquered countries containing the aboriginal people still vitally alive, and on the Webi Shabeli, as all over Somalia, they drew their knives in 1941. They had to, for an order had collapsed around them.

It is very hard for Europeans to realize how dull, how heavy is the crushing boredom of the order, the habit, the daily round of the work-day which they brought with swords into South America,

66

Africa, India, Ireland, everywhere where a completely different set of appreciations had been at agonized work for centuries. That the Irish tribe-families slew each other gave the invaders no right to take their country, while churls by the thousand groaned in Britain. That the Aztecs piled up mountains of hearts in bloody temples was not why Cortes went there and wrecked the world he found. He went for gold, just as the English went to Ireland for land, to Africa and India for raw materials, for money and power. Most pathetic of all was why the Italians went to Somalia, because there was nothing else left of Africa to take, the Nordics having carved up the rest among themselves. Yet ironically enough, while the conquered everywhere resented losing their country and their freedom, they nearly always took advantage of the policed peace forced upon them, nearly always relaxed, their swords left at home, yet they wanted their country back for themselves, while enjoying the 'peace of the grave', as Pandit Nehru once called it, in which they now toiled under aliens. And they revolted when they saw a hope of success. But time is always on the side of the original owners, if they can only survive.

On the Webi Shabeli river in 1941 the tribes refused to give any more labourers to the Italian plantations, for, having been liberated from Italian rule, after long British propaganda telling them to help the preparing invaders break the Italians, they could not see why those plantations must work again to give food to the world that was still at war outside. They said they were finished with working for white men, and they went amok among the Italian plantations, until some of us appeared with platoons and weapons and started to lay down the thin cement again. When I told them that I had come to find labour for the plantations they took off into the bush. Africans hate work for its own sake. They cannot understand how it can be a virtue to toil regularly at dull tasks, keeping to a piece of tin and glass called a clock. I sympathized with these people who had had enough of working on plantations, and then sent out scouts to bring in their chiefs. The first chief to appear was a fine, tall old man, old enough to be my great grandfather. As a young man he had fought long and stubbornly as a warrior of his tribe, the Bimal, against the Italian invaders. He was grave and stern, most concerned to hear that I had come here to the first clearing beside the river to ask the chiefs to send labourers to the deserted plantations. He stood in front of me, a staff polished by years of handling stuck in the brown soil in front of his sandalled feet, his bald head shining in the sun, regarding me solemnly as he listened to my request, which he knew would become an order if not acceded to as a request.

'The young men will not go back to the *colonia*, Signor Tenente,' he told me, shaking his head. 'They will not go back to those heavy Italian tasks and live in those *colonia* villages. Your coming here as an army was the very thing that freed them from that life. I cannot ask them to go back to it.' Here was a real chief, one who did not rush to offer his people and get a medal, a certificate, a reputation for 'reliability', 'loyalty' (that word which has sent so many to their deaths when the revolt against the alien comes).

'*I* will be organizing the work contracts,' I told him. 'The *colonia* is finished. *I* will regulate the work tasks, and the pay, and I will see to it that they are not ill treated in any way.' Most of the Italian plantation managers had been good to their labourers, but there had been the usual small quota of white gods from over the sea who felt better when Africans were slaving for them. As I finished speaking to the chief another old man came in, dramatically, pointed his finger at me, and shouted, 'You can shoot me this minute, but I will never give you one of my people as a labourer on a plantation.' A crowd formed behind him, drawn from under the far trees by his fierce, declamatory shout, one with him in his anger.

'I cannot shoot you, old man,' I told him. 'Go and sit down again under the trees until I send for you. You have made your point and your people are proud of you.' When I smiled all the people laughed, not unkindly, and the old man narrowed his eyes and stared at me for a few seconds.

'I mean it,' he said. 'I would die rather than give you my men to work on the plantations. I thought you had come here to put an end to that.'

'There is a difference in being made to work, and wanting to work,' I said. 'It's right that your people are enjoying freedom from being taken to work which they had not chosen, but soon a time will come when they will want to earn money again, and it will be on the same plantations but under different conditions. I am here to look after you, to prevent raiding and killing, not to make you work, yet I have been asked by the new military government to get food from here for the soldiers who are fighting to end *colonias* everywhere, and we cannot get that food unless your men will help to grow it on the plantations.'

'We do not want to work for the Italians anymore,' the old man said.

68

'You will actually be working for me,' I told him, 'just as the Italians will be working for the military government. The food must be grown somehow. Think it over for a day and then come and see me again and tell me what you have thought. I am not here to arrest you, or force you. I am asking you to find men among your tribes who will work on the plantation under new contracts which I will arrange.'

'We will think over what you have said,' the first old chief said to me. 'We are glad you are giving us time to speak this matter out.' He beckoned to a man nearby, who came over obediently, a tall youth with a shock of thick woolly hair. 'Take off your cloth and show the officer your back,' he said sharply. The young man slipped the cotton cloak off his shoulders and turned to show me the healed, shining, grey scars of whip strokes on his back.

'That was done at the whipping post at Shalambot,' the chief said to me. 'My people wanted to kill the Italians when their army was retreating, but I would not let them. Are *you* going to kill the Italians or not?' He stared into my eyes.

'No,' I said. 'They are defeated. One cannot kill those who did not die in the battle. One gives them a chance to live another kind of life. Would *you* kill unarmed people after a battle?'

'No,' he said. 'I wouldn't. We wanted to hear you speak on that subject. It was said that the new army would kill all the Italians. Do you now say that work and pay will be just?'

'Yes. Discuss it and we will meet again tomorrow.'

When men, Spaniards, Englishmen, Frenchmen, Russians, or those wearing their insignia, sit at desks in countries not their own, but borrowed by gunfire, or bribes, or handy accident, tell the inhabitants (the actual winners), what is going to happen to them tomorrow, they cannot help acting the strangers, as if they, and what they feel they represent, are going to last for centuries here, in this country which is not theirs, and may last for all eternity. They cannot help feeling that. They have to feel it, or go, resign, be court martialled, cease to believe in what they only half believe anyway—that they have come here with a special message; in fact they must administer the accident they find themselves involved in. And it takes acting. Acting is important to kings, barristers, administrators, judges, officers, all who assume cousinship to God. And I felt it that hot, sweaty day beside the Webi Shabeli when I sat with six chiefs and listened to their decision.

Of course they were going to send the labourers. They had numbered them off already. Of course they saw that the two white races had fought each other in Africa, in front of their eyes, one white race being downed, and of course they saw that this made no difference at all in who owned the plantations, and who slaved on them in the heat. The Italians owned the plantations, and would own them as long as the new conquerors backed them in their ownership (though the actual owners were sitting around me in the sun that day, and would never forget it), so they would supply the labourers. I told them I was very happy, for them, for me, for the government, for the Italians, and for the human race in general. Men must work with one another, tolerate each other, help each other, etcetera, and I meant it, though not quite for the reasons I gave at that time and in that situation. I began to understand politics, government lying.

Yet there is something touching about being an administrator, and one can see how easily it can become a habit, and then a conviction, a way of life if carried on long enough with enough power behind to ensure its continuance. And it had been the history of the human race up to then, this taking of other people's countries, the setting up of incomprehensible governments, the governing, the policing, the pensioning, the retirement, the memoirs detailing the failings of the governed (who yet might rise to civilization).

Even then, in 1941, 2 and 3, I sensed that just as it was about to die, the British Empire had almost risen above the cash and factory image which it had so long worked for, above even its stuffy racial prejudices sometimes, and it was too late then. But it was not till I got to the Fourteenth Army in Burma, with its many races, that I saw what the British Empire might have been, despite the fears felt by those upstairs in London about the servants downstairs. Too late after too much cant.

It was the oldest of the chiefs who, when the first drafts of labourers for the plantations came in, said to me what I had always known I felt, but had never heard spoken by one of the subject races.

'We are lending you the labourers,' he told me. 'But only because you are living with us here on the river, and because you have spoken well, and not because we recognize this new government which has replaced the Italians. We do not want to be ruled by any strangers anymore. They beat us with cannon, but every inch of this land is ours. Ours. It can never belong to any strangers. Men cannot live under strangers who have taken their lands. Never. If

70

I had a spear and you had nothing and I came and took your house from you, and made you work in your own garden for me, you would not like that. That is what they have done, these governments. And it must come to an end now. You can tell them that, for that is what we all feel.' There was a good opportunity for some cant here, to tell him about the docks, the roads, the harbours, and all the handout material about how good it was to be ruled by clever white men, but I let it go. I agreed with every word he had said, while looking grave, and enigmatic, and non-committal. These chiefs, when young, had fought against the Italian invaders, and this tribe had been difficult to subdue. All these people everywhere would have to be let free, left alone, lectured to no more, or this war would be as useless as the last one.

CHAPTER FOURTEEN

About a thousand miles north from this crowded street in which Ali and I were walking in the sunglare Humf lay buried. He was killed while I was in Burma, a friend I grieve over, and it was over there in that palm shaded house, its white stucco shabby and greying now, that I last met him, in 1943 when I was certain I either had cancer of the throat, or something like it.

Fear is interesting in the way it can either drip in slowly, given time and circumstance, or blast in like a flash of flame in a millionth of a second. But I did not know that the body and mind can make their own arrangements for you by forcing buried fear into an actual lump, a rocklike lump in your throat, until Humf explained it to me.

'It's just strain,' he told me laughing. 'Strain caused by fear, and fear caused by the fear of going wrong, of balancing a situation too long, as you have been doing lately up country.'

Humf was a marvellous doctor, and greatly interested in the effects of the wilderness on each of us. He knew the breakdown signs in the eyes immediately, and *always* fought to get leave for an officer when he saw these signs.

'Isolation among the wolves,' he used to say, 'can bring about exactly the same effects as a good long drenching of shellfire. The body has to find some getout.' He always referred to the desert tribes as 'the wolves', rather fondly.

'But listen, Humf,' I protested, 'this is an actual *lump*. Here.' I showed him. 'I can't swallow. I can actually feel it there. It hurts.'

He shook his head patiently. 'I'm telling you,' he said, 'it's just strain. If you hadn't ended the operations when you did, you'd have cracked up completely. This 'lump' as you imagine it to be, is merely your body's getout, its effort to help you crack up and get sick, and—' he grinned—'have the right to desert your post among the wolves, honourably. That's all. Now do what I tell you. Go and get drunk with your friends. They're in the bar now. Get drunk for a few nights. Talk all night. Go to a few parties. There's no actual lump. It's quite normal to get apparently ill, when you're ready to have a rest and you can't.'

He was right. I woke up with a hangover about a day and a half later, the sun burning on me through the open window of the room, the bed soaked with sweat, and while in the shower clapped my hand to my throat and found that the lump, which had been hardening there for about two months, was gone. And I sat down after drying myself and thought about how remarkable that was.

What would have been the strange machinery of emotion which could have caused that actual lump in my throat, which had got worse, so that I had to make an effort to swallow towards the end of my term in that worst of all places from which I had just come, emptied, sickened, tired, and shattered after a truly demoniacal malaria? It was true that I had not enjoyed what I had had to do up there, nor had the others. That was why drink was good at night. You could feel the fourth drink slowly melting the iron tension in the head and body, and you could feel your frame sighing with relief. It was the third year that that lump had gone, and I had never had a nice soft job on the coast, in the gin belt, and had begun to want one, and to resent wanting one, preferring to belong up there with the friends who preferred it too, and who all wanted a nice soft job for a while on the coast.

I did not like to think that my machinery could invent that psychological lump for me, preferring to believe that one was in full control of the emotional works all the time.

It helped me to understand the crackups, that lump, and the suicides. It became obvious to me that when you were done, and ready to bend, you would not know what you were doing, and would do it. It was obvious that you could not live in violence and threat for overlong periods and not be diverted into those side lanes of fear and doubt. It was all too personal, too close, too tiring to one's reverence for charity, and pity. It was having to live like a savage for too long, becoming casual about brutality, revenge, bloodlust, which set up intense inner struggle, disgust, while all the time you had to stay the wary, watchful, confident white stranger who revelled, apparently, in this warrior world where the standards of fighting spirit had been set by the 'Mad Mullah' twenty-odd years before. Many of one's opponents, proud to be known as *Dub-Ad*, had been in his ranks. For a time it was feared that another 'Mad Mullah' might arise, but those of us close to the Somalis knew it was unlikely.

73

'Well, how's the cancer tonight?' Humf asked me in the bar that evening.

'Gone,' I told him. We laughed.

'But of course, it's not funny,' Humf said. 'I've asked for a psychologist to make a report on the officers up country. It's not just the general tension of living among "the wolves", it's the long stretches, a year and more, you're having to do up there without proper food, without civilization in fact. You'd be surprised what other forms of "lump" in the throat I've dealt with during the past couple of years. Symptoms, that's all, of used-upness. But there's nothing I can do about it.'

I told Humf that I actually enjoyed living among 'the wolves', while hating it too, that when I was away on my annual twenty-eight days leave I longed to go back again. He nodded.

'That's because you're a romantic,' he said, 'like your friends. You've learned a common unit feeling, living a life that only a few of you live. It can get so bad that officers have to be *ordered* to go on leave. In other words, if you've got to live rough, then live the roughest, with your friends. That's romanticism, and highly necessary in an army, of course.'

He then explained to me some of the forms of mania he had glanced at in some of the other officers who had consulted him. These manias and tensions were dissolved quite often by action or leave, but it was usually responsibility involving the possibility of a wrong decision at any moment, especially among a volatile and violent people, which found the hidden cracks in one. A decision, no matter how many hours, weeks, months, it has been coming up, or considered, takes a moment only, and there is usually no going back, and probably fear comes from the fear of making the wrong decision, and a wrong decision could mean a disaster too far away from base to be, well let's say it, safe. So it probably came down to a rationalization about personal fear in the end. However you try and shape it, personal fear, of disgrace or death, must lie behind this kind of neurosis. The root of the erosion, though, lay in the fact that one sought so hard to keep peace among tribes who despised it, while one often waited, through frustration and anger, stoked by climate and living conditions, to have it out with them in the way they wanted it, through violence. One swung between pity and rage, while slowly one eroded. When the violence came, however, one hated it, and one came to know how it damaged one's slightly phoney ideals about how Man longed only for goodness and peace,

74

whereas, actually, he loved fighting and knew he shouldn't. Hypocrisy is the keystone of civilization and should be cherished.

Greater than your own petty anxieties and fears, though, was the sense of desolation when you saw the nomads dying or dead on the hot bitter rock of their prison, the wilderness; and made worse by the realization that they did not resent it, did not want a washing machine or to live forever, and that they despised pain and death, perhaps the true nihilists, these famished wanderers of the wastes come to their bloody rest by treachery. Their scorn of death was both depressing and exalting, as your civilized and primitive selves tried to be truthful.

They always made me feel, those nomad dead, as if they announced to the world that there was no purpose after all behind life, and that it was all like this beneath the tapestry, loneliness and vengeance and waste. I think that that was what I hated most about their wilderness; that it showed you how the world had once been, everywhere, and could be again if the compassionate will of civilized men was ever finally defeated by the spirit of death, which the scientists have packaged at last, and who know, far better than the warrior generals, that there can be no next war, only the last one.

CHAPTER FIFTEEN

I recognized Finn's house across the busy sandy street, the lattice work still faded green, the yellow walls still cracked and scabrous, the palms as wilted and as dusty as ever, and I wondered where he was now, tall, lean, patient, hospitable Finn in his dark glasses and big upturned moustache. The sun beat down hard on his house, and if I knew Finn, at all, he was now in some African wilderness, stroking his moustache and listening to a tribesman explain some finer points about a murder (known as 'a killing' to the tribesman).

'Who lives in that house?' I asked Ali.

'A merchant,' he said. 'Do you like that house?'

'Yes. It is very attractive,' I told him. It had been two o'clock in the morning when I had gone to that house for the last time, invited there by a telephone call from Finn. He had wanted me to interrogate an Italian who had been found wandering in the desert, a kettle in his hand, by an askari patrol.

Finn was in one of his very stiffly starched and pressed khaki drill uniforms, buttons glittering, thick dark hair brushed back, great moustache sharp against his haggard, big-boned handsome face, tall and massively shouldered, the living embodiment of the linen-shirted Gaelic warriors who had met the English with a crash on many an Irish field, warriors and strangers, until time had melted down their race memory into Tom Moore's honeyed songs for drawing rooms.

'He's in there,' Finn said, pointing to his living room. 'He's round the bend, poor fella. A kettle, mind you, that was his kit for the desert. Let's give him a drink and you can question him. He's in a hell of a state.'

The Italian was even bigger than Finn, a man of about six feet three inches in height, grey haired, tragic-eyed, sitting at a table and staring at the wall with tears in his eyes. He looked at us accusingly and when I greeted him in Italian and asked him how he was he shook his head wearily.

'I must go home,' he said. 'I *must*.' He rose to his feet. 'Give me

76

my kettle and let me go home. I will bother nobody. Nobody, signore. I will walk it and bother nobody. But I must go.'

Finn poured a shot of O.B., Cioffi's local brandy, and handed it to the Italian who held it in a trembling hand, and when Finn and I had a drink we both sat down, and the Italian sat down too and stared at the wall again.

'Where is home?' I asked the Italian.

'Italy,' he said.

'And you were walking there?'

'I am walking there,' he said, nodding sadly. 'It is the only sensible thing to do. I cannot rot here any longer in this hell. My family are bombed, Italy is being destroyed, and I am here in this hell in misery. I must go home. I must. I will bother nobody.'

'You are not bothering anybody,' I told him. 'We will do anything we can to help you.' He jumped to his feet, smiling, his hands held out to take ours in friendship, a sad smile on his lean, red face.

'Then let me go,' he said. 'Just let me go. I had left this hellish town and was in the desert with my kettle when your soldiers arrested me. Give me a pass and let me walk home. I cannot stay here while Italy is being destroyed. Please give me the pass and I will go.'

'Finish your drink first,' I told him. 'We have plenty of time yet. Sit down and finish your drink. What were you going to do with the kettle? Had you nothing else but your kettle?'

He sat down again, sighing, staring at the wall, thinking. 'The kettle,' he said, 'was for condensing the sea water. That's all you need, a kettle and a small tin. The askaris took my small tin.'

'You were going to walk along the sea coast right up to Egypt, and then sail across to Italy?' I said.

'That's my plan,' he said. 'It's the only way.'

I asked him if he had ever seen these wild, burning coasts, and if he knew of the thousands of miles of it peopled by dangerous tribes all the way to Egypt. He looked me in the eye and laughed.

'Such things are nothing to a determined man when he is walking home,' he assured me. He was trembling and sweat had broken out all over his face and hands. I opened one of those round tropicalized tins of fifty cigarettes and offered him one. He could hardly hold it in his hand he was trembling so violently. 'This war,' he cried. 'This useless stupid war, what can it ever achieve for anybody in the world except suffering and death? Why have they started this war, these Generals and politicians with their lies? What about my wife and my children?' Finn went to telephone the Italian hospital for a doctor while I tried to soothe the weeping grey-haired giant who had had enough of this savage coast, of separation from his home and family, and who had gone insane with despair.

'They'll be here in five minutes,' Finn said, coming back into the room.

'You have contracted malaria in the desert, signore,' I told the Italian. 'You see how you are shaking? That's malaria. We will get you well first, and then we'll do something about your plan to go to Italy.' He looked at his shaking hands, nodding, saying, 'Si. Si. Si. I am eaten with malaria. The world is eaten with it, war and malaria and suffering.' We gave him another drink and a cigarette. Under the table the Italian was sawing at his left wrist with the jagged edge of the metal diaphragm I had cut from the tin of cigarettes, and we saw him at it and I tried to snatch the piece of metal from him. He drew back, his wrist bleeding slightly, wild eyes looking at Finn and then at me.

'Give it to me,' I said, holding out my hand. 'Give it to me, or we will take it from you. Give it to me.'

'Let me do it, signore,' he pleaded. 'Let me finish it now. You have sent for *them*. I know you have sent for *them*. I will be locked up. They will not believe that a man could walk to Italy with a kettle. They have heard about my kettle. I have been laughed at before about my plan. Let me finish with it all.'

'Give me that piece of tin,' I said. He handed it to me and laid his head on his hands on the table and wept, his shoulders shaking. I could see him, tiny on the edge of that great desert, the moonlight on the sea, trudging through the sand with his kettle, on the way to Italy, a wild happiness in his head. Finn and I could hear 'them' arriving and I went out to meet them, an Italian doctor and his assistant. I showed the doctor the weeping Italian through the lattice work and he nodded, shrugging one slow sad shoulder, saying, 'Ah, si. He is mad, this one, poor fellow. A financial crash with his friends here in the town. *Italia, il bombardamento, la famiglia, la guerra, il sole, disperazione, povertà, etcetera.* The formula for collapse.' He shrugged his shoulder again with kindly Italian cynicism. 'Who is not liable to run off with a kettle from this pesthole we are all trapped in?'

'I've told him he has malaria,' I said. 'It will help you to give him an injection of sedative, if he thinks it is quinine. He calls doctors "*them*". He is afraid.'

'How long do you think this war is going to go on?' the doctor asked me.

'Ten years.'

'Ah. An optimist.' The doctor shook hands with me with comic gravity. 'I had settled for twenty years. You have cheered me up, Signor Capitano. Let us proceed.' They took the struggling Italian away, the doctor whispering and coaxing, the assistant quietly tough and strong.

'Maybe we should have let him go on with his kettle up the coast,' Finn said to me when they had gone. 'That's what I'd want if I went round the bend here, with a kettle. They'll put him in a strait-jacket, I suppose.' We had a melancholy drink together in the hot, still night, talking about many people who were going round the bend in Somalia. (Everybody thought everybody else was going round the bend.)

'The Italians are a marvellous people,' Finn said. 'The way they've stuck it out here in Mog, defeated, broke. But it's better than Italy just now, I suppose.'

Yes, better than Italy. '*La Macchina*,' as the Italians called the Germans, was just then starting to drag its fiery, destructive way up Italy, but even so the Italians in Mogadishu wanted to go home. As the *vecchi coloniali* liked to say, '*Un anno in Somalia è come cinque anni in Italia*,' so cruel was the climate, and it was worse in defeat before the Somalis. Nevertheless the Somalis liked the Italians, when all was taken into account; most people did when they got to know them.

CHAPTER SIXTEEN

THERE is a feeling of threat in the air of some Islamic places in certain parts of the Middle East, and particularly in Somalia, which you seldom feel in Muslim India. There is a tindery dryness and a harsh flintiness in Muslim Somalia which you feel might go up into flames at any moment, with hoarse screeching and knives, as a relief from the relentless pressure of the sun and the glare upon the frustration which haunts this tortured landscape. Fanatics abound, and I remember one of them who had gone down in action against us, dying on a straw mat in the blue lacework of shadow from a thorn tree. His thin beard stained with henna, withered and dried-out after the long campaign in his wilderness, which had once belonged to the 'Mad Mullah', he had stared up at me with the eyes of a wounded leopard. He had led the attacks, sword in hand, supervised the hacking to pieces of over two hundred men and boys, and was dying happy, old and full of corpses, ignorant, brave, frightful, a victim of the murderous ghost which seemed to live in the sand, in the thorn trees, in the ravines and rocks and waterholes. Bravery and courage and steeliness of heart was all that mattered to his generation, but already some of the younger warriors were restless with this generation's old monster of blood which had ridden their backs since childhood.

Perhaps the most unforgettable of all the fanatics I had come across was a young warrior dying on an enamel-covered table in 'the surgery' of the fort at Galkayu. I could smell him through the open window ten yards away in that still heat as I walked through the sand to talk with him. It was at the beginning of the operations in the Mudugh when we were assembling to hunt down the roving killer-bands who were haunting the waterholes in the bush. This one had been carried in to Galkayu tied to a camel with bloody cords and the camel led by a silent little boy wearing a dagger. They had been three days on the way under the fiercest of suns.

The warrior lay on the table absolutely still, the only sound his slow, hoarse breathing and the soft rustling of the thousands of maggots which now formed his chest.

The officer who was with me rushed out to throw up while I stood there with my craw heaving, ready to follow him, but perhaps it was the two large fierce eyes which rolled to look at me that helped me to stay there. The two black eyes studied me. I went and looked down into his face. It was narrow, strikingly handsome like all the faces of his group, but grey and damp now, the fine, thick lips covered with a dry whitish sediment. His hair was the usual shock of dusty wool. He had been speared through the chest days ago, and I knew, had it been I who had received that spear-wound, I would have been dead in a few hours, never mind the terrible journey tied to that camel across a bush waste full of his enemies. And I could not forget the courage of the little boy who had brought him in here, too late to be saved. But the warrior was not worried about being saved.

'Tell me who stabbed you,' I said. 'Which sub-tribe was he of? Tell me what you know and I will avenge you. You are going to die here in this room. So tell me who did it.'

'I will kill him myself when I am well,' the warrior said to me in a whisper, baring his marvellous teeth in a grin of ferocity. 'I will get well and I will kill him myself. He was treacherous to me.'

'You will not get well,' I said. 'You are going to die. Be prepared for that.'

'I will live,' he told me, his wild eyes rolling as they took in the whitewashed room. 'I will take my own revenge.' The air was whistling through the sea of maggots which hid the hole in his chest. 'I will live. *Hrun sheg!* I tell you the truth. I will live to kill him.'

'So you know him?'

'I know him.'

'And you will not tell me who he is?'

'It is my affair. Give me medicine and let me go.'

He was buried the next day in the hot sand on the edge of the fort area. I have never been able to forget his terrific will, his tragic, innocent belief in the magic of health. There is no one alive as tough as the Somali nomad. No one.

An askari wounded in a fight in the Haud country walked fourteen miles holding his guts in his hand, was sewn up and lived to soldier again. And the women are as spiritually strong as their men. One day I came on a poor old hag crawling in the sand, dying of thirst where she had been left by her group when unable to walk anymore. 'Give her water,' I told the askari with us. When time has used you up, and you cannot rise one morning from the sand, you are left to die.

'But she is finished, Effendi,' he said. 'Left here to die. Old. Finished.' My concern for her irritated him. She was used up. Why waste the water? He was not cruel. He was a nomad.

'Give her some water.' The askari knelt down and took the water-bottle out of his webbing sling, removed the cork, and the old woman smelled the water and came at him like a cat, seizing the bottle while the askari laughed and fed her the water. Then he poured water over her head and shoulders. She died the next day, all her senses intact, silent, acceptant, sadly splendid after her pointless life of servitude to camels and men and waterholes.

The noblest and most touching gestures can be made by these nomads, some of them efforts which only the brave and patient would attempt when the difficulties and dangers of their world are counted.

One day during operations north of the Mudugh Jaysee and I were driving through thick bush, our eyes ranging for sight of the killer-bands who were known to be moving across this piece of country. Bullet wounds had been increasing and I knew that these tribesmen were moving their rifles out of the way of the patrols harrying them towards the Ogaden. I suddenly saw two armed men running, about two hundred yards off on my left. They saw me jump out of the truck with a rifle and race into the bush to cut them off. Jaysee went the other way to get behind them. As the two men vanished into the bush I saw their weapons flying through the air where they had thrown them. I ran all out until I knew I must be ahead of them, and, with a round up the spout, I moved slowly through the thorns in long quiet steps, eyes watching for a movement. I knew where they must be, lying in the thorns watching for me. I went silently in my sandals through the thorn bush and suddenly saw the black-red gleam of Somali flesh in the sunlight, and stopped, ready to shoot, and could hardly believe my eyes when I saw a beautiful Somali girl sitting under a thorn tree with her back to it. She was naked and was holding something in her arms. I saw her teeth glisten like snow in a smile, and quite mystified I called to her.

'Where are the men?' I shouted. 'Call the men. Tell them to come to me. I won't shoot if they come unarmed.' And she called out for the *ninkan*, the menfolk, and I saw the two of them rise out of the scrub about a hundred yards away. They held their hands in the air and came towards me. I walked to the thorn tree where the girl sat and saw she was holding a recently born baby. Milk was dripping from her beautiful breasts. Her whole perfect body was shining. She was radiant, so happy that she raised her right hand and greeted the white man in the khaki shorts and sandals with the rifle in his hands. I greeted her too and knelt down in front of her and admired the baby and she was too happy to even worry about the evil eye, but stole dark glowing looks at me and enjoyed my admiration for her baby. The two young men stood in front of me, warriors wearing strips of reddish cloth about their loins and daggers in their soft belts.

'Were those rifles you threw into the bush?' I asked them. They said no, they were spears and sticks. I told them to bring them and they came back with them in a couple of minutes and showed them to me. What were they doing wandering with a girl and a baby through an operational zone they knew to be dangerous just now?

'We had to come,' they told me. 'We were taking our sister here to her tribe to have her baby, but we were too late, and she had it here, just here under the tree. We were out there guarding her when we saw your truck and we knew you would think we were *shifta*, so we ran.' They both laughed and I praised them for their courage and goodness in taking this risk. They had come over two hundred miles with this girl, and this was her first baby and she had borne it in the easy nomadic way under this tree within easy reach of the savage war-bands, to whose tribe they were aliens. They might have pleaded *Magan*, protection, '*Adigaba magantaida*,' but the *shifta* were usually merciless.

I gave them an escort of two askaris to see them across the Mudugh to the girl's tribe. The girl was so absorbed in her baby that she hardly knew where she was, and she reached her tribe.

The easy-going Somali capacity for adventure and endurance is very closely woven into their contempt for pain and death, particularly for death, death which you feel they would like to meet and kick in the teeth, contemptuously. On the desolate northern coast of Somalia two castaways were once brought to me by an old chief.

'Give them a piece of rag each to cover their loins,' the old chief said. 'They have come out of the sea naked this morning.'

The two castaways were innocent, hopeful youths with thick hair, their hands over their groins while the swarms of little boys yelled laughing at them.

'What happened to you?' I asked these grave, worried youths

83

who sighed with relief when they wrapped the cloth I gave them round their waists. They told me they had stowed away on a British ship at Aden, a ship bound for India, and all had gone well for a day until they were found. They were then thrown over the side, a plank following them into the sea. They floated for two days on that plank in a sea full of huge sharks until they were washed ashore near Bosaso, where I was going slowly round the bend at the time.

'Did the captain give that order?' I asked them, incredulous, 'the order to throw you into the sea? Or was it done by the bosun, the *nakuda*? Who did it?'

'The captain,' they told me. 'He was very angry with us. The ship was in a hurry. He could have thrown us off nearer the coast than he did, but he was too angry to think of it. If he had thrown us off nearer the coast we might have only had one day instead of two on the plank.' They bore no resentment for this strange, brutal captain. I checked on this story and was satisfied that it was true, and sent a complaint about it by dhow to Aden. It takes a really hard man to throw two stowaways into the shark-swift Gulf of Aden, a man as hard as a Somali but with much less excuse for it. The old chief was laughing so much about the captain's action, when the stowaways had gone clothed into the village, that I thought he was going to hurt himself. And when he stopped laughing he was indignant about the business, both reactions being heartfelt.

'What are we going to do about all these starving *maskin* children, these orphans?' I asked the old chief one day. 'The town is full of them.'

'We?' he said. '*I* don't want to do anything about them. They seem quite happy to me. What do *you* want to do about them? What are you going to do to them?'

'Feed them,' I said. 'They've got to eat. There are too many of them running about in the *Suk* and stealing. They are becoming a tribe on their own. Call the elders.'

'What's the use of that?' the chief said. 'The *maskin* are quite happy, I tell you. We've got to have the poor so that we can give charity. I was a starving *maskin* myself when I was a child, and they threw coin to me now and then at the mosque. What harm has it done me? Leave the *maskin* alone, Effendi. They're necessary for charity. It is the religious law that we give charity to the poor. If you abolish the poor you attack religion.' He had been serious until he thought of that last part and I could not help joining him in his screech of laughter. He was a hard, cynical, laughable old criminal, who would have cut my throat for pleasure any night, and the throat of any other *Galka*, had the situation been safe enough. I once made him get out of a bogged truck in a flooded river bed of the Daror, and haul on the rope with the rest of us. 'But I am a chief,' he told me, enraged. 'I cannot possibly pull on a rope with these ordinary men.' He pointed to the Somali askaris, sodden and muddy like myself.

'I give you ten seconds to get on that rope behind me,' I warned him. 'Or I'll throw you into the flood.' He could see I meant it, and that the askaris were longing to seize him, and he joined me on the rope. That incident had formed a sort of angry friendship between us and he told everybody he met that not until he had joined us on the rope was the truck able to move out of the mud, which was true.

He fought my plan to help the *maskin*, fought it to its death, and I could not help admiring the way he helped me in public and sabotaged me in private.

Once a year the rain floods up in the Abyssinian foothills came down the hot desert valley behind us and turned everything green for a few days. I planned to dam the water, and hold it long enough to grow millet for the starving children. I sent for the seed and it made its way slowly up through the wastes from Mogadishu until it reached us on the Gulf of Aden, and well in time before the rain in Abyssinia.

The population of the huddle of huts turned out to see me un-load it. 'It's getting serious, this business,' the noble warriors said to each other. 'But I'll die before I'll take a digging tool in my hands.' This was their fear, that I would force the spear-carrying nobles to labour with their hands. But I had a respect for their traditional prejudices, with all of them except killing.

We built the dam, the swarms of children and myself, and when the rain came they put the seed into the mud, and when it sprouted the warriors used to go out to look at it.

'It's getting worse,' the warriors told each other. 'These brats are now becoming intolerable with their vanity. The stuff's actually growing.'

'There's money in it,' the merchants said.

'You're ruining these children, you know that?' the old chief said to me. 'They are of noble blood and here you have them working like slaves. No good will come of all this madness. I tell you I was

85

a beggar outside the mosque myself as a child, and has it harmed me? Has it?'

'It has,' I told him.

'How?' He nearly took me by the throat in his anxiety to know. 'In what way?'

'I'm not going to tell you that,' I said. He almost pined away during the next few days, continually asking me to tell him what I had hinted at, but I assured him solemnly that I could not tell him. On my very last day at that place, when I presented him with a permit I had promised him for the first post-war pilgrimage to Mecca, and he gave me a beautiful Muslim rosary, a *tusbeh*, which I still have (he had always hoped I would become a Mohammedan), he was still pining. He asked what it was that I had hinted at that day months ago, but I said I could not tell him.

'Tell me,' he shouted. 'Tell me. You can tell me now, you're going.'

'I can't. I'm sorry,' I said. He saw me explode into laughter, and all the elders bent and laughed with me, still bent as they followed me to the truck, still laughing as I drove away, the chief frowning and puzzled in the middle of them.

By the time the merchants and that old chief had finished with the grain-market after the *maskin* had reaped what remained of the crop, there was about twopence halfpenny left for the poor. They beat me there, I had to admit it, and I never quite discovered how, but the money found its way into the usual pockets, the trained pockets of the merchants. All one could say was that the children had enjoyed themselves, but nothing changed. Only the Somalis can change things, when they want to, which is the way it should be.

It was in Bosaso too that the old men of the Omar Suleiman tribe, the magicians of that northern area, called a girl to them for a ceremony, out of her sleep, every night for ten days. I would not believe it when I first came across it.

I had had to put a curfew on the town after a number of stabbings, friendly enough stabbings in their way, but one of them had grown into a riot. Anything to break the hot, stifling boredom of that coast.

One night an askari came to me with a beautiful girl and reported that he had found her breaking the curfew while she was asleep. He had seen her walking, asleep, through the sand towards the other side of the town, had woken her up and brought her to me.

'Were you asleep?' I asked her, thinking she must be a sleep walker, though one could not, somehow, imagine sleep-walking

86

among the Somalis. She told me she had been called and had had to go. The old men often called her and now it was the curfew which had caused the trouble for her. I sat her down on the step of the company office and got her to tell me about the business. The askari was laughing. 'It's those Omar Suleiman, Effendi,' he said. 'They're at their magic again.'

CHAPTER SEVENTEEN

AFRICAN magic is real, quite often, and at other times it is the application of practical human psychology by the medicine-men or druids.

I had first come across the respect and fear of the Omar Suleiman during a long safari with a young and brilliantly intelligent, impatient and ambitious Somali called Abdi Karim.

We were spelling each other during the long drive from Galkayu to Bosaso, a distance about half the length of Somalia, and I had a brand new three-ton truck loaded to the top with kit and askaris, with no room for even a small boy to get aboard as an extra passenger. Abdi himself was adamant that we could not even load one extra kitbag aboard, and we took the truck carefully over the rocky surface of Somalia, while Abdi poured out story after story of the days of the 'Mad Mullah'. We drove through the Mudugh, the Nogal, on towards the northern coast, refusing many wanderers on the way who begged for a lift. We were about a day from Bosaso when Abdi slowed the truck as three bearded and turbanned men waved to us and came running to the two sets of tyremarks on the hard sand, which was the road in Somalia.

'Get on with it,' I told Abdi. 'No lifts, remember?'

'But these are Omar Suleimen, Effendi,' Abdi said, shocked at my uncaring attitude. 'We can't refuse Omar Suleimen. We don't want a curse on us, do we?'

'Now listen, Abdi,' I said. 'Get that thing into gear and on to Bosaso.' I waved refusal to the three tall men beside the track, pointing up to the stack of askaris smoking Crown Bird cigarettes on top of the cargo of kit. Abdi stopped the truck and begged me to reconsider the matter, to remember what I was doing, and not to risk a curse on us all by refusing the Omar Suleimen, the greatest magicians and sorcerers in Somalia.

I had just had a long and interesting lecture from Abdi on modern thinking among the Somalis, on the necessity for the ending of all tribal differences, even tribal designations, so that there should be one Somalia with one Somali race who would take up politics and modernize their country. Abdi was an early and devoted member of the Somali Youth League, a body designed to bring about the modern, tribeless, feudless Somalia he had described to me. I did not use this as a weapon on him now, but I refused the Omar Suleimen a lift.

'Drive on,' I told Abdi. 'The springs won't take one more person aboard, and you know it. Drive on.' Grieved and strained he leaned out of the cab and shouted a stream of apologies to the three grave men and we drove on. What happened next went into the folklore of the Northern Mijertein. About two hours after passing the Omar Suleimen the truck began to yaw, right out of control, and it was obvious that the steering had gone. We braked carefully to a stand-still. Abdi stared through the windscreen and then looked at me.

'I know what you're going to say,' I said. 'But it's the steering column. It's broken. Do you think the Omar Suleimen broke it with a curse?'

'Yes, Effendi,' he said, looking accusingly into my eyes. 'What else could have done it? Have you ever seen a new truck do this before?' I had to admit that I had never seen the steering of a truck, and I had driven hundreds, give out before. All the askaris were perturbed, but Abdi ran about like an old hen, fretting about what we had done to the Omar Suleiman, and then wailing about what they had done to us, because I had not listened. I should have listened.

We were stuck there for two days and when we finally got into Bosaso Abdi worked his way round the town and received free coffee on all sides as he told the story of the curse on the truck. I have often wondered about that curious coincidence, which had so suited Abdi's fears.

There was no doubt about the girl who got up out of her bed each night, and walked obediently, asleep, to the old men who had called her from the other side of the town. I gave it a meticulous examination and was satisfied that it was magic. I had to tell the askaris to let this girl walk in her sleep whenever she was called, until the end of the curfew.

Some of the Rahanwein medicine men in the south of Somalia have another way of calling a person. They drive a nail into a tree each night and chant the person's name, and they say he comes no matter how far away he may be.

The Rahanwein put on a show of magic for a friend of mine

89

which affected him so much that he could never bear to look again at anything out of the ordinary performed by Africans. I found this out one night in bright moonlight when we were having a rest from patrols in the fort at Galkayu. The askaris were performing a dance which breaks the spirit called *Mingis*, a form of possession in a person, and one of their number was certainly possessed, I thought then, filled by a malevolent *jinn*. If I had only known it he actually had meningitis, which led to a horrible situation in the end, in which several of my askaris died, and I sweated quietly as I waited for my own infection, but luckily escaped it.

For the *Mingis* dance the men form two lines, each line facing each other, their feet bare, and they strike their flanks with their flat hands for rhythm as they sway and chant. The possessed man lies on the ground between them, this one with his back arched, resting on the ground on his head and heels, the body quivering and shaking as the dance went on. One of the dancers will eventually pick up the *jinn* and go spinning about, foaming at the mouth, but if anyone wearing sandals should come close before that happens this person will take in the *jinn* first. We sat in the moonlight and watched the dance, my companion telling me he did not like any of it, and after one of the askaris had gone shaking and shuddering into the darkness, full of *jinn*, a little, black withered and demonic looking Rahanwein cook came on carrying a pot made of white soapstone full of redly glowing and smoking *luban*, the gummy incense of the Mijertein which gave Somalia the name of the Land of Punt in ancient times, many believe. A drummer followed him about and played to him as the old man whirled around with the pot in his hands. Then he placed the pot in the sand and danced round it, and as the drumming got into him he would throw himself on his knees and try and burrow his head into the sand, howling and gibbering. Finally he stuffed the burning *luban* into his mouth until it was full, and danced while he sucked in air, and his open mouth shone almost whitely hot with the blazing incense, a human fireplace drummed out of his ordinary mind.

'I want to go,' said my companion, about to rise. 'I've had enough of this. I'll tell you why afterwards.'

'One more dance. Watch this one,' I said to him. Two tall slender black askaris ran on, both Hawiya tribesmen, each one having in his right hand a six foot, iron-hard rhinoceros hide whip. They faced each other like fencers, smiling proudly, while three drummers began to boom out the rhythm for them and the two men began to circle, waving their whips over each other, dancing slowly and beautifully into a gradually hastening movement. The moonlight flooded down on to them, and we sat up with shock as the two men struck each other across the naked bodies with their whips, the blows they had given each other so hard that they rang like pistol shots. They struck each other again and again, the blows timed to slide between the drum beats so as to add to the rhythm. The watching askaris were swaying and clapping to the rhythm. The whips curled about struck harder and harder and the sweat came out on their chests and faces with the exertion they used in striking each other. Of the various uncanny things I have seen this terrible rhythmic flogging with the rhinoceros hide *kurbash* was the strangest, frightening and disturbing, yet at home here, part of Africa. How could they bear such pain? How could they go on with this lashing of each other, their senses acute enough to do it to rhythm, and they laughed as they did it. This dance is called *Kurbash*, the Whip Dance. It finished in a rain of blows struck with all their strength, the askaris with their feet planted firmly in the sand, their bodies swaying and undulating as they struck each other, and the drummers leaned towards them and thrashed out a final crescendo of drum-beats. The dancers ended their frightful exhibition by pointing the whips at each other's hearts like swords, and uttering a fierce laughing sound. They had not a mark on their bodies, but there had been no trickery. They had given each other a fearful beating and showed no sign of it, nor was there any mark or stiffness next day when they ran out on parade with the rest of the troops.

'It's weird, isn't it,' I said to my friend as we strolled back into the fort and the askaris went to their lines under the N.C.O.'s. (It was a few days later that the *mingis* turned out to be meningitis, and our miseries began.)

'It's not as weird as what they put on for me down below Janali,' he replied, 'just after I relieved you there last year it was. Just seeing that stuff tonight gave me the creeps and took me back to that night at Janali again.'

That was the country of the Malablei, the men who slowly spun to drums in goat masks, the men in touch with something right down below the skin of the world as we know it, a swarm of black ecstatic divers who plunged down into unknown darknesses, which somehow seemed to be their real world. And they had shown some of it to Sydney, my companion, shown some of the mysteries the divers could bring up out of the mindless depths they could reach, through drumming and a sort of take-off from the so-called real world of soil and water and trees about them.

Their river swarms with crocodiles and you must be very careful when you move along beside that river at night. One day a crocodile had come up and taken an askari who had gone a few yards from the parade ground beside the river, and his comrades could not get him back, even with rifle fire. They had had to watch him pulled down into the brown waters, down to the larder somewhere below. And a young officer, brand new and pale from Europe, transfixed, had watched it all happen and end, in a few seconds.

'Come and we will show you some of our secrets,' the little black glistening men had told Sydney, and thinking he was to see some dancing he had gone, taking a few of his askaris with him to the village near the river. Drumming had begun once he had seated himself beside his askaris. Before them was a patch of red sand, an arena in the middle of the village, and around it were the Rahanwein with their drums, an old man as master of ceremonies, announcing each secret before it happened.

'What would you like to see first?' the old man asked Sydney, 'We will bring it. Ask for it.'

'An Arab dhow,' he had called back facetiously, and the Arab dhow sailed slowly into the sandy arena while the hair on Sydney's neck stiffened and he stared at the dhow full of cheering Arabs.

'No lights of any kind,' the chief had warned him. 'You will spoil the magic if you use a light.' But Sydney had a cigarette in his cupped hand and he burned his leg with it to make sure he was not hypnotised. He burned himself and it hurt. The dhow sailed slowly off. Then a dog with flames pouring out of its mouth appeared, its eyes two smouldering coals. It stood in the arena and growled and snarled, lashing its long ragged tail. Then it disappeared. Next a truck full of askaris drove into the arena. The askaris beside Sydney were terrified by now, and so was he, his hair prickling.

Sydney was a man with a deep and unwanted feeling for the occult, hating what he possessed, an attraction for the ghosts and spirits which do not bother people like myself (though I have seen others in terror of things visible before them, and which I could not see myself). When the lorry full of ghostly askaris had driven off into the darkness Sydney got up and left, and never asked to see any Rahanwein secrets again. Perhaps the Rahanwein knew that he was their man, a man they could reach immediately with their magic. He was a deeply religious person, with a hard mind, a police officer of many years experience in Africa. And he hated African magic.

Until I lived on the Webi Shabeli I had thought that the 'talking drums' were purely West African, never having come across them in Eastern Africa myself, but they were there on the River of Leopards among the small black forest people. Once, two officers from Mogadishu had decided to pay me a visit on that river, to hunt elephant, and, not telling me they were coming, had set out in a fifteen hundredweight truck.

Two of the river tribesmen came in to tell me that two officers were lost, their truck broken down, far up the river. They said the two officers were ten miles away, stressing that the truck had broken down about an hour ago. After questioning I put this time statement down to exaggeration, but I sent a corporal off in my truck and he found the two officers wandering in a swamp, lost, over ten miles up the river. It was wild country, a few tracks running through it, and the two officers were mystified, as mystified as I, by the unexpected help they received. They themselves had heard the drumming, and I found later that news of them had been drummed down the river, though the Rahanwein were not too anxious to discuss the matter.

My African sergeant, a tribesman from Tanganyika, feared and hated these river tribes. One of them had threatened to turn him into an idiot (not difficult with some of the herb mixtures known to the medicine men). I hated the place myself because of the constant malaria I suffered while there. The whole population was malarial, the oily heat sickening, and the old stone building in which I had my headquarters seethed with millions of black cockroaches two inches long. The askaris used to sit, for pleasure, hour after hour spraying the trains of cockroaches with kerosene. I used to get old men to come in and talk to me in the evenings. They would tell me old stories, legends, customs, winding up with the genealogy of each tribe. Again and again I came across the story of the snake which carries a blindingly bright jewel in its mouth by the light of which it makes its long journeys through the night across swamps and savannah. 'Look out for it,' they would tell me. 'It is a great fortune to see it.'

Down the river and near the southern Juba there is a dance tradition called *Sarlugéd*. You, the guest, sit watching as the tribesmen dance with their spears about twenty yards from you, dancing to and for you to the drums. They advance slowly in the dance until they are only a few yards from you; they then spin and charge, plunging the spears at you in one determined thrust, the points resting, halted, on your chest, and you are not supposed to flinch, even at the savage exultant shout that goes up from all the throats around you. When the women dance to the long drums, all of them decorated with fresh green leaves, in the rhythm called *Mudundu*, forbidden by the Italians, and allowed again by myself, they go out of their minds, thrust their heads up into the hollow ends of the drums and shout, line up again and shiver their way across the sand, and then when the true dance ecstasy seizes them they jerk their necks so that the tight bands of coloured beads break, the beads showering among the dancers. The old men and the children get up and move in on the rhythm, and the drummers increase the beat until the sweat flies like thin rain from the dancers in the fire-light.

The last time I went down with malaria in that piece of country was the day I disbanded the last Abyssinian troops of the Italian Colonial army. They had been used in the operations along the Juba and now were aching to cross the enormous sands to their mountain homes in Abyssinia. I had a surprise 'loot inspection', and found the usual dozens of wrist watches, Italian automatic pistols, ammunition by the thousand rounds, left them the wrist watches as doubtfully theirs by right, (they had looted madly), and then lined them up for a last ration issue before they climbed into the big diesel trucks for their journey.

When the diesels carrying the homesick Abyssinian soldiers had gone, I went to see the seven malaria cases in my platoon, carried out the light machine gun drills with the rest of the platoon, and then felt the iron weight of malaria filling my bones, the beginning of the longing to die which that horrible disease brings on, and I remember saying to Sergeant Lehani Baruti that he was to wrap me in soaking wet cold sheets when my temperature hit high, like last time, like I had done for him, and then I vaguely recall wandering through the palm trees towards my headquarters where I had my camp-bed. I was trying to go fast, for before the war I had once passed out on the edge of a swamp with malaria and had lain there for a day until found by the Kavirondo *neapara* of the plantation block. I remember leaning against a tree and then hearing Sergeant Lehani's voice saying in my ear, 'Come, *Effendi, wewe na tetemeka sana sana*,' and he took my arm. The shakes had begun. You can get the shakes so badly with high malarial fever that you can shake your way out of bed on to the floor, again and again. You feel these shakes are going to break your bones.

I woke up a couple of days later in a military hospital in Mogadishu, having my thick, long hair cut by a Rhodesian nurse, and I have never seen that stone building again among the palms with its millions of cockroaches, its whining mosquitoes, and its one smoking hurricane lamp. Now, it is confused for me, that building, with other things belonging to malarial delirium. That is one of the curiosities of malaria, how real people and things about you during the delirium, can occur again in another malarial delirium, perhaps years later during a fresh infection. But malaria is a very strange disease, and it affects people in many curious ways, like hashish, depending, it seems on your personality type. Hashish used to make me laugh. It makes some people cry.

CHAPTER EIGHTEEN

WE had walked about Mogadishu now for two hours, Ali and I, he talking to me about his life, and I thinking about everything which the sight of certain buildings, clumps of palms, and old Italian monuments evoked for me. But I knew it was finished for me, all that wilderness, all those safaris, and that I would not want to live that life again with this small sprawl of decaying Italian and Arab buildings as the longed-for paradise behind us a thousand miles south. One had been drunk here with excellent friends, people like oneself, the scattered fraternity of The Shag, drunk more with talk after long separation than with liquor, and they were scattered now, all over the world. A few had stayed in Africa, but there would only ever be one Africa for them and that was where the silent scrub began at Isiolo in Kenya, the scrub which stretched through Sudan to Egypt, to the mountains of Abyssinia, and to the Gulf, Aden and Gardafui. About fifty or sixty of us had controlled two hundred thousand square miles of that scrub and rock.

All through my wanderings there I had sought to find someone who would show me how the powerful arrow poison, called *Wabaio*, of the small Sa'ab tribal group was made. It became a goal for me but I noticed early on in my enquiries that the Somalis themselves, the conquerors of the Sa'ab group who claimed to be the original inhabitants of Somalia, did not want me to take an interest in these people.

I read about *Wabaio* for the first time while idling in a troopship early in the war. Sir Richard Burton, that marvellous person, pauses for a few lines in his *First Footsteps in East Africa* to say he had heard that somewhere in the Somali wilderness he knew they made a virulent arrow-poison called *Wabaio*. He was on his way to Harar in Abyssinia, disguised as an Arab, when he heard of this poison, but he never found out much about it.

I finished *First Footsteps in East Africa* in a captured Italian fort in a bitter nook of Somalia which Burton never reached. When I asked an ex-askari of the Italian colonial forces about *Wabaio* he lifted his thin black hand, cracked the long fingers in the particularly Somali way and said, '*Molto, molto velenoso.*' Yes, but had he even seen it? 'No. Only a fool would want to see it, and anyway you would never see it, only feel it on the end of an arrow-head shot into you. They would never show it to you as a *thing* to look at. They are full of secrets, and anyway they are only a kind of slave race.'

'Who are *they*?' I asked him.

'The Midgan,' he said. 'A race of impudent dogs of the Sa'ab group. Never trust them. Never believe anything they tell you. Nail everything down if they come near your possessions. They are not really a people. We will not even allow them to have a chief. But we have had to bear with them ever since we, the noble ones, first came to their accursed country and the secret is never to trust them. Such is the race which has invented *Wabaio*. That is all they could do, mix a poison.'

After the dramatic warnings given me by the ex-Italian askari, I sought hard to find a Midgan, but was never allowed by the Somalis to see one, for I was too interested. When it became obvious to me that the Somalis had come to an agreement about this matter, I questioned the headman of the village near the God-forsaken fort in which I was living.

'Why is it,' I asked him, 'that I am always being put off about the Midgan? Why is it that you don't want me to meet one?'

This man was an old, subtle and battle-scarred veteran of the long struggle to keep the white man out of his violent and happy world. He had a short grey stiff beard which he plucked at with both hands while he thought about this approach I had made so directly and brutally.

'It is because you are young,' he said at length. 'We want you to be our friend. Why should you take an interest in the Midgan? It is *us* in whom you should be interested.' He placed his black claws on his thin chest. 'Us. We are the ones in whom you should be interested. *Our* ways and *our* customs, not those of the slaves who have no chief. They will only lie to you. And you will make them proud by questioning them and showing interest in them. For they have nothing to show you or give you. That is why men are unwilling to bring you a Midgan. They say to me, "The white man is asking again about the Midgan, about their language and their poison. Why is this?" So you have worried them. That is what I have to say in answer to your question.'

'This is a waste of time,' I told him. 'You can't prevent me for-ever from meeting the Midgan. What are you afraid of?'

'We don't want to help in the matter,' the old man said. 'There is no harm in that, is there? We do not mean to insult you. It is only that men wish you would not ask them to bring you Midgan people to talk to. A Somali does not want to go to a Midgan and say, "Come, a white man wants to speak with you," and then bring him to you. It would make the Midgan proud. He could well say to the Somali, "So, it is me, a Midgan he wants to see, eh? And he sends *you*, a Somali of the Darod race to bring me." The Midgan could laugh then and a man could want to kill him for that. That is my answer.'

'It is a very good one,' I said, impressed. The old man relented a little then. He said, 'If ever you go to Donkukok or Garowei you could arrange something there on your own, perhaps. But not here. We do not want the Midgan to become proud here.'

As it turned out the old man had a very good reason for his un-willingness to make the Midgan 'proud'. They had never been allowed a chief, and now they had plans to influence the new con-quering government of the British to grant them one. When they thought of such a possibility the Somali could not sleep. They told me about it later when the great danger had passed and the excited hopes of the Midgan had died along with other enthusiasms which the British military occupation had kindled.

The first Midgan I ever met was lying in a patch of blood-soaked sand, stabbed through the shoulder. He had got in the way of a tribal raid near a well and had not had a chance to defend himself. We brought him in to the camp and a medical orderly, a man of a noble blood, sniffed and mumbled while he dealt with the outcast's wound.

The Midgan was small and black and cheerful, wearing a scarlet turban tightly wound round his shaven skull. He bore no malice for the terrible spear-wound in his shoulder. He knew which tribe his attacker belonged to but he made no claim for revenge. He was too wise for that.

A white skin is no help at all in the acquisition of military secrets among the Somalis, though a Somali woman, if she loves you, can help. It was not for a long time that I found that this Midgan's family group had been making spear and arrow-heads for the traditional rivals of his attacker's tribe. The wound was all part of the business risks, and it was better than being killed.

The Midgan belonged to a group, he told me, called Sa'ab. The

Sa'ab are a sort of outcast people made up of four groups called Midgan, Tomal, Yibir, and Yaha. 'We,' he said, stabbing a long finger against his bare glistening black chest, 'we, the Midgan, are the most important of the Sa'ab. Without us there could be no Somalis.' Then he burst out laughing to think of it, like all conquered races when they consider the proud masters who are frightened of them.

When there were Somalis nearby he was silent. When they were not actually present they hovered nearby, fretting, thinking of ways to end my conversation with the outcast, chatting worriedly in small groups. Any white man who imagines he has got very far under the surface of the remains of warrior Africa, when that Africa has plans, is deluding himself, perhaps even in Rhodesia, maybe in South Africa too, even now. But if he skims along the surface with it, and is interested, he can learn as much as the warriors feel is good for him to know, and they are quite right not to trust him. They know that his ultimate aim cannot fail to mean the end of their particular world. The white man wants order in which to go on killing other white men in Europe, they suspect.

Four days after being stabbed the Midgan disappeared, leaving behind a quiver of arrows and a beautifully made long-bow. A merchant called Hersi brought these to me.

'A present for you from the Midgan,' he said when he gave them to me. He saw my surprise. I had met Hersi on a few occasions when he came to arrange about the importation of sugar into our fortress-village area which was like a small sprinkling of mud-pies on the enormous Mijertein desert.

'He asked me to give them to you,' he said.

'Why you?' I asked.

'Because I am a Midgan,' he said.

I was amazed and Hersi laughed. 'I know,' he said. 'I know you have sought a Midgan for months, and I know you did not expect to find a Midgan-merchant.' Then he grew serious. 'I have had a long struggle,' he said. 'But I have come to help you.'

'Ah!' I said, all caution at once. Like a sounding-board he responded to me immediately. He raised his small pudgy brown hands and said, 'Do not fear, Effendi, I have no snare in my tongue. I am no Somali. I have no plan to lie about. I am a merchant grateful for your interest in my people.' He had superb manners, great character, fit to mingle anywhere in the great world of Islam, from the Maghreb to Chittagong and on.

I was impressed, though still cautious. In the lands of the Somali you need quick-silver in your mind in order to keep pace with a Somali plan for greatness, money, revenge, in which your aid is sought with steady, subtle and admirable patience. Things might be at stake which are of the greatest importance to the Somali, tribal position and pride, rights to a water-hole, camels (the greatest single possession of a man in this world) or the removal of an insipid chief. The longing to kill in the terrific excitement of a raid, the protracted and fascinating negotiations afterwards about blood money, these are real and important things.

Later, across this ancient tangle of feuds, the newly formed Somali Youth League cut like a bright light. No more would there be *tribes* of which to be proud to kill for or ashamed to die for, only one united Somali people.

But meanwhile what did Hersi want? He must want something. It might take many hours to find out, for again, among the Somalis the matter in the real plan is not brought to the tongue until the white man has been tired, brought to a stop by long talking, the keen caution dulled and the official brightness dimmed by several arguments about unimportant things.

'I want to talk about *Wabaio*,' he said, flashing a bright smile, and laughing when he saw how the word had worked.

'You are not going to try and make a bargain with me?' I said.

'Effendi,' he said, 'these lying Somalis have made you very suspicious. I assure you that I have no plan hidden, no Somali trick to try on you.'

'All right, Hersi,' I said. 'Tell me something first. Why are you, a Midgan who has known for a long time of my interest in your people, and of the Somali effort to block my way, why are you now here, ready to say you are a Midgan and to talk about *Wabaio*? Tell me that.'

'Because of the war, Effendi. The Allies *are* going to win the war. That is why.'

The Allies were going to win the war. That was now obvious, he said. There had been a time when it seemed that the Fascisti officers might come back to rule the Somalis, and then the tribes might take revenge again upon each other in the massive way they had done when the British drove the Italians out. Now, if a man, even a Midgan, showed his real hand he could be safe. The new government seemed settled and permanent. Men were no longer nervous. That, said Hersi, was why he was now here before me, as a Midgan, to talk about *Wabaio* or about anything else I wished. Did I not see this? It was purely a gesture from the heart.

Somehow, one had never connected the Somalis, or the Midgan, with 'the war'. In this howling wilderness silence had fallen again following the swift East African campaign of 1941. The war was in another world altogether.

'As a merchant,' Hersi went on, 'I have to think of the war and of trade, Effendi. Men need sugar, salt, coffee, cloth. Once Africa is quiet again, why trade will begin with Kenya, Abyssinia, India, Arabia. The latest news that Abyssinia is completely cleared of Italian soldiers has made me realise that I need no longer fear to show my hand. Before now I have had to go slowly, carefully. The jealousy of the Somalis is like a wound in the heart. It burns them night and day.' His hand, which he was showing now, was only that of friendship.

Hersi was a small fat man with indoor Arab skin, yellowish-gold and well nourished. He wore the Somali *lungi* or sarong, a khaki drill jacket and a small brightly-coloured Arab skull cap. Clean shaven, he had large intelligent black eyes, and his whole face had calm and wisdom in it.

'So you have known for a long time of my interest in the Midgan?'

'We all know of it, Effendi. We have discussed it. It is a surprising thing to us. As you are interested in our group I have given orders that when the time comes all must help you in your questioning and writing down.'

No, he said he was not afraid of the Somalis now. He had watched carefully the problem of the world war and the feuds and fears and plans of the Somalis. But he knew now that I would protect him and his people. He looked hard at me and saw the flicker of suspicion again in my eyes. He laughed aloud, and said, '*Sicuro, Effendi, che non ho detto anche una bugia,*' he spread his hands, selling me the truth of this statement with his wide eyes; he had no plan. His interest was my interest. I believed this at last, never looked back from it, and made a friend.

He promised to bring a Midgan who was 'a man of the desert' and who would tell me all about *Wabaio*.

Not long after this conversation, killing began on a large scale some miles away and the tribes tried once more to settle their ancient accounts with each other; camels and water and honour, the dreary trinity of the Mijertein desert. They slew each other without mercy in the first few days and we hunted them through the wastes for weeks, disarming raiding groups and picketing the water-holes. It was during this period that I met the Midgan as nomads. They came pouring into camp, little lithe men with information about Somali raiding groups. Hersi, they said, had ordered this. They were to help the officers in every way with information, as guides, and trackers.

The ancient tribal hate, a terrifyingly determined force when it drew its long pitiless dagger, flickered down into a smoulder after a time, but revenge for injuries received during the Italian collapse had been taken and for a time the fanatical tribal honour was satisfied. They were willing to pay for the dead, in camels, and they paid, sneering.

'I,' said one of the Midgan trackers, 'I am the one chosen by Hersi to be your teacher. I am to tell you everything you want to know.'

'Even your language?' I asked him, delighted. The Midgan have a secret language of their own. 'And the way you make *Wabaio*?'

'Yes,' he said. 'That is Hersi's order.'

His name was Hirad. Burned by that fierce sun to the colour and lustre of coal, he glowed with heat, as if his skin had sucked up a million years of sunglare. His hair was as thick and wild as a young Somali warrior's, standing up from his head in a thick woolly halo. He had great black eyes which flickered fiercely and which saw everything. He wore only a *lungi* and old worn sandals of camel hide sewn with thick white sinew. In his soft, tanned leather belt which was hung with magical talismans, was a long bone-handled dagger. Under his left armpit was a small skinning-knife which was as sharp as a scalpel. He looked the absolute spirit of that savage lunar landscape, his big white teeth wet with saliva when he laughed. He was, I was to find out one day, the nearest link to a wild animal in his nose, his sensitivities about water, beasts, and the right track to follow in a trackless waste, that I ever met.

There was a great pile of curved swords, spears, daggers, bows and quivers of arrows which we had taken in the operations. I took some arrows from one of the quivers and showed them to him. They were war-arrows with the long cruel barbs which would lock them in a man's guts. They were smeared with a dry khaki-coloured paste.

'Is this *Wabaio*?' I asked, showing him the arrow-heads.

After scratching the dry stuff on the arrow-head, he tasted it, his eyes staring far off as he nibbled at it.

'That is *Wabaio*,' he said. 'But it is dead.' He spat out the dead poison and threw the arrow back into the heap of weapons.

'It is a long way to where the tree grows, Effendi,' he told me. 'Near Yillig in the mountains.' That was days of driving by truck across the bone-shaking rocks and sand. There was no possibility of my making such a journey just then, during the operations. I told him I could not go. Could he not bring the stuff and make the poison in the fort?

'No,' he was definite about it. 'We have never before shown any *Galka* how *Wabaio* is made. It is secret. I would not bring it to you here because the Somalis would find some way of making trouble about it. And anyway the root would die if I brought it down here to cook. It is best cooked on the hills where it is cool, near its home. It is happy there, and when it is made and brought down here on to the desert it must still be kept happy. We have a thing for that.'

I did not argue. I did not want to look this gift-horse in the mouth, something Burton, who saw so many rare things, would no doubt have given a lot to see made. I also felt a very young white man's pride in being chosen as the recipient of such a secret. I trembled lest I spoilt it and seal off this gateway by some stupid move.

'All right,' I said. 'When I can come to Yillig, you will be ready?'

'That is Hersi's order,' he said. 'I will be ready when you are ready.'

It was four years before I got to Yillig, for not long after meeting Hirad I was transferred to another piece of wilderness hundreds of miles away on the south eastern Abyssinian border, and then, after long and involved effort, to the Burma campaign. In India in October 1945 I had a letter, a splendid surprise out of the Somali wilderness, from Hersi. He had taken great trouble to trace me and had even found the number of the infantry division I was with. The letter was full of news of trade. His business was happy. Now that the war was over was I going to come back and study the Midgan and write it all down on paper? If I were to come back he was there to help. May God protect and look after me (he was, of course, a devout Mohammedan) always. Peace had come again to the world and men could again turn their hands to trade. '*Non sabbiamo la futura di nostra Baese*. (He, like most Somalis, always used the letter b for p in Italian.) *Gli Nazione Unite sanno, sberiamo*.'

A few months later I found myself again in the eye-searing glare of the Somali desert. 'This time,' I told myself, 'I will fill in this small gap left by Burton. I will see *Wabaio* made if I have to walk

103

all the way to Yillig.' If there is anyone I would like to have known, travelled with, learned from, especially of his enormous knowledge of the lore of Islam, it is Burton.

In early 1947 I was at Bosaso, the place of the winds, on the Gulf of Aden, and one day while I was drinking a melancholy gin on a verandah overlooking the shabby huddle of skin huts and rickety houses which dribbled wearily to the sea's edge, Hirad appeared, dressed for the wilderness, *lungi*, sandals, and dagger. He gave me his lean dry hand, laughing, and said, 'I have arrived.'

He had come on a trade truck from a fort over four hundred miles to the South. Hersi sent greetings. He was well, and more prosperous than ever.

Was I ready now to go to Yillig? We were nearer now than ever before. A day in a truck. A walk up a mountain. Burton had passed near Bosaso. Had he known he was that close to the *Wabaio* which interested him? But he had no truck in those days, and he was in great personal danger.

'Yes. We will go,' I said. 'In a week from now.' Then I said something which I had nursed in my mind for a long time. Now it was so close, could *Wabaio* really be so powerful a poison?

'This poison,' I said, 'it cannot be as powerful as they say. Will I be seeing the real and true poison?' Surely such a secret must be lost by now. Like many things in Africa might it not be exaggerated? I was afraid of disappointment.

Hirad shook his head gravely and cracked his fingers in disapproval. 'I will show you,' he said. 'It is true *Wabaio*, stronger than anything you have ever seen. Even tribes beyond Kismayu buy it if we will send it to them.' Kismayu is on the Kenya border, many days' journey south by truck from Bosaso. 'You will see, Effendi,' he said, 'and believe'.

Hirad wanted to make his way among the buildings of Bosaso, the only 'city' he had ever seen. Bosaso is a crumbling sun-beaten village to which the dhows come from Aden and Mukalla, taking away hides and incense, the *luban* which the Somalis chew like an aromatic cud, and over which whole families fight, generation after generation, not being able to decide about the rights and title. (And I had to decide it; another sad story.)

Bosaso lies stunned most of the day in the blinding sun, and the only really active people are the whores and their pimps who make great play with one like Hirad come out of the desert full of wilderness and with a longing to be a sophisticate for a few hours. Arabs stride through the narrow sandy alleys, throwing alms to the herds of starving Somali orphans if the voyage from Mukalla has been profitable, a few coins, a kind of sop to the Prophet who said that we must never forget the poor, the *Maskin* who forgather near the mosque, and whom I had failed to save from poverty by my petty effort at millet growing.

In the morning Hirad came, smelling of charcoal-brazier smoke and Arab perfume, a ring on his finger, the nails of his right hand varnished with scarlet paint. He was to tell me about the Sa'ab group.

He claimed that they were the original inhabitants of the Somali-lands who had lost the great and final battle near Hargeisha and were then taken into slavery until they became Mohammedans. After that they were Mohammedan slaves instead of mere slaves. They became metal-workers, carpenters, herbalists, hunters, leather workers.

Every Somali woman, when she was ready to bear her child, liked to have a Midgan woman present. Weddings and dances were not complete without Midgan dressed in their gay colours and bringing luck to the nobles.

Hirad came of a family of hunters. He and his younger brother, who had come with him and was in Bosaso, had been taught the skills of the chase by their father. In Somalia more skill is needed to hunt and kill meat than in Kenya and Tanganyika, where, even now after years of slaughter the game is still plentiful, and stupid and lazy compared with the rare game of Somalia's deserts. Even the lion in Somalia is smaller and thinner compared with those of Kenya. The plains leopard of Somalia is a yellowish haggard creature compared with that of Bantu Africa. Everything in Somalia is thinner, more nervous, sharper minded, than in the fat lands of grassy Kenya and Tanganyika.

'He has taught us nearly everything,' said Hirad, speaking of his father. 'He teaches us more and more as he grows older and slower.'

The old man would not give all his wisdom until he was too slow to use it. In that way he would keep some power, some respect and mystery. He was a hard master, said Hirad, and if a boy made a mistake he would beat him severely so that he should never forget. 'He once beat me as one would beat a woman,' Hirad explained. 'And he did that until I was a man, when he knew I could kill as well as he.' Kill what? A man, a wild beast? Probably both. I did not ask.

'He taught us how to stand still, without even blinking in the sharpest sun. For you must stand until you are ready and the shot is ready, then you bring up the bow, drawing the string as you do so, in one movement, with no mistake.' The *Wabaio* did the rest.

Not like Kenya, where in the rains, the panting hunter who has run his fat eland to a standstill in the heavy mud, stabs him to death. Here in Somalia the game is moving away before you have got within rifle-range. For the bowman it must be a work of art, of great patience and with a thrilling reward for a hungry belly. These nomads live in a state of continual hunger. They can get drunk on camel milk and poetry, the declamations of some genealogically demented elder who will stand up and cry the glory of this tribe's particular genes, perhaps the Midgan standing by, listening, older genealogically on this bitter sand and rock, but now without a chieftain.

The nearest approach to the Midgan are the Wandarobo of Kenya, the hunters, though they are forest dwellers and not nearly as tough and resourceful as the Midgan. They too brew an arrow-poison, but they will use the *Wabaio* of the Midgan in preference, when they can get it.

We left a few days later, before dawn, heading the truck for Karin, an old and deserted Italian post, but Hirad was not in the truck. His brother had come instead. A long and mysterious story had not cleared up the reason of why Hirad could not come. He just could not. Certain things were not right. No, he could not tell me. It was a matter of deep shame, he said. He could not explain. But I must believe in his brother, Jama, who knew everything about *Wabaio*.

I had waited by the truck in the first light, smoking many cigarettes, and no sign of Hirad. The youth who came, carrying a bundle wrapped in a dirty white cloth, said, 'I am Hirad's brother. Hirad cannot come.'

'They've got at him,' I thought. 'The Somalis have fixed something.'

'Where is Hirad?'

'He is ill,' Jama said. 'I am to show you how to make the poison.'

'You are too young, Jama,' I said. 'You can't know as much as Hirad.'

He was not annoyed. He smiled and shook his head. 'I know more than Hirad,' he told me solemnly. 'I am my father's best son. I have killed more in one day than Hirad has ever done. My father has said that I am his best son.'

I made him take me to see Hirad. He was lying on a heap of palm-leaves in the corner of an old hut near the market where the butchers sold their fly-wrapped goat meat. He looked like a malaria case, sweating and racked, though very far from delirious. He had been taken ill in the night. He swore that Jama was as clever as himself. I could not believe that the noble race had not in some way reached out a hand to spoil this opportunity to see the making of this famed and mysterious poison. You get into that way of thinking in the Somali waste. You think that way because the Somalis bitterly resent the white man, and struggle continually, and admirably, by lies and intrigue, to fight off his influence which spells the end of their peculiar world. You cannot beat them. They have no inferiority complexes, no wide-eyed worship of the white man's ways, and no fear of him, of his guns or of his official anger. They are a race to be admired, if hard to love.

From Karin we drove into the rough stony hills towards the borders of British Somaliland, the country moonlike in tumbled rock and grey bushless loneliness, not a beast or a man for hundreds of miles. We were topping a rise when Jama pressed his hand on my arm and said, 'Meat.' His eyes were staring into the grey distance. I stopped the truck and it was some time before I saw the oryx bull standing beside an enormous boulder about two hundred yards away, greyish-yellow, lonely-looking, perfectly camouflaged, and, as far as Jama and I were concerned, doomed. Fresh venison after the starved leathery goat-meat brought up in me as much of the ancient wish to kill as ever Jama knew.

'Will you let me shoot it, Effendi?' Jama asked.

'Are you good with a rifle?'

'I am an expert, Effendi,' he said. 'I will show you.'

He did not want the sporting-model I had with me. He preferred the Italian army rifle as carried by the two Somali askaris accompanying us. Grudgingly, one of the askaris handed over his rifle to this inferior man whom the white man was favouring and spoiling.

'These people cannot shoot, Effendi,' they complained, pointing at Jama. 'They lie. They boast. It is waste of ammunition.'

Jama ran forward then, for the oryx was moving, bulky and fast, his long tapering curved horns set back, and a thin trail of dust at his feet. Jama did not aim or use the sights at all. He simply swung the rifle up, moving it left as he did so, firing as the butt came into his shoulder. The oryx slithered forward and fell in a heap on to his chest, rolling then in that slow upward lift of hooves which the heavy antelopes often favour when mortally wounded.

He was stone dead when we reached him, the small red hole glowing in his dusty shoulder. Jama cut its throat with his sharp knife, the 'halal' for the Prophet's sake, a deceitful 'halal', for the beast was dead, but good enough, just as sand is good enough for a ritual wash before prayer in the desert where water is scarce.

'Now, we will have to lift this fellow's kill for him,' the askaris said to each other, angry with admiration and jealousy.

'Where did you learn to shoot like that?' I asked Jama.

'We have a rifle at home,' he said in a low voice. 'But I swear to you we have never fired it at a man or taken part in any raiding.'

We paunched the oryx and loaded it into the truck and drove on to the mountain of Yillig.

I was full of excited anticipation now, wishing Sir Richard Burton was alive, so that tomorrow I could write him a letter saying, 'I have seen them making *Wabaio*.' Surely he would have been interested. Solitude causes such wishes, just as once I had sat down to write to Gogol after an all night sitting reading *Dead Souls* near Isiolo before the war, twenty years old, before remembering with a deep regret that he was long, long dead. If you read Gogol's foreword to that novel, (in which he asks for letters), in a really lonely part of Africa, *after* you have finished *Dead Souls*, you will definitely want to sit down at once and write your gratitude to Gogol.

The Italians had left a grass-roofed stone hut on the mountain near Yillig. A group of Somalis was camped nearby in tents made of grass mats, the *kariya* of the small family group, young warriors carrying spears, a couple of tired wives, hags already at thirty or so, for the nomad life in that climate quickly takes away the bloom of these most beautiful women in Africa. The family were naturally suspicious of me, apprehensive about a white man in that isolated spot they had chosen for their camp. A white man means orders, questions, or some unknown governmental plan for the eventual ruination of the nomad's life. There must be some particular reason for this particular white man coming to their camp, and I was the only white man in hundreds of square miles. So why was I here? The young men stared sullenly at us, exchanged tribal names with the two askaris, found they were as noble as they looked and then began their questions. When the askaris told them that I had come to watch a Midgan make poison, an elderly withered man with a wall-eye came forward and said to me in Italian, 'I am of the Omar Suleiman. We are magicians. We know more than the Midgan. We are the wisest. Men are frightened of us. And we will never show anybody our secrets, because they are powerful. Why then is a Midgan ready to show you his poison? I will tell you. For money. You will pay him for a lying trick. That is all.' The rest nodded in satisfaction. The two askaris were respectful and without argument. I told the old man that I was very impressed by what he had said, but even so I had my own wishes to consider.

It was Jama, the Midgan who was angry. He went up to the elder of the Omar Suleiman and said, 'We will see about the poison. You believe I am lying to the white man? In the morning you will see the poison. Give us a goat and I will show you. I will use the poison on the goat.'

They did not like that. They talked in low voices for a long time among themselves, Jama standing by, watching them proudly and contemptuously. Why did *he* not fear their curse? He laughed when I asked him later. 'It is I who can curse,' he said dramatically.

'So you want to trick us as well as the white man?' one of the warriors said when they had finished their low-voiced conference. 'And you want a goat into the bargain?'

'Yes,' said Jama. 'If my poison is no good why should you fear for your goat? If it does not die under the poison you can have it back, sound and safe.'

He laughed pitilessly while they considered this, for he had hurt their pride. They began to shout among themselves, arguing angrily as to whether such a risk was worthwhile.

'You see them,' Jama said to me. 'They are like children.' Then he goaded them and the elder said with heat that he would give a goat. When was the poison to be made?

Jama said that only the white man would be allowed to see the poison made. It would be made at dawn.

'And you will not show *us*?'

'No.'

'Will you not show the askaris?'

'No.'

A long bitter argument began and I left them, preferring to watch the plains from the hut doorway while sipping a gin. They enjoyed the wrangle for about a quarter of an hour and then Jama came to say that he was ready to go to the poison-trees. There was something, he said, he must now tell me about why Hirad had not been able to come. Hirad had gonorrhoea.

'But nearly everybody in the towns of Somalia has gonorrhoea,' I said. 'What is important about gonorrhoea and *Wabaio*?'

'No one who has gonorrhoea or syphilis must go near the *Wabaio* tree, or be present while the poison is being cooked,' he replied. 'And Hirad is very unhappy to have got the disease. He got it at El Lagodei from a girl when we were coming up on the trade-truck. "Lucky it was that I brought you," he said to me. "God did it. Otherwise between the angers of the white man and Hersi, our rich King, what would I do?" That, Effendi, is why it is I and not Hirad who has come here to show you the cooking of *Wabaio*.'

It said a lot for Hirad's beliefs that he should stay away because he had contracted this disease, for he would have to confess it to Hersi eventually. He would have to confess that a youth, though his own brother, still a youth, had replaced him in the exhibition of wisdom for the white man who was so interested in Midgan things, a white man who had nagged for so long about this *Wabaio*

'This disease would kill the poison, Effendi,' Jama told me. 'A man with this disease in the presence of the tree I will take the bark from, or nearby when the poison is made, would kill the power of the *Wabaio* at once. So Hirad is sad.' He smiled. 'And Hersi will shout at him when he hears of it. A man must be clean when he makes the poison.'

There were many things which could destroy the poison, he explained. Some of these things he could not tell me. They were magic, and he would have permission from his father to tell me about them.

So the making of *Wabaio* itself was not magic. But there was a great deal of magic built about it for its protection.

The Somali, like many throughout the Muslim world, will drink the ink washed from certain Koranic writings to get strength, to empower his dagger-hand, or to win a potency for a time, but I never found what the Midgan's own magic is made of, though he too will drink a Koranic potion in a pinch, just in case.

The tree was about eight feet high, dark strong-looking leaves thick on it, nothing very remarkable or sinister about it. Only its green health was strange in a land of starved grey tormented thorn brush and snarling spine-covered creepers.

The tree itself is called *Wabai*. The correct name for the poison got from it is *Wabaio*. Jama explained this and then said that a truly powerful tree was the one on which the birds would never sit, for it would kill them. On the other hand a tree with many dead birds under it, skeletons, feathers, or even freshly dead birds, was a tree to choose when you were going to make the poison. We went into this for a long time but got nowhere at all. In loyalty to the unmade *Wabaio* I decided that it was up to the birds, the difficult part being that there was not even a feather beneath the clump of *Wabai* trees before which we stood. Jama could not see anything curious in his description of a tree's power and a bird's choice of resting place, and a complete absence of bird-relics to back his lore. I felt depressed then. Perhaps the poison was only a legend.

In Kenya and Tanganyika the hunters brewed a thick stew of euphorbia juice, snake venom and bug-essence, which can kill meat or men efficiently. Somehow, after this lore about the birds and the *Wabai* tree, the Wandarobo of Kenya seemed much nearer to the mystic killers of fairy-tale than Jama with his calm contradictions about the strength of a *Wabai* tree.

'Now I will begin,' he said. He took the heavy matchet we had brought and began to dig into the harsh flinty soil at the base of the chosen tree. He dug for a long time until about a foot down he found a root which pleased him. Then he took a coloured cloth from his belt and wrapped it about his face so that his mouth was covered. Expertly he chopped long pieces of bark from the thick twisted root, placing each piece on a growing heap. There must have been two or three pounds of it when he had done and said he was satisfied.

He showed me the bark. It was hard, though bleeding a thin colourless sap where his matchet had cut it, and on the inner side of it it was a dark shining blue, like gunmetal, and it had a strange lethal glow. It gave off a sharp bitter scent and Jama drew it sharply away from my nose when I sniffed at it.

'Be careful,' he said. 'Your skull will ache and you will go blind if you smell it like that.'

'Is this all we need?' I asked him. No, there were other things. A poor unlearned kind of man would be satisfied with this, he held up the pile of bark which he had wrapped in the coloured cloth, and would complain to God when the wounded beast went on and on across the country, its death delayed. Swift and sure death was the hunter's ambition, and for that only a proper and careful making of the poison would do.

'There are many kinds of men,' he said. 'Just as there are many kinds of Midgan. Our old father was the greatest hunter of all his family-group, because he had knowledge and he took care. He was beaten by his father when learning as we, his sons, were beaten. He taught us every wisdom there is about making *Wabaio*, for, as he said, 'What is the use of the good bowstring and the right arrow and the patient waiting for the beast, if the poison on the arrow is made by a fool who does not know the secrets, or who, knowing, is too lazy to give care to the making of it?' "

When we got back to the hut the sun was sinking. A very old man with a loaded donkey was waiting. He saluted Jama and was as respectful to him as a young Somali would be to an old man. Jama spoke with him in their own tongue, which sounds like the hard, brittle Somali language, but is very different, their secret language. This was an old Midgan whom Jama had sent to cut a special wood called *shillin*. The old man, I found, had been waiting at Yillig for days on Hirad's orders. God knows how the word goes out across these vast Somali wastes, how the old man had heard the order, who fed him, where he would go after this making of *Wabaio*. Jama brushed my questions away by saying, 'He must obey my father's group. He belongs to a *Kariya* of the Omar Mohamed tribe and where he is told to go he goes. Pay him little, for he is old and they eat little.'

He treated the old man like a servant, ordering him to put the wood by the hut, and the old man obeyed with a deference that was touching, for he did not know, despite all his years, what the youth knew of the tribal lore.

'*Shillin* wood is not always used for the fire on which we cook the *Wabaio*, Effendi,' said Jama. 'But it *should* be used. Its smoke makes the poison happy. The smoke of this wood when it is burning will blind a man. Always I use it, as my father said we should.' The wood looked like ordinary, dry, twisted thorn branches.

That night we broiled some of the oryx meat over a glowing ash-bed of wild olive wood (the very best wood for a cooking fire in the bush) and Jama told me stories of the days of the 'Mad Mullah' which his father had told him, and he sang several Midgan songs. One was about the *angarara*, the black centipede which comes from the earth after the rains.

He told me how a Midgan could live (if he had listened to his father) when hungry and thirsty, without meat or water, in the wilderness.

I had seen *hangeio*, a smooth greyish creeper which grows in the crevices of rocks, and had been told it was eatable. Jama said it forms a satisfying pulp in the mouth when chewed, fills the stomach and sustains life 'until you can reach other men and cry "*Magan!*" ' He laughed, saying, 'And a Midgan cannot be *Magan* with a Somali. But he can cry for food.'

Magan is a word a warrior will cry to a man of another tribe, even an enemy, who, spear raised, is ready to kill, and the man cried to must protect and feed the crying one for a certain time. I had an askari who was *Magan* to a tribe which hated his, but he had satisfied them by claiming protection. It is not surrender so much as a temporary admittance of need, and it satisfies the one who is proud to accept the hostage.

Yoho is another plant which will yield enough moisture when chewed, to keep you this side of thirst-madness. It makes a wet sponge in the mouth, 'and is paradise when you are dying', as Jama put it. As he talked one had a look into the hopes and fears of the nomad, who did not know when he might die suddenly in the dark with a spear blade between his shoulders, or perish far from a water-hole with only the certainty that God will remember him, for that is what he must think as the sunglare fades on his dying stare. That is the law.

We ate meat and drank black tea until a thin wind rose in the dark desert and sighed in the thorn trees, making Jama restless and uneasy. He rolled his black eyes and smiled when I asked what worried him. He would not tell me. He said it was nothing for a white man, only for a Midgan. When I nagged him he rose and said he must go now. Before dawn he would be ready to start the cooking of the poison. He would wake me at the false dawn, and before he went to sleep he had one request. Would I ensure that no Somali would be present during the making of the poison? Yes, they pretended they were too proud to want to know any Midgan customs, but, secretly, they had a great wish to find out what they could. They liked to stand idly by and pretend not to watch. They were cunning men.

I promised that we would cook the poison on the stone floor of the broken down kitchen next to the hut and that no Somali would be allowed to see a single part of the proceedings.

'Then that is good,' he said. 'They are jealous because you are interested, and angry because I know what they do not know.' He was going into one of those passionate sermons about jealousies, hatreds, tribes and wisdoms, which the races marked down by the other races for conquest are always making to their friend, the agent of the conqueror, trying to help, to explain—Sermons which become 'Int.I. Tribal. Tensions' in a file for some future day, which may never come. If there *is* oil there, of course, that day will come.

The sun was quivering in soft pink and green veils when Jama and I lit cigarettes. The dawn threw slow wings of brilliant light beyond the mountains until the soft flux of darkness and false light began to retreat and revealed the shabby dessicated world, and the jagged rocks stood out, flinging long shadows on to the surface of our particular barren world, the enormous silence undisturbed by a single cough, or by the first exciting religious cry of Mohammed's special world. Our cigarette-smoke hung in the fierce gold light of the dawn as it climbed. Jama smoked like an Indian, sucking the smoke up through the closed fist, the cigarette hanging down from the base of his curled palm, like one who missed the *hukkah* and must make do with a cigarette.

'All is ready,' he said. Then he went into a detailed description of *duk'neya* (and *habar-daar*), which he had walked two miles before dawn to cut. Without *duk'neya* the poison would not kill. *Duk'neya* was the great killer, the real killer, not the killer who actually extinguished life's delicate light, but the substance without which *Wabaio* could not come to sinister fruition. *Daar* is an aloe but the word *habar* interested me. It is the word for a curse, in Somali, but the names of the materials used for the arrow poison are Midgan.

'*Duk'neya*,' Jama said, 'is like salt in the food we eat. It draws the strength of the good.' He showed me the white sap melting from the thick coarse green cuttings in his hands. This sap threw off a thin malevolent smell, acid and bitter, pointless until you knew what it was for, until you were a Midgan. It was like a part of a terrible salad which could be cut up with crisp fresh sounds, for it was innocent to see despite what Jama said.

'It is the salt,' he told me. 'It is what draws out the final poison. Without this the poison is useless.'

He used an iron pot for cooking. When he unwrapped the necessary parts for the mystery the scene had a kind of tawdry grandeur, the grandeur given to it by Jama's quiet gravity. The iron pot was black, bent, pitted, yet scrubbed and shining inside, like a rifle barrel after a gauze. A few large, heavy, yellow sea-shells, a long peeled dry twig, some rags of multi-coloured cotton which he tied to a string and hung round his neck. There was something subdued about him. He was nervous. He was afraid, possibly that the poison was no good. I was only a white man, but I had been promised.

The whole bitter smelling mass of *Wabai* root he poured from a sack on to the black stone floor. He took a large flat stone which he laid between his crossed legs. In his right he held a piece of jagged rock, the pestle. He laid the pestle beside the *Wabai* root and then, taking a thick black and yellow striped cummerbund in his hands (a waistband of an Italian army Colonial battalion) he said, 'Cover up your mouth and nose now, effendi. I am going to crush the *Wabai* root, and if you breathe it in you will be in great pain.'

I was tense and nervous now, wondering if the *Wabaio* would work. I wanted it to work because I so admired the Midgan. I believed that the Midgan had once made it, and that it was as powerful as Burton had been told. But I did not believe that this wisdom had survived into 1947, for so many tractors had been driven across so many folk-wisdoms.

Jama wound the striped scarf tightly about his mouth, binding it above his eyes so that he was staring through a slit. He was about to begin pounding the coarse bitter-smelling pieces of *Wabai* when he looked sharply at me. He put down the pounding-stone, loosened the scarf and said, 'Effendi, wrap up your mouth and nose while I am crushing the *Wabai*. You will have pain otherwise. I tell you you will have pain.'

You couldn't make a white man do anything if you were black, in Africa. You suggested. Then you left it when you got the reply I gave.

'I'm all right,' I told him. 'You carry on with the *Wabai*.' I did not believe the pounding of the *Wabai* root would affect me.

Jama beat each piece of *Wabai* into a heap of trash which sent off a sharp, wet, acid stench. The iron pot was boiling on the fire now, the spring water in it rippling and bubbling. When all the *Wabai* was crushed Jama put it into the pot, handful after handful. A thick stifling steam poured from the pot while he pushed the mass of poisonous bark below the surface of the boiling water.

He then chopped the *duk'neya* into pieces with his dagger. He lifted the dagger which was now smeared with the thick white sap.

'That sap would blind you,' he said. 'One drop in your eyes and you are like the very old, begging for alms.'

Now he stuffed the pieces of *shillin* wood under the pot, and as they caught fire and crackled they began to send off clouds of thick blue-grey smoke. My eyes filled with tears and began to burn and Jama laughed.

'I told you,' he said. 'Let us go until it has burnt down. You can blind a man with *shillin*.' Covering his eyes with the scarf he put all the chopped *duk'neya* into the pot, placed the lid on it and then came with me into the hot fresh air.

'Do you know about *dunkál*?' he asked when we had lit cigarettes. When I said I had never heard of it, he shook his head and said, 'It is a wonderful poison. One of the best there is. No good for the hunter, but for killing a man peacefully you cannot find anything better than *dunkál*. You can kill a man with it hours after he has drunk milk or tea with you. You give it to him in his drink, and if you have measured it properly, he goes into his final sleep several hours later. He longs for death, he is so tired. No one can keep him awake, or alive, for he must sleep. Yes, that is *dunkál*. They say it is an Arab poison, though the Arabs deny that, as they deny every-thing until they know why you have asked them about it. *Ju'us* is theirs too. You know *Ju'us*? It will give strength where there is none. That is an Arab thing too.' He threw back his head and laughed. 'Always in our stories the Arabs are the cunning ones, but *are* they as cunning as we Somalis and Midgan? No. They cannot be.'

Occasionally we looked at the simmering poison in the pot. It was thickening to a brown bubbling soup and giving off strong rank acid fumes. The smoke of the *shillin* wood had thinned now but could still bring a rush of tears to the eyes.

While Jama was telling me of how, wearing a donkey's head to which oryx-horns had been strapped, he had sat for hours near oryx, waiting for them to approach, my head began to ache. It was no ordinary headache. My gums and teeth felt enormous and full of dull heavy pain, as if swollen after a beating, and pain grew in my jaws until I could no longer feel my teeth when I simulated chewing. The pain in the skull was terrific and when Jama saw me holding my jaws and in obvious pain, he said, 'I told you, Effendi, to cover your mouth and nose. Now you are hurt because you did not do it. The *Wabai* dust is poisonous.'

'Well, what is the cure for it? There must be a cure.'

'There is no cure. It will go away after a time.'

The headache stayed with me all day.

Yes, Jama would sit wearing his donkey-head, poisoned-arrow ready in the bow-string until an oryx came near enough for a safe shot. Then the twang of the bow-string, the soft thud of the arrow striking, the rush of the oryx while the fire of the *Wabaio* hissed in his blood, then heart failure, a stumbling and a shivering as the oryx died. How long before it died?

'Well, there is no rule, Effendi. It depends on how old the poison is, how big the oryx. It depends on many things.'

'So you can't say how long?'

'I could, Effendi, but only for this or that oryx. It differs.'

'Well, roughly how long?'

He would not say. The hunter was not worried about 'how long', but was satisfied to follow the animal until he fell. 'How long' was a typical white man's question. 'How sure?' was a Midgan's question, and once that *Wabaio*-smeared arrow had gone into the beast he was as good as dead. After death the poison all came back to the wound. The hunter cut that portion of the meat out and the rest of the beast was safe to eat. How explain that? Jama could not say, but it was so.

'If the game is afraid and will not come near the hunter, no matter how clever and patient he may be, then we have another way of killing him with *Wabaio*,' said Jama. 'There is a plant which the game like to eat. We scoop out the centre of the plant and put *Wabaio* paste into it. Some time after a buck has eaten it he will die. But it takes much longer than an arrow-wound.'

When the pot had been bubbling for about four hours, Jama took one of the big sea-shells, called *dalla*, and decanted enough of the thick dark brown soup from the pot to fill the shell. He placed the brimming shell on the hot coals and when it sizzled and boiled he stirred it gently with a peeled twig. As it boiled the liquid turned to a thick blackish gum. It looked like hot tar and it now gave off a heavily sour perfume.

'It is time for the first test.' Jama went to the doorway of the hut and called the old withered man who had been so ready with the *shillin* wood. I heard Jama use the word '*shimbir*' (a bird) and when the old man went hobbling off to Jama's sleeping place I asked, 'Why *shimbir*? What *shimber*?'

He said the hunter always used the new poison on a bird first. It must be tried on a bird. That was the tradition. The old man brought a dove in a small cage made of twigs. 'Must it be this bird?' The dove was so peaceful, so harmless, I was wanting to be coaxed.

'Always it must be this bird.' Jama looked steadily into my eyes, as if he knew the great sentimental complication of the white man who would spare a bird and massacre a city full of men and women, (from the air preferably for then he does not know what he is doing!

117

The 'savage' has known all about this for a long time. Will the white man forgive him for knowing?).

'We are ready?' he said. He opened the dove's beak and inserted a drop of the *Wabaio*. The dove closed its beak, sat still, obediently, and then fruffed all his feathers so that he resembled a ball of grey-lilac fluff. He closed his eyes, shivered, and in a few seconds fell dead on Jama's hard pinkish-yellow palm.

'There,' he said. 'The *Wabaio* works.' He stared triumphantly at the bird. 'Now for the goat.'

The desert goat is tough and could live on a diet of sandpaper and thorns if necessary. When even the camel is desperate for a meal the goat will find sustenance. He helped to make the desert and the desert can support him. To see a goat chewing a mouthful of grey sharp thorns is always a surprise, and they thrive on it. I once watched a goat eat a packet of cigarettes, remembering from my farming days that nicotine is splendid for wireworm and for other parasites. The desert goat will eat anything, staring ahead with those strangely beautiful insane eyes, tougher by far than the camel.

Jama wanted to stab the goat and then insert *Wabaio* deep into the wound, 'like an arrow would'. I said it was needlessly cruel, and anyway was not a fair test.

'Cruel?' he said. 'Why is it cruel? It is a part of the thing we are doing about the *Wabaio*, is it not?'

I fell back on the fact that it was not a fair way of testing the poison. The blood carried the poison to the animal's heart. It was not necessary to put the poison deep into the animal 'as an arrow would'. The poison smeared on a cut would do, if the poison was any good. It would be the best test of the *Wabaio* I had so long waited to see made.

This perplexed Jama, and he did not like it. 'It will not work then,' he complained. 'When it does not work that way you will laugh and say the *Wabaio* is no good. Then you will tell the Somalis, and they will be glad. No, it is not a proper way of doing it.' He held the *bilau*, the long sharp Somali dagger in his right hand while the goat, seeing the knife, and knowing its purpose, struggled in the crook of Jama's left arm.

'No,' I said. 'The *Wabaio* is good. It killed the dove. I want to see if it will kill the goat in the way I have suggested.'

With a razor-blade we shaved the coarse hair from a square inch of skin on the goat's shoulder, made a small incision which bled, and Jama then pressed as much of the tarry *Wabaio* as would cover a teardrop on to the wound. While doing this, he told me of the curious way in which a hunter will test *Wabaio* made by another. He makes a cut on his inner arm, lets the blood stream down to his wrist, places the tip of the arrow-head, which is freshly poisoned, in the blood at the wrist, and if the poison is good it will race up through the trail of blood ('you can see it go') and as it travels 'it burns up the blood' until it reaches the cut, across which the hunter has pressed his finger. After such a test the hunter will use it. Bad *Wabaio* will not race up the blood. It will do nothing.

The goat stiffened, ran backwards, its eyes closed, beat its fore-feet on the stone floor for a few seconds, sat on its hindquarters, and then opened its eyes to stare with a sort of sad amazement at us and then fell over dead on its side. From the time Jama had applied the *Wabaio* it had lived one minute and forty seconds, and Jama was disappointed, while torn by gladness that anyway the *Wabaio* had worked.

'It is much swifter than that when it is done as the arrow does it.'

'But if it will kill an animal when it is smeared on a cut doesn't that show you it is even stronger than you knew?'

This time it was Jama, and not the white man, who was worried about 'how long'. I told him that the blood moved like a river and that it had carried the *Wabaio* to the goat's heart because of that, but he was unable to decide whether he was relieved because the *Wabaio* he had made had worked for the sceptical white man, or whether he had not had a real chance to show what it could do 'as the arrow does it'.

So there it was. A root out of the earth contained a toxin powerful enough to stop an animal's heart in one minute and forty seconds after it was laid on a small cut made in the animal's skin. How much stronger is it, I wondered, than the *curare* of the South American Indians? If that *curare* could be used as a medicine, why not *Wabaio*?

I like to believe what Jama told me, that I am the only white man who had seen *Wabaio* made. But am I? Surely some Italian officer, bored in those wastes, had been invited by the Midgan to see *Wabaio* made. The Somalis liked the Italians, even if they did not like their rule (a very important distinction about 'empires' and 'occupations', not always appreciated by the white man up on the hill, who thinks he represents some abstract mystique and not just himself), and there is no reason why the Midgan should not have shown an Italian this curious ritual.

When they heard that the *Wabaio* was good and that it had killed their goat, the Somalis in the *Kariya* refused to come out, not being willing to be amazed, or discomfited, or convinced. They stayed quietly sullen in the shade and we left them to it, for after all it was their country, and the Midgan were their parasites and their problem, and in some way I had disturbed an accepted fact, unwillingly, but I had done it out of a curiosity awakened by Burton, long dead, while reading one of his books in a troopship.

I never saw Hersi again, that subtle, warm-hearted uncrowned chief of the Midgan. When I next saw the fort of El Lagodei, surrounded by its tatty sun-beaten slum of crumbling huts, he had gone—'into politics, Effendi'. What politics? I hoped he would become the leader of his ancient tribe.

The Somali race, the most interesting, the most proud, the most courageous and intelligent, and the most 'difficult' of the races of Africa, has gone into politics, for if they don't others will, in this age of turmoil, and if by some strange chance Hersi should read this (he was always in touch with 'the West') I would be happy to have contact with him again.

We put the *Wabaio* into a special container, and Jama sewed it into a piece of khaki drill ('a soldier's colour which *Wabaio* would like') and then he stitched about the neck of the receptacle all the gayest colours in wool he could find (plucked from the bright 'pom-poms' worn by the Banda of the Italian colonial soldiers, who had taken Wal-Wal for Mussolini when he decided that ancient Rome was right about empires). These colours would keep the *Wabaio* contented, wherever I might take it in my travels. When it was sewn up in its khaki and decked in its black, yellow and red woollen collar, Jama burned the wood of two different thorn trees, mixed the grey ashes and then, after placing the gay *Wabaio* container in one of those English cigarette tins which hold fifty cigarettes, packed the mixed ashes tightly about it. Why? Because if one ever carried the *Wabaio* to territories near the ocean, the poison would 'turn to water', melt and be useless. The ashes held a peculiar magic which would prevent that. My white mind guessed that the ashes would absorb the great moisture of the Indian Ocean which washes Somalia's coast, the great water known to Jama, but who knows? Who knows what magic really is?

When leaving London for India in 1950, I was over-burdened with baggage. So I buried the *Wabaio*, with nostalgic thoughts for Somalia, three feet deep, in a garden in London, where it now lies, 'happy' in its khaki and colours.

CHAPTER NINETEEN

'ONE more fresh lime and water before I go back to the ship,' I suggested to Ali. He agreed and we walked through the crowds back to the Croce del Sud. Perhaps it was the old taste of the swift violent spirit of this land, of the threat of melancholy coming over me, which made me want to leave Mogadishu now. Perhaps it was the memory of the seven suicides I had known personally (there were many more suicides than that), and how many cases of madness and breakdown I had counted up in memory as I had walked these streets with Ali. Fifteen or sixteen of them. People who, if they had never been tried out in that restless threatening country, would be alive today, or would never have cracked in the loneliness that was too much for them. For every one of us there is a situation, a crisis, a place, a commotion, which will force us into what we cannot do, will find us out as lacking, or unable, and most of us spend our whole lives without being trapped in that particular set of circumstances which will break us. You do the wrong uninspired thing, rushed and fearful, a moment's decision, as the tangle of mess piles up, until there is a moment after which nothing can go right again.

Some of us have been mad without knowing it until later, much later, though the mask may not slip off completely. There may be only a little odd behaviour which hints at the turmoil, the shaking of reason behind. It used to be after the sixth month, on bully beef and biscuits, with tea in which the condensed milk would not dissolve but floated about in sickening lumps, because of the well water; after long and varied threats by the chiefs, strings of killings, the situation aching more angrily every day in the heat, with the possibility of massacre (and your own little, enormous death as well), that the loneliness fell like a wolf on a will here and there. One fine officer, cut off, surrounded by thousands of the warriors of two tribes who were about to fall on each other (and he with his few askaris in the way), tried everything he could think of to bring the two sides together, coaxed, pleaded, reasoned, and the two murderous chiefs, knowing that here was an honest, trusting, gentle person who thought only of their good, put on the pressure, each for his own side, and watched the young officer slowly lose his way among their threats. They finally broke him, for he became so obsessed with the need to bring them to peace (without the violence they loved to use, and feared if you used it on them), that he forgot that he was in a jungle full of splendid animals who understood emotion better than reason. The real panic-bringer is to remember that you are absolutely alone, and that you are not sure even that your askaris, if they are of the tribes you are tangled with, will stand by you. But it is the all out gambling gesture that often saves the day (which is so often your life disguised as duty), the feeling handed out by the gesture that the gesturer will follow his threat or his order right to the end, no matter what it costs.

One day, during operations in the Haud and Ogaden, a subaltern, Steve, promised me that he would outpace the raiders and get round them, driving them down to me about fifty miles south west of him. He was tougher than his Somalis, for after three days of the forced march in that glare and rock, thirteen of his platoon, the only askaris with him at that time, mutinied, backed off with their rifles and stood in a line fifty yards from him. He had a .303 rifle in his hands, the magazine full but with nothing up the spout. The thirteen askaris, he knew, had full magazines, but with nothing up the spout, and they threatened to shoot him if he did not give in to their demand for a day's rest. The argument became angry. One of the askaris pulled back the bolt of his rifle (the emotional storms which come down on the desert Somalis are total, blinding, frantic), and this officer held up his hand and they listened.

'You've seen me shoot,' he said. 'I'm good, and you know it. I'll kill five of you before you get me. Five. And I've chosen the five. I'm ready. Put down your rifles, or open fire. Take your pick.' He was a very good shot. It was one of those moments when no mistake can be made, and they knew he was willing to die, but that he would kill five of them before they finished him. The storm of rage collapsed, the moment was gone, and they sought to bargain, but he refused. 'Ground arms,' he ordered them, and they grounded arms. With their rage finished they knew they were out of these operations now, anyway, and under arrest. They said they would soldier on if he would forgive them, but he refused their offer. This officer was a gentle, sensitive person, but with a will which nothing could break; no isolation, crises, threats, ever climbed over his cool ability. The Somalis admired him, but it was when it looked to the

122

ringleader of the mutineers that the officer was, unintentionally, tougher than themselves (and the Somali is vain of his staying powers) that they mutinied. That was the only time I ever knew a white man to outlast Somalis in their own geographical hell.

I knew a cynical old Irishman who tried everything he knew with five raving bloodthirsty chiefs (they shake their fists, scream, threaten, if you once let them start), and these chiefs, at loggerheads with each other over the waterholes, were ready to send their tribes against each other. And they had come in to the old officer to frighten him, and each other, and to work up to the point where the meeting would end in hatred and rage. Then they would rush off to their tribes, who were waiting to kill. The five chieftains shouted each other down and then looked at the old Irishman, and he knew he had tried everything and found no solution to the problem of the waterholes, and to the generations of quarrel which had gone before him. He said the first thing that came into his head, gravely, ponderously, and perhaps it was his white hair and his age which gave it the poetic and sagacious weight it had for them.

'Remember,' he said, looking into all their eyes in the pause, 'remember that it is the elephant asleep in the long grass which defeats the greatest men.' He had no idea what he meant (though he used to invent wonderful, idiotic tribal proverbs), and told me he had said it cynically, out of weariness, exhausted anger, but the chiefs stared at him, exchanged glances with each other, and nodded, went on nodding, and sat down, saying, 'Let us thrash this matter out again. That is a splendid thing you have said.'

Finn of the big moustache and the dark glasses, in a crumbling fort in the Ogaden one hot tense night, had talked two chiefs, who hated each other, into signing an agreement not to fight, and their powerful tribes were armed, ready, and he had the paper on the table there in front of them, the purple ink pad beside it ready for the two hard right thumbs of the chiefs to sign their agreement to the peace. He had wooed and coaxed them for hours, sometimes telling them of the millions of troops who were waiting to swarm to the attack, from far south, if their tribes went to war; sometimes reminding them of their age, responsibility, religion, better natures. Then, in the fort behind him, a single pistol shot exploded across his soft voice. The officer representing the 'millions of troops' who could be called up into these wastes had just shot himself. The wilderness had used him up at last.

'Just here,' said Finn, pointing to the paper, taking the thumb of each staring chief in his big hand and pressing it on the bottom of the agreement. 'That'll do for tonight.' He dismissed them and went back into the fort. The officer was alive, with a bullet hole through his head. He had fired the round from his .38 through his forehead, but he was alive, *and* talking, from where he lay back on his bed. He told Finn that he had just crashed his truck and was injured, badly injured. 'Got to get him right out of here,' Finn decided, 'for two reasons, to try and save his life, and to keep any of the Somalis from knowing what has happened.' He drove all night with him across the wilderness towards a fort where he knew there was a doctor, but just before dawn the officer died.

Some characters are made for wilderness and strain and privation, come to their happiest in that dry sterile loneliness. It is a fact that barren wilderness grows on you far more mysteriously than can any lusher landscape. Often, staring at the rocky horizons far off, at sunset, sitting under a thorn tree while the camels fed and the askaris brewed their tea, I wondered what it was that fascinated one, that captured one in this threatening loneliness. I loved the soft, thin whistle of the evening breeze in the black ant-hollowed bulbs of the thorn trees, the almost friendly groans and howls of the hyenas sneaking round the camp, the monotonous low-voiced arguments of the askaris squatting over the glowing fire, and, despite my weariness of their bloody feuds, I understood the mindless happiness of the Somalis who had known and would know no other life than moving like ants across these wastes. I liked to squat with them and drink the cold salty camel milk, their eager eyes watching to see if you enjoyed this particular milk (for camel milk has a thousand tastes for these desert experts), and to listen to them tell me the histories of their tribes. I enjoyed sitting back and hearing them argue a point, about divorce, about punishment, about the abilities of one kind of camel against another, about the true, severe *shariat* law of ancient Muslim times compared with the milk and water law which was allowed now.

Frightened of nothing on earth, willing to try anything anywhere, the Somali is never over-impressed by what he sees in the West, and they are great travellers. If he sees New York, or London, or Paris, the sight of these places with their superb machinery in no way diminishes his love of his desert home. He will go back there one day and wander with camels again. Once, in as blasted, dried-out and stark a piece of scenery as I ever sighted in Somalia, I met a tall lean Somali who spoke to me in American. He had lived in

America, after sailing the world as a stoker, and had been a cocktail barman in Baltimore for some years. He spoke of it casually, even contemptuously, as just something that had happened to happen to him. This was Jibreel, Willie Ritchie's interpreter. He was glad to be back here, with nothing except a piece of cloth round his loins, a knife and some camels. Like the two stowaways at Bosaso, who had survived the sharks on the plank so thoughtfully thrown after them into the sea, this Somali who had shaken cocktails in Baltimore, who had seen all the things so many millions sigh for in the West, saw it all as mere happenings, mere pictures walked through and seen with the eyes. As avaricious as can be, about camels and money, the Somali is never blinded, like the Bantu, by the big show, the white man's 'magic' and power. And they are obsessed about their rights, and about justice. Anyone who has commanded Somali troops, and lived with them for a long time in the field, sieved and shredded thousands of complaints brought to him by Somalis, dealt with their delicate prides and vanities wounded by some feather of unintended injustice, can put up with almost anything afterwards, even himself. But they only fret and nag for kit or equipment, or some luxury like sweet pepper, if they know it is there somewhere, to be had, within arguable reach. If they know it is unobtainable they will wait until they are near it and it is gettable, and then cry for justice.

I could never hear the word 'ghee' (*subuk*), for years after Somalia without a tightening up of the whole nervous system. They used to cook their food in ghee, clarified butter, and when the ration ran out in the bush and I knew we would get no more, perhaps for months, I used to drag the rags of my will together and get ready for months of anguish about ghee. Like white troops without cigarettes, they talked about the ghee all day and night, but unlike white troops, held conferences about it, drew up statements, compiled measurements of the ghee they had not had, and must expect from me when the time of ghee came again, and some of them would come trembling with fury to me about the ghee, after having worked each other up over the campfire.

'There is no ghee here, or for hundreds of miles,' I screamed one night at them, a deputation who had not even got a word out of their mouths before my scream, and they were convulsed with laughter, and I laughed with them, and it passed off in further laughter. But the next day they came again, the corporal sternly holding up his hand to silence any scream from me before they had said their piece, about the ghee. I once threw a ghee party after some operations in the Nogal, throwing the ghee about with a wild carelessness, having crookedly managed to get far more than I was entitled to on the ration scale, and the askaris ran about with their huge ghee issues in four gallon petrol tins in such a state of childish delight it was almost pitiful.

If you have the patience and use the slow, steady drip technique, keep your temper, stick to your points, and never let yourself be rushed, you can beat a Somali in argument. I have never known a Somali to admit he was wrong, once he has taken up his position, but I have managed to exhaust quite a few, when it mattered. And I have crawled away, completely worn out, after many a bout with the chiefs on the finer points of justice.

You develop manias in the bush after a time, various manias which may last for some weeks on end. I once worked up a mania about rags being used as plugs in the ends of rifle barrels. I used to tell the askaris how this made the barrel 'sweat' and damaged the rifling, and how in other ways it was unsoldierly and dangerous, even if it did keep the desert dust out of the barrel. I went on about this until there was only one askari left in the unit who still sneaked a rag plug into his rifle muzzle when on the march. One day I sent a patrol out and this askari was one of the number. He was carried back a few days later with his right eye missing and a good deal of the bone of his right cheek as well. He must have been in terrible pain when I stood over him and had a look at the frightful wound. I knew what had done it but said nothing. It could wait, but the askari started on it right away.

'You think it was a rag in the end of the rifle muzzle, don't you, Effendi?' he said. The other askaris standing round the bed smiled and looked at me to see what I would do with the possibilities in this piece of brazen nerve.

'*I* didn't say anything about any rag,' I said innocently.

'There was no rag in the rifle muzzle,' the askari said sternly. 'I don't want you to think that. When I opened fire there was this explosion and now my eye is gone. It's going to cost the army a lot of money.'

'The bullet blew the bolt out into your eye, didn't it?' I said.

'I didn't make the rifle or the bullet,' he said. 'It's your rifle and I know nothing about what made it knock my eye out—' The corporal of the patrol came in then with the smashed rifle and showed me the split muzzle, the shattered breechwork, and it was quite

obvious to all of us that there had been a plug in the muzzle, forgotten in excitement until the explosion and the tragic wounding.
The corporal told me that the askari had already admitted he had
had a plug in the muzzle when he had fired, but had said he was
determined never to admit it to me.

'Lies,' the askari moaned on the bed. 'Lies, lies.' All the askaris
laughed.

'I'm sorry about your eye,' I said. 'We'll get you down to Mogadishu as quickly as possible.' He was a fine looking, healthy Mijertein
tribesman but he was not in any way upset about the pain and
disfigurement he had suffered, only about being right.

He called me as the truck carrying him to Mogadishu crashed
into gear, gripped my wrist and stared into my eyes with his one
splendid eye.

'Don't believe the corporal or the others,' he said to me. 'They're
all against me in this. There was no plug in the rifle. You told me
never to use one, didn't you?'

'I did.'

'Haven't I always been an obedient askari?'

'Always,' I said, 'except for that plug in your rifle.' He turned his
face away, disgusted, weary of me and the whole effort of the
miserable business. The other askaris, like hawks about the truck,
listening to this final passage, looked sharply at each other as the
truck drove away and left us there in the sand outside the fort.

'You won there,' the corporal said to me.

'It's not a question of winning,' I said. 'It's a question of discipline.' (A lie. It was a question of winning.)

'No, but you won. You beat him. You got him right down there
with that last bit. He thought you were going to give in. But you
won.'

'And he was a good liar too,' an askari said, thoughtful and
admiring.

CHAPTER TWENTY

ALL during the walk through the town, and while Ali and I sat for the last fresh lime and water in front of the Croce del Sud, I had been watching for faces, for the face of Mohamed Saad, Ahamed Hussein, Hersi, Elmi, just in case they *should* happen to be in their capital, Hamar by the sea, but I did not see one face I recognised. And they did not belong here anyway, among the smells and the thieves and the town men who had forgotten their tribes, who did not know who they were anymore.

I brought a savage here once to this town, a fierce, impetuous youth whose parents had been killed near El Wak during the fighting; El Wak, a blinding sheet of white rock away up in the north where Kenya meets Somalia and Abyssinia. He had come quietly to the convoy in the warm darkness and stood over me where I lay on a blanket, smoking and watching for the moon. He had six bottles of Italian Aranciata, green conical bottles wrapped in a dirty cloth. He knelt down and showed me one.

'You want that?' he said in a low urgent voice. Want it? I nearly tore his hand off grabbing it. I had the top off in a couple of seconds and poured the delicious cold fruit drink down my throat.

'Where did you get that?' I asked him. It was magical, this production of cold fruit drinks in the middle of the wilderness after days of dazzling heat over those rocks. 'More.' He handed me another bottle. 'You got it from an Italian army dump,' I said. 'Where is it?'

'This is the last of it,' he said, coyly revealing the other four bottles. I gave him two shillings for the four bottles and he gripped the money in his narrow black fists and said, 'I'll work for you. Take me with you.' He spoke good army-type Swahili.

'Impossible. What is your tribe?'

'I am a Garrei,' he said, and he looked it, black face like a ferocious eagle, two enormous black eyes, and a shock of woolly black hair that you could have filled two cushions with. He was about fifteen. All he had on him was a piece of white cloth round his loins and a long dagger. He was ready to go anywhere, tomorrow, now.

The Garrei are even harder, fiercer, more emotional than the Somalis (to whom they are related through the Hawiya tribal group), but this lad, Mohamed, was like a quivering black harp which burst into flames during emotional stress. He turned out to be the most savage, hysterical, loyal and dangerous human being I ever had with me in the bush. If he felt rage he acted upon it at once, with a knife, or with his nails and teeth; if he felt generous he gave everything away in sight, most of it yours. He stole, lied, made many enemies.

I should not have taken him with me from his own hell-home of El Wak, and I refused to do so, though weakly after long argument with him, but he stowed away in the convoy before dawn and it was five hundred miles afterwards that he showed himself, with his big burning, serious eyes.

'I have done it,' he said. 'I have come with you. Thank you. I will serve you. I have always wished to travel and now I am travelling.'

'It will not be like you imagine,' I said. 'Your life with me. You think it will be in houses in towns, but it will be like your own life, safari, safari, safari, on rock and in thorns. You will be sorry you have come, but it will be too late. It is too late now. When will you see your home again?' Among the Somalis he was like a Swede trying to be a Greek in Greece, and it was impossible.

'Some day,' he said. That was savage freedom, for a boy to jump on a truck and disappear, perhaps forever, without needing to run and ask his elders, without knowing where he was going, or how he would live, or even what he would earn. He just wanted to go and he had gone. The next day he stabbed an askari who upset him, and the askaris took hold of him and beat him until he fell down unconscious. Then he came to me to report, after the stabbed askari had shown me the knife wound through his shoulder.

'Give me your knife,' I said. He was shaking with anger, his big eyes devouring the askari's face, as if he wanted to kill him right there. He hesitated about giving me the knife.

'I must speak,' he said. 'I have a right to speak.'

'You stabbed before you spoke. Give me that knife.' He handed me the knife and I turned with it and threw it far and high and we watched it fall into the thick grey thorn bush.

'If I ever see you with a knife again, without my permission,' I told him, 'I'll beat you myself, with a whip. Do you hear that? And then I'll take you a hundred miles from wherever we are and I'll drop you in the bush, naked. I'll leave you with nothing. Have you heard that, and believed it? Do you still want to work with me?'

'Yes.'

'And remember about the knife?'

'Yes.'

'Then finish. The *shauri* is finished. The askaris flogged you. Next time I will do it.'

'He insulted me—' Mohamed began.

'I don't want to hear now what happened. You used your knife. That cancels all your case for me. No more talk. Finish.'

In the camp, among the Somalis and Abyssinians he was a complete stranger, and they jeered and laughed at his strange efforts to talk their languages. A true savage has never had to control his angers and appreciations. He has never had to keep silent when in the wrong, never had to hold back when insulted, never had to behave in stages of childhood, boyhood, manhood. Mohamed was a headlong type, who screamed aloud with fury when upset, and the askaris goaded him, and it looked as if he might have to learn to control himself. But I cursed the night he came with that Aranciata and attached himself to my caravan.

I stopped the convoy half a mile out of Mogadishu so as to wash and change into a clean bush shirt and shorts, and we could see the white flashing buildings below us on the edge of the Indian Ocean, glittering silver and blue water with a horizon flatter than even Mohamed had ever seen. He was standing, as if in fear, his head forward, staring in unbelief at the ocean and the buildings. And the askaris were watching him and laughing. He had never seen anything like it in his life before, and there was no doubt that it scared him, all of it.

'The water is moving,' he said to me, not taking his eyes off it. 'It's like milk boiling.' He was watching the surf swell and burst on the rocks far off in snowy foam, and the surge of the ocean catching the golden sun, and to him it looked as if the whole safe universe was in motion.

'Let's take him down to see and feel the water,' I said to the askaris. We piled into the trucks and drove hard until we came round Mogadishu and I stopped my truck not far from the waves. The sharp, salty, almost rotten, bitter stench of the Indian Ocean filled the nostrils, and when Mohamed got down off his truck he was paralyzed, rooted there in the sand and trembling from head to foot as he watched and listened to the great tumult of the ocean rolling to him. He had never visualized anything like it and he could not speak. Even the askaris were silent as they watched him study it all with his rolling, worried eyes. It was a most solemn moment.

'What's the matter with it?' he said to me. 'What's it for? Why does it smell like that? Where does it go to? Is it boiling?' He could hardly speak with fear and wonder.

'There's a big fire under it and it's boiling,' one of the askaris said, and all the others laughed at Mohamed and took pleasure in their worldliness and knowledge, but for me it was one of the strangest experiences I have ever had, seeing a desert savage shivering in front of the ocean for the first time, as if expecting the ground to melt and swallow him up at any moment. We must all have been like that once, in a time of thunder or storm, a million years ago in innocence.

He was silent for hours afterwards, looking almost crushed by the experience he had had. But that very evening he vanished into the town and I warned police patrols to watch out for him.

They found him in a mosque arguing with an old man who was threatening to have him hanged unless he took his savage self off the premises. He had been chased there by a crowd of Somalis with whom he had begun a quarrel, God knows what about.

As a Garrei, Mohamed thought of himself as the bravest, cleverest, noblest human being alive, and he took a great interest in fighting with the Somalis whom he had said he hated.

'It'll be easier to handle in the bush, all this,' I thought. Had there been a convoy travelling back the thousand miles to his home I would have put him on it, under guard, and yet I knew that in the bush, in trouble, he would be good, headlong, and perhaps might become tamed enough for him to enjoy his new life.

I had to go after some raiders on the other side of the Webi Shabeli shortly after arriving in Mogadishu, and I was given a *gogli*, a guide and messenger who knew that country and all the elephant herds in it like he knew the back of his hard slender black hands. This was Ibrahim, a tall, grave man, the finest looking human being I have ever met, and the most fearless. He once brought me two killers through moving herds of elephants, in darkness, and laughed while we went over the incidents. He had had to run, the two murderers tied to his left wrist, between the screaming elephants whom he had disturbed, with the murderers trying to bite through their bonds as they stumbled in fear beside him.

Ibrahim was the only person I ever knew to frighten Mohamed, who challenged Ibrahim to fight after the older man had rebuked him for impudence. He seized Mohamed, lifted him high in the air, and hurled him into a clump of thorns, and then went after him and seizing him again, dragged him through the thorns by his ankles. Mohamed, bleeding and humiliated, got up to fight again, with his nails and teeth, but Ibrahim flung him back into the thorns. I heard the high shouts of rage and the threatening cries from my camp under some thorn trees, and Ibrahim came, dragging Mohamed through the sand by one foot. He left him at my feet, saying, 'Unless this one can be restrained, Effendi, a man will kill him outright. He has the tongue of a snake. I have not met one like him before. I have had to be hard with him. I would kill a man for less than this snake said to me, but he is your servant and I merely chastised him, for his sake and ours. I have presumed, I know, but I could not help it.'

'What have you to say, Mohamed?' I asked the lad who was glowering at the whole world and wiping his body which was crisscrossed by long white and bleeding scratches.

'I was wrong,' he said. 'And then *he* was wrong. He has threatened to kill me. What do you think of that? Would you let him kill me?' It was his admission to being wrong which astonished me. I had never expected to hear that from him.

'So you were wrong, were you? You admit you were wrong?'

'I could not help being wrong. These people want to treat me like a slave. I am no slave. I am of a fighting race. I am a Garrei. I cannot be expected to put up with the insults I am treated to by all these people.'

'But you admit you were in the wrong this time? That is good, to say that.'

'I say it because I know this man will kill me unless I say it. He said so. He will stab me in the back some night. I know these people.'

'Don't you know Ibrahim is an official, a man of learning and years of experience who cannot be expected to stand by and listen to a boy insult him? I tell you you will get killed here if you go on like this, and I want you to live, and to learn. You must control your temper, or you will be killed.'

'I will try again,' Mohamed said, scowling at Ibrahim. 'I will shut my mouth, even when I am insulted, if that is what you want.'

'The *shauri* is finished,' I said.

Then Mohamed went down with malaria, the shattering illness which the Webi Shabeli gives generously to all who linger by its brown flood and its gloomy thickets. All the askaris rallied to save the savage, their goad, their whipping boy. It looked as if Mohamed would die at one time, for he had the shakes so badly that you could feel the heat coming off his wet skin in waves. On the morning he came out of his delirium and was lying in that post-malaria state when you feel like a twisted, wrung-out steaming towel, light in the head and quite careless about dying (in fact it would be a pleasure), Mohamed sent for me.

'I have not died,' he said when I sat down on the floor beside the straw mat on which he lay.

'No, you are alive,' I said. '*Wallahi.*'

'Ibrahim brought fruit to me.' He peered into my eyes as he went on, 'Is that a good thing, to bring fruit to your enemy? I do not understand that kind of thing. What am I to make of it? What is the meaning of it?'

'It means,' I said, 'that Ibrahim has accepted other customs than the old ones, of killing and revenge, and never forgiving or for-getting. When I am angry with you I am angry with you, and then it is finished. I do not go on punishing or shouting, do I? The anger is only for that time, for that particular time when you have caused some trouble through losing your head. The anger is not for always. It is finished, forgotten. We begin again immediately afterwards. That is what Ibrahim has done. He is a man, a man who could kill, but does not. Open your thick skull, Mohamed, and understand. Let your *akili*, your intelligence, show you what is simple. You have no enemy if you refuse to have one, and Ibrahim is like that. He is a true man. Have you understood that?'

'No,' he said, shaking his head. 'I understand your angers when I have been foolish, and your forgetting of them, because you are a white man and have no time for remembering these things. You have the rations, the drill, the patrols, the bundles of papers to write on, the looking after of the askaris and the remembering of all the things that have to be done, with the corporals and the sergeant listening to you. But I cannot understand my enemy, a black man like myself, coming with fruit when we have made enemies of each other. I would not eat his fruit. I gave it to the old woman who sweeps the camp.' He sat up, his teeth bared, 'And I will never eat his fruit, or the fruit of any man like him. That is my custom.'

'You are only a boy, and a stupid boy,' I told him sternly, trying not to laugh aloud. 'But God will give you wisdom one day and you will look for friends and not enemies.'

'I am learning things,' he said to me. 'New customs, and lies, and troubles, and I will not always be a boy.'

'Do you want to go home?' I asked him. 'Would you like me to send you to your country again? I did not want you to come here. This is a hostile land where nothing much matters, and where you are a stranger. Do you want to return to El Wak?'

'So you are finished with me? You have had enough of my work? You want me to go?' He looked accusingly into my eyes. 'Where is the fighting, the trouble? You said there would be fighting. Have you seen me fight? Have you?' He challenged me to wait until I saw him fight.

'I have seen you stabbing and making fights,' I said. 'But I don't want that. You are a servant. Serve, or leave.'

'I will serve,' he said. 'But you think I cannot fight?'

'The askaris and I will do the fighting,' I said. 'That is our work. Yours is to clean and bring and make fires. When you are a man you can become an askari, if you like, but not now. Serve.'

'I will never be an askari,' he told me.

'Why not?'

'I would not allow a sergeant to call me the names your sergeant calls the askaris when he is angry. I would not put up with it. That is no life.'

'It is only a custom,' I said. 'The askaris know it. It is something you do not understand unless you are a soldier. The askaris were not forced to be soldiers. They asked to be soldiers, and they know what it all means.'

'I cannot understand any of it,' Mohamed said, sullenly. 'It is all madness, all of it.' And he never said a truer word, though I shook my head, patient and sighing.

Three months after this, wildernesses away from the Webi Shabeli river, he stabbed my cook, a fat, cynical man who lived only for ghee, and who had a tongue like a knife. He gave Mohamed a public genealogy which sent Mohamed running screaming for a knife, which he got, and came back into the kitchen and drove the knife right through the fat arm of the genealogist who had gone too far. ('Son of a sick hyena, grandson of a noseless thief, descendant of vultures, father to be of a hermaphrodite baboon, filth and refuse untouchable, animal without religion'—and so on.)

I felt this was the end. It was over two thousand miles of nothing until you got to Mohamed's country, but I was by then up to my neck in more serious troubles. Yet even so, I was tired enough of Mohamed to carry out my threat, to take him and dump him, yet I knew I could not do it, though he volunteered to be dumped.

'Finish with me,' he said bravely, defiantly, while the bandaged, enraged cook gave his screeched, emotional evidence over Mohamed's thin shoulder. 'Take me and throw me into the bush, as you said you would,' Mohamed went on. 'For it is right. I cannot put up with what these beasts and imbeciles say to me here. So I must go. Let it be so. There is no other way, for I cannot put up with this pig here—'

'Now he is calling me a pig,' the cook screamed, wringing his fists in the air. 'You heard him, this beast-child, this insolent little filthy boy. I cannot stay here. I cannot cook. My brain and my heart are aflame. My stomach is burning.'

'Get out, both of you,' I shouted. 'I'll think it over and do the punishing when I've thought. If either of you raise one finger I'll kill you. Do you hear, I'll kill you.'

'Kill both of us,' the cook yelled, 'kill both of us.' He was dragged off to his kitchen by the askaris and the orderly corporal took Mohamed by the ear and led him to the lines.

'And if I see either of you today in front of my eyes, anywhere,' I yelled after them, from the doorway, 'I'll shoot you both, I swear before God. I swear it.' A silence fell over the camp. Then I called in the manic chiefs for one more effort to make them give up the Italian rifles their tribe possessed.

It was the askaris who pleaded for Mohamed, the askaris who had goaded him and who had been threatened so many times by this savage from the rim of the Somali world, a nomad like themselves but who was so maddeningly and pointlessly proud of being a Garrei, when all knew that to be the chosen of God here was to be a Somali.

'He is sitting at the edge of the camp, silent and without food,' the deputation of askaris told me the next morning. 'He will not speak to anyone. We have decided that we are sorry for this little fool, Effendi. We know now that he cannot understand anything. He should be sent away forever, but we have come to ask you not to send him away. There he is. Look.' One of them went to the doorway of the company office and pointed into the whitish yellow glare. I went to look. Mohamed was sitting like a yogi, about two

135

hundred yards off, about twenty yards beyond the line of white rocks which marked the boundary of the camp.

'He has been there since first light, Effendi, and says he will stay there until the cook is punished. He is mad, this boy, Effendi, and God likes the mad. What will you do with him?'

'So you accept him at last, do you?' I asked.

I still do not know, and perhaps will never decide if what I did after that was the right thing, but that it was the right Somali thing, the right thing for the desert Muslim world of rough justice, I have no doubt. And it finished the feud between the poisonous-tongued cook and the ferocious Garrei youth.

I took them both into the stretch of hard shale we used for a parade ground, and when they saw the rhino-hide whip I had in my hand they both stared.

'Justice,' I told them, 'is a kind of official revenge men can perform on each other, and you both need justice. Say nothing—' they were going to unload another million words about their case against each other. 'You,' I said to the cook, 'called him vile names, after he had insulted you, and after you had insulted him, and so on. Say nothing! I will go on. And you,' I said to Mohamed, 'took a knife and stabbed the cook. So you have seriously wronged each other. Lie down,' I said to the cook.

He pointed to his wound which the dresser had dealt with again that morning. 'Lie down?' he cried. 'After I have been stabbed?'

'This thing is being ended here and now,' I said. 'Lie down, or do you want the askaris to put you down?'

'What happens after I lie down? Do you mean to beat me?'

'No. Mohamed here will give you six lashes, and then he lies down and you give him six back. And after that, if I ever hear one word of quarrel, *one single word* I'll flog you both until you can't walk. I have no gaol here, and no transport to send you away from here, but you will give each other justice instead. Now lie down.'

He lay down and I threw the whip to Mohamed, who seized it and shook it over the cook, who stared up at me and said, 'I agree to this as long as there is no trick.'

'There is no trick. You shall beat Mohamed as well.'

'Remember that, beast,' he shouted up at Mohamed. 'Remember it. Now strike.' Mohamed lashed him six times and the cook lay in silence with his face on his hands, stiffening as the whip came down each time. Then he got up and said, 'Give me that whip now and lie down there, *yiro*, little impudent child.'

'If I hear you utter one more insult from this moment,' I told the cook, 'I'll beat you. Do you hear that?'

'I hear,' he said. Mohamed had hurt him, and Mohamed did not want to lie down now to get the other half of the justice we had set in motion here.

'So that is the Garrei way,' a corporal cried at him. 'To punish and then to run when it is your turn. Lie down,' and with burning eyes Mohamed lay down. The cook gave him six lashes which he took in enormous and powerful silence. Then he got up and the cook threw the whip down on the sand.

'Are you satisfied that you have had and given justice, you two fools?' I asked them.

'I am satisfied,' the cook said. He knew he had hurt Mohamed.

'And you?' I asked Mohamed.

'He cannot walk properly,' Mohamed said. 'I hurt him more than he hurt me.'

'No, I hurt you more than you hurt me,' the cook said angrily.

'It's finished now,' I told them. 'That's an order. And remember if there is one more word between you I'll flog you until you can't walk. Now get back to work.'

They never spoke to each other again, though they worked together often, and I think it was the beginning of Mohamed's first try at controlling himself. But some months later, in Mogadishu, he attacked an Italian in a repair shop, who gave him such a handling in return that Mohamed could not eat for three days. The Italian came to me and apologized, though puzzled by the sheer savagery of Mohamed's attack.

'Where is he from, this animal, Signor Capitano?' he asked me. 'From what tribe is he?' I explained and the Italian said, 'I am glad I never soldiered in that country, then, for this creature is of a kind quite new to me. Like a leopard. A leopard. I had to defend myself as if against a leopard.'

Mohamed's explanation of the affair was, 'He is your enemy, an Italian, who insulted me, so I would not take it, from your enemy.'

'This is the finish,' I told Mohamed.

'I will try again. I will try to be good,' he said. 'I will.'

'No, it is the finish this time,' I assured him. 'I am sending you to El Wak.'

'I don't want to go back there,' he said. 'I will try again.'

'*I* want you to go back,' I said. 'More than anything *I* want you to go back.'

'What about my work? It is good work. You have said so.'

'It is splendid work,' I agreed. 'But you are mad. Mad. And one day you will kill somebody and hang for it, or somebody will kill you first. And I am weary of this situation now. I have other things to worry about. Many other things.'

But I did not get rid of him. He appeared again after I had arranged his transport to Mandera, near El Wak, and in despair, and fury, I took him on again.

He disappeared in the Ogaden one night, and at that time I felt certain that the local tribe had taken him and killed him. He just vanished, after being in trouble with the local headman, in an area where it did not pay to have trouble with local headmen. I think they must have killed him, that quivering savage whose knife hand moved faster than his brain, for it was a very long way from El Wak, and in a country where you can get your death, free, at any time, especially if you are a stranger. None of my enquiries for him came to anything. I was silent and let the time slide and pile over him, but I never forgot him, or those moving moments when he stood transfixed by the sight of the heaving blue Indian Ocean. All over a bottle of Aranciata brought one night to a white man lying smoking beside a convoy where Kenya, Somalia and Abyssinia meet on the map.

CHAPTER TWENTY-ONE

THE two best Somalis I ever knew, and I mean men who can take the city for what it is, a pleasant experience for a time, and be at home in the wilderness again, after missing it, were Mohamed Saad and Ahamed Hussein. With these two I weathered all kinds of situations all over Somalia, and I would give a lot to meet them again. I put out feelers during my few hours in Mogadishu with Ali, but nobody had ever heard of them. The wastes had swallowed them up again.

Mohamed Saad was one of the best friends I ever made in the bush, or anywhere else for that matter.

He had fought with the Italian army as a member of the ir-regulars called the Dubat (*Quinto Gruppo*), and what was good about the Dubat was that they were not drilled and broken down into infantry, but were allowed to stay Somali, operating like raider bands, living frugally and never dependent on truck loads of ghee, flour, and the usual mass of requirements required for the usual infantry troops. We more or less continued the tradition of the Dubat in those wastes, from necessity, turning to camel and goat for food as soon as the rations ran out. The Dubat irregulars were very proud of themselves and their traditions, and cherished the memory of their Italian commanders, particularly of Colonnello Becchis, and Maggiore Cimarutta, of whom they often spoke to me. I recruited as many ex-Dubat as I could find, and the word went round in the bush that if you were ex-Dubat you could always get a job with me.

I first came across Mohamed Saad at about three o'clock in the morning when about to leave on a raid with a section of askaris. I wanted to be at a certain waterhole far into the bush at sunrise so as to surprise some armed raiders who would be watering their camels there before moving north.

One of my askaris brought Mohamed Saad to us as we were sitting in the warm moonlight oiling weapons under a tree. The askari told me that this man knew the waterhole as well as the fastest way to it. I told him to sit down and he squatted down in front of me on the thick red sand.

You cannot mistake human goodness in a face when you see it. You can be mistaken about all kinds of other things but never about real goodness in a human face, and Mohamed Saad was good, I knew, as soon as I saw him. He was a lean, well dried-out bush type, about thirty, with steady, honest eyes.

'I need work,' he said. 'I am starving since my tribal section was raided and all the camels taken. If I take you fast to the waterhole will you give me work? I am a good tracker and used to weapons. I will serve you well. Maybe you could use me as a servant.'

He had fought in two battles, the last of them on the Abyssinian border a year before when the Italian army was collapsing. After that he had been captured and had spent some months in a prison camp. When he was released he made his way back to the Mudugh country to find his tribe being raided and looted by more powerful tribes around, the tribes we were then trying to disarm and subdue.

I gave him some rations and cigarettes and he led us through the bush in the darkness at such a pace that my shirt was ripped to pieces on the thorns and my bare legs lacerated, but I could not complain. It was I who had pressed for haste. We took three prisoners who gladly and proudly admitted that they had taken part in the big killings of a couple of months ago. I signed Mohamed on as my servant and he taught me the construction of all the tribal groups in the Mudugh, as well as teaching me the camel brands used by every tribe. Hour after hour we would sit over the dying camp fire and talk, askaris of every tribe telling of their service as Italian soldiers against the Abyssinians and the British, recalling the failures or virtues of this and that officer, a loot, of good eating times after a victory, and of bitter retreat with thirst and wounds. And then, like all men of action, they would begin to argue as to who had suffered most, endured more, outdone other men, except Mohamed Saad who smiled and listened. He was wise, and he had compassion for men, while possessing the vanity which made him tough and tireless.

'Do you like this life?' I asked him one night when we were marching behind the camels. The wastes rolled and glittered all about us in the fierce moonlight and the only sounds were the scuff of the askaris' sandals and the clink of rifle barrels. You felt you could see to the ends of the earth, so far off were the jagged moonlit horizons around us.

'There is no other life, Effendi,' Mohamed said, smiling. 'What more can a man ask than to be young and to have health and to be

140

free? When the sun comes up we will drink fresh camel milk and then we will sleep, and then we will get up again and pray and eat, and then we will walk on. I am contented.'

He would check all my possessions, my web equipment, pistol and ammunition, grenades, sub machine gun, clean and oil them all. He would examine my shirts, sew on buttons, launder them with the foaming root called *gasangas*, a fine replacement for soap but liable to leave painful splinters behind in cloth, and high up in the hills on the old Abyssinian frontier, where it was very cold at night, he would lay out my bedroll on the scorching earth at four in the afternoon, so that when I crawled into it at night it was like entering an oven. He sewed and repaired sandals, trimmed the frayed edges of puttees, and then, one day, revealed casually that he could repair truck engines. He was a good shot with a rifle, and he could cover amazing distances with messages at a tireless, steady lope.

Imagine the trust a servant placed in his wandering employer in the great spaces of Asia and Africa, the total commitment involved in travelling enormous distances, sometimes thousands of miles from his tribal home, to some outpost, malarial or parched, where he may be thrown out of his employment by his master. They have done this for centuries for men of all colours and creeds, and asked very little in return. In a way they place their whole life in the hands of the stranger, who may be cruel, or mean, or thoughtless. They never know. These servants were the true adventurers, the men who gambled all, took all kinds of chances, survived all sorts of dangers, forgave and were forgiven, and usually possessed little more when they were finished with their master than they had set out with. In the chaos of the worlds in which they were born and raised they found a kind of safety, a kind of anchor, with the man they went to work for. They knew far more about their masters than even the women their masters returned to one day. They had no trade unions, no fixed hours, no scales of wages. They pilfered, drank, used their masters' position to raise small loans in far off places, often enough, but in many ways were far better people than their masters.

Mohamed Saad stayed with me for two years and when I was transferred to the Burma campaign I smuggled him into Kenya with me, hoping to take him with me to Burma which he wanted. He was a subject of the Italian empire and should not have been in Nairobi at all, which was ridiculous, as he was a Somali and had as much right to be anywhere in Eastern Africa as any other Somali, and more right than all the white men. But I could not get him into military service, or even take him with me to Burma as a signed up batman, though I knew one officer who had managed to get an Italian Somali to Burma with him. So we said goodbye over a coffee in an Indian *duka* down River Road one morning.

'If ever you come back, Effendi,' he said, 'to Somalia, just send for me. I'm going back to my tribe.' He did not like the green jungle battle dress I was wearing. He said it would not iron well. I told him that ironing had not been going on in Burma since 1941. 'Uniforms should be ironed,' he insisted. 'We are in a city, remember.'

When the war was over I went back to Somalia but I never found Mohamed again, though I sent messages right through the Mudugh and the Nogal. He had vanished.

I never found Ahamed Hussein again either, the brilliant linguist, expert corporal, all round mixer and subtle handler of varied problems. He too had vanished into the two hundred and fifty thousand square miles which had been our parish.

Like all Somalis, Ahamed had had no feeling of inferiority, no complex about being black, no worry about proving anything to the white man. All Somalis stroll up to you to talk. They do not hesitate or straighten themselves, or look haunted by any doubt as they approach a white man. They treat you like a Muslim, a brother. The rest is with you.

Ahamed was of a holy tribe called the Shekál. No one must ever attack or raid this holy tribe. There are two Shekál groups, one in the Ogaden, and one down south on the way to the Juba river. They are respected by even the most rapacious camel collectors.

Superbly intelligent, witty, philosophic, Ahamed never moaned when we were in difficulties, say, marooned for a couple of days in a rare flood when the rains exploded up in Abyssinia's foothills and sent brief raging rivers coursing down dried-out dongas far south in Somalia, or isolated for months in some God-forsaken litter of hot rocks and burning sand. Since his country's independence I have always hoped to come across his name as a member of the Somali government, for that is where he should be. He had compassion, firmness, sensitivity, a marvellous character. How strong this character was I was able to understand in 1947 when the Somali Youth League was becoming a great and vital force all over Somalia.

It was then astonishing to sit and listen to a Somali deny that he was a member of anything called a tribe, and to hear him acclaim that he was a Somali only, and that there was only one Somali race, and that there were no more tribes which had separated men and had made them enemies. While it made administration as we had known it, and still had to make it, impossible, it was wonderful to see this new movement among a race to whom tribalism had become a curse.

It was a part of the great stirring of all the peoples of Asia and Africa, set in motion by Gandhi and hastened by the Japanese army. Nothing can stop it now, luckily, and I have always counted myself as lucky to live in a time which saw this tremendous revolution, when even the coolie decided it was time to see what he could do outside the shafts of his rickshaw.

The Somalis wanted freedom too, and it was an Englishman who set the idea of the Somali Youth League in motion, and it was strange and exhilarating to see the speed with which the idea raced across the Somali wilderness, reaching the farthest primitive nomads behind their camels and giving the young men something to feel about beyond the length of their spears.

The askaris were not supposed to take part in this feverish movement, but they did, quietly. They had to, but Ahamed Hussein would not join, much as he believed in the movement. He said he would join it as soon as he was out of his uniform. He would join then because he was ready to do so, on his own decision, but he would not do so now, in uniform, when he was being threatened if he refused. Askaris told me that 'they' would kill Ahamed Hussein if he went on refusing to join.

We were in a lonely little town on the edge of the deserts, a straggle of white buildings strewn along the coast and dribbling into the warm, blue Indian Ocean.

'They' broke his jaw one night, while trying to kill him. They looked upon him as a person of importance and felt that his refusal to join the League would in some way discredit it.

Ahamed used to sleep in a room on the edge of the barrack area. In those areas you sleep lightly, especially if you have slept for years under the stars in places where it pays to wake quickly, and Ahamed told me that something, he did not know what, caused him to turn quickly in his sleep and jump off the bed. He swore he had heard no noise. As he turned over and moved off the bed an iron bar smashed down and caught him on the edge of his jaw and neck.

Had he not moved it would certainly have broken his skull. He went for the attackers in the darkness but they got away. I bound up his jaw and sent for 'them'. 'They' in no way represented the best of the League, but were old men who were trying to cash in on the new movement which was taking the youth away from their old and bloody hands. I knew the old man behind this violent deter-mination to enlist every askari into the League. But I could prove nothing, and Ahamed told him he would still not join the League.

Several times I had told Ahamed he should join the League, for soon Somalia would be free anyway, but he had always refused, and now he refused again, and refused the offer of a transfer to Mogadishu which I offered to arrange for him. Young members of the League came in to see me and to apologize for what had happened to Ahamed, swearing that they had had nothing to do with it. But they told me that the old men were trying to keep control of the League, old men who had sworn when the League first appeared that they would forbid it to function because it denied a man's most precious possession, his tribe.

'It will take years for men here to forget their knives and spears, Effendi,' Ahamed told me. 'They were stupid to want to kill me. They still think that killing changes things.' He used to laugh at my perplexity caused by the impossibility of trying cases when the accused would not divulge their tribal status to me. The League almost brought administration of justice to a standstill. And it could be very funny too.

I remember one old hardened bandit in his turban and loincloth, a man who could lift your clothes off without your knowing it, so able was he as a thief, laying his withered old claws on his chest in the court and saying cynically to me, 'Tribe? My tribe? I have no tribe. I am a Somali.' The whole court shook with laughter, for many could remember how those claws were often pressed against the lean chest when the old man had screamed the name of his tribe in pride, before the League came. The old man had to join in the laughter himself, unable to contain it. He went on refusing to name his tribe.

'Very well,' I said. 'I'll put you down as a Rahanwein tribe,' naming one of the 'slave tribes' of the river Juba, knowing this would incense him.

'I am not of that tribe,' he screeched across the court, again joining in the laughter. 'I am not of a slave tribe.'

'How do I know that?' I said. 'I've got to put you down as some tribe so it's going to be one of the Rahanwein.' Because of the nature of the case I had to have him declare his tribe. He lost his temper, forgot his plan, and screamed the name of the tribe across the court at me, and then stared round him as everybody in the room howled with laughter. I had to close the court for the day.

Genuine members of the League I eventually allowed the right to refuse to give their tribe names. This rallying to the League in that great wilderness, among such tribally obsessed people, was one of the most wonderful things to witness, (and yet, that senti-mental reverence I had for tradition silently mourned).

The League ran an administration of its own, preparing for self government. It was touching to see the young men trying so hard to put an end to the tribal strife which had been their curse for so long. But I could not believe that that marvellous fervour could last, and the pride with which the three police askaris in Mogadishu twenty years later told me their tribes made me think that it must have been easier to stick to tribalism. The blood feuds of tribalism have been their curse, and the blood price, *diyya*, which must be paid in camels.

When it was time for me to throw aside my uniform and leave Somalia behind, I asked Ahamed Hussein what he would do with his life. He said he would go back to his tribe and the camels. He spoke four languages fluently, could read and write them perfectly, and could have gone far in many a career away from his desert, but he was going back to that lonely life of the nomad. Perhaps this is a real strength in the Somali. He does not think there is anything discreditable in being a member of his primitive living group. They do not have the sad longing of the Bantu and the white men for a collar and tie and a desk, yet it will be the Bantu who will soften and civilize Africa, because he longs for comfort and ease. The Somali never surrenders to the armchair or the big house. In fact, in the small Italian settlements in southern Somalia when the Italian army was collapsing in 1941, I noticed how the nomads who broke into the big cool Italian houses used to shit exactly in the centre of every room, and then leave. I have never come across this strange form of savage wit anywhere else. The Somalis swore that the Abyssinian deserters from Italian units were doing it, when I asked them the reason for this custom with its almost mathematical care for the placing of insult.

I went after some of these marauding Abyssinians when hunting down a band of them who had broken into an Italian house where an Italian woman was alone with her children. They had thrown hand grenades into the lonely house, then broke in and had smashed in a beautiful little girl's face so horribly that I had to go out to vomit after seeing her. One of them had done this with a club. The mother, whose husband was a prisoner of war, was out of her mind, holding the silent, stupefied child in her arms. Well armed, some of these Abyssinians liked to fight it out when they were tracked down in the bush. Italian East Africa was a place of turmoil during the time of the Italian defeat, and rough justice of all kinds was dealt out on all sides, and, much as one had an understanding for Abyssinian sentiments towards the Italians who had invaded their country, I found I did not wish to extend it to the animal who had destroyed the child's face when we ran the raiders to earth one night in the bush.

There were more pathetic Abyssinians than these armed bandits, men who had been rounded up in Addis Ababa after the attempt there on Graziani's life. Some of them were in terrible physical straits, many of them being unable to hold down food which was given to them, and these I looked after in a disused barracks for some weeks until I could get transport to start them on the first move of their long way home.

I asked Ahamed what he thought of Abyssinians. 'There are always too many flies about where Abyssinians camp,' he said.

The Abyssinians liked to hang strips of raw meat in their barrack rooms. They liked it high, and raw, and the flies swarmed. I recruited some of the healthy Abyssinians as askaris and fought a losing battle against the raw meat in the barrack rooms. In the bush it never mattered. When I armed them and lined them up in threes for their first march into a deserted Italian barracks the right hand man at the head of the marching unit broke ranks, ran a few paces ahead, raised his rifle and began to leap in the air and declaim in Amharic, and the troops answered him in fierce shouts. This was a custom allowed them in the Italian army and I was sorry when I had to forbid it as it seemed a sensible way of dealing with the boredom of long marches. The Italians seemed to me to have been very understanding in the way they tended to allow colonial troops to retain some colour in their lives. The British tend to flatten everything out into a disciplined sameness which gets on the nerves of exuberant peoples, though it pays off in action.

'It is not fair,' a Somali chief shouted at me when we made him and his raiders prisoner one night at a waterhole he was sure we would never reach. 'It's not right that officers like you should be running across country like this, and in ragged clothes too, standing to eat your meals out of a tin with a fork, and behaving like us instead of officers. The Italians never did this. It is not right and it isn't fair. Why don't you behave like officers, like the Italians used to?'

This old chief spoke good Italian and had received a medal and a rank from the Italians for his loyalty during their war in Abyssinia, and he tried hard to convince me of the ungentlemanly and improper life we officers were living in Somalia. 'We cannot have a proper respect for you,' he said again and again, fretfully, querulously.

He asked me what the whole war was about anyway, and I can remember sitting by the waterhole that night and wondering how it was that the war I had joined because it was against fascism had landed me in ragged shorts and shirts in a geography like the moon where fascism had vanished like a thin mist and the war had rolled far away into distant silences.

It was an interesting conversation we had beside that waterhole, for I learned for the first time how world news penetrated to these nomads, and how much it interested them. They hungered for and cherished news from the outside world, and the best of it seemed to come from Arab dhow captains on the coast far away. They were very much interested in the future of Palestine, and the old chief liked to hark back to the days of the Turkish empire. The average Somali, I found, had more of an idea of the *shape* and extent of the world outside Africa than had the Bantu in the bush of Kenya. This may have been because they regarded themselves as a part of Islam, an ancient empire, whereas the Bantu remembered nothing equivalent, though they too had a long but now forgotten past.

The old chief asked me to tell him about Hitler and Mussolini. His summing up on various white races was interesting. German and British rifles were excellent, finely and strongly made. Belgian rifles, (from the old Ethiopian army) which could be found among the tribes where the Ogaden met Abyssinia were good too, but Italian rifles when compared with the others were cheap and poorly made. 'As soon as I realized this,' he told me, 'I began to worry, for I knew that the Italians must lose, and my pension would go with them. What are you going to do about my pension, Signor Capitano?'

'Nothing,' I said, regretfully. 'I am going to arrest you for raiding and stealing camels, for now. Years from now, when the war is over, you will be able to go into the matter of your pension. I will make a note of it on your papers when you are tried.'

'Will the Italians come back here when you have gone from here?' he asked me.

'If you want them back they'll come back,' I told him. 'There is a thing called the United Nations, and one day you will all be able to tell them your story. The world will be rearranged, shaken up. All will be changed everywhere.'

'I have seen it all change before,' the old chief said to me bitterly. 'You are too young to have seen anything change yet. Change is not always for the good.'

'It depends on who and what you are,' I told him.

'Yes,' he said. 'It does, and it does not pay to lose, either. I had honour under the Italians, and now I am a prisoner. That is what change has done to me. And you still haven't explained to me why the white men are all fighting.'

'That,' I said, 'goes back for about two thousand years. *E' un abitudine adesso.*'

'War is all right,' this old embittered warrior said. 'But it is good to know what the war is for. White men do not seem to know why they fight. We Somalis fight for camels, and here you are chasing us about and annoying us for doing it, while you, the white men are fighting all over the world. Do you expect us to understand that kind of thing?'

'No,' I told him.

'Men fight for power and honour,' he said. 'That is why they fight, no matter what they say. You win or you lose. Do they feed you well in a prison?'

'Quite well.'

He got up and brushed the red dust off his *lungi*. 'Remember what I have said, Signor Capitano,' he finished. 'Dress like an officer, and behave like one. Stop this running about in the bush. I cannot respect you for this kind of behaviour. May I sleep now or are you going to start walking back to your fort at this hour of the night?'

I had many conversations with this chief while he was a prisoner. He finally admitted to me that he was tired of tribal fighting and only wished there could be a Somalia in which old men could live in peace. I hope he has it now.

CHAPTER TWENTY-TWO

'WHEN the Europeans go from Kenya,' Ali said, 'what will happen to the Somalis who live there? They will not live under Kikuyu rule. They will refuse.'

I told him I did not know what would happen to all the Somalis in Kenya, but I agreed with him that it was unlikely they would be willing to live under what he called 'Kikuyu rule'.

Africa is like an enormous Europe, full of people of one colour, but who differ like Swedes and Spaniards, Greeks and French, Czechs and Italians.

The Somalis, whether they live in the place still called French Somaliland, or what was British and Italian Somaliland, and in the Ogaden which is now ruled by Ethiopia, and in the Somali country of Northern Kenya, are all one race with one language and one religion and one way of life, and eventually they must all unite as the pencil lines drawn by European powers on the African map a century or so ago blur and vanish.

I had once tried hard to get the Somalis to give up their contempt for Bantu people, at a time when we had Nyasa soldiers in the scattered garrisons of the Somali moonscape. But they broke the hearts of the softer Bantu soldiers.

'We cannot obey slaves,' Somalis told me. 'It is impossible for us to live under slave people even when they are in uniform and have arms.'

'We cannot go on living here among these people,' a Nyasa askari had cried hysterically at me. He was charged with causing a riot in a coffee shop in one of the more sun-blasted of the desert outposts. 'They despise us, they sneer at us, they hate us,' the Nyasa told me. I knew all this but could not change the Somali feeling of superiority over these chunky, black people from the lush south, nor wipe out the memory they had of a time when these Bantu people were slave material for the Muslim world to the north. That was the trouble, the curse of race, looks, noses, lips, eyes, legends. Colour has little to do with it.

They liked to taunt the Bantu askaris, and the Bantu innocence had little chance against the sharp, splintered wit of the nomad Somalis. Fights were frequent, and the unhappy Nyasas pined for home. They also had the misfortune not to be able to go long without water compared with Somali askaris, and the Somalis used to enjoy baiting them about this, especially on long patrols in the fierce heat.

But the average Nyasa soldier had a staunchness of personality which took a lot to bend and break it, and the Somalis, and their wilderness, were able to do it in the end.

Many of the Nyasas fell, insanely sometimes, in love with the beautiful Somali women, and when they got them they worshipped them, to the amusement, and anger, of the Somali males who watched it all. Far more beautiful than the Bantu women so far away, the Somali girls first laughed at this worship, and then grew to like the strange experience of being precious to a man. Somali men knew how to love, but not with the hopeless tenderness which the Nyasa soldiers brought to it.

The Somalis never treated the Bantu as their equals, not even when they soldiered together in the same units. A slight warmth might be shown to a Bantu who proved that he was a Mohammedan, though even then there could still linger suspicion and hostility. A great deal of it had to do with looks, facial features, and the Somali, lean and handsome and hawknosed, felt himself to be more becoming than the Bantu African. In fact the Somalis resented being considered Africans at all, and they demanded different treatment in rations and uniform than that given to the Bantu. Bantu troops like discipline. Somalis resent it. Every individual Somali fights to stay himself, a person. The Bantu liked the certainty and safety of unit life, and functioned well as a receiver of orders. The Somali fumed under discipline and loved the irregular life, the scattered patrol and the lone effort which might bring him to individual notice, to recognition for what he might achieve on his own. The Bantu had patience. The Somali had to control himself, even when learning how to handle weapons, which he loved and cherished. I have seen a Somali tear a machine gun out of the hands of an instructor and prove on the spot that he needed no more instruction, that he knew it all and could handle and strip and assemble the weapon after one lesson. He had resented the very implication that he needed the long dreary lessons which the instructor seemed resigned to giving him.

When the Somali battalion sailed for the Burma campaign they demanded Indian scale rations, and uniforms with collars on them, 'like Indian troops'. They did not want to dress like the Bantu troops, who wore collarless khaki blouses. They all went into green jungle battledress anyway when they reached the front.

When the Somali battalion, after a shattering artillery bombardment from the Japanese guns, finally attacked with the bayonet, they went headlong and their officers could not keep up with them. One of them who was decorated for bravery in that battle, a Degodiya from the Northern Frontier of Somali Kenya, told me that he had enjoyed it, and that he admired the way the Japanese infantry liked to stand and fight it out. But he was not satisfied with the ghee ration they were getting. We had a long conversation about it, and it made me think of the ghee problems in Somalia, and the Somali askari could not understand what I was laughing about.

In the deserts of Somalia the Nyasa soldiers were all right for about six months, but after that, worn down by isolation and heat, insult and hostility from the Somalis, they deteriorated. They could not understand this continual challenge, this nomad *machismo*, or the sharp, impatient bloody mindedness of the Somali.

CHAPTER TWENTY-THREE

'IT'S time for me to go,' I told Ali. We had one more fresh lime and water and then we got up and left the hotel.

I did not like all the memories that those hot streets had brought up for me out the world which lay behind Mogadishu. Many of the memories awakened I had suppressed, but they kept trying to break through and be inspected for what they were, mere memories of brutal things which quailed if looked at directly, like all evil memories of the silent area we call the past. There is no such thing as justice, only the effort towards it, and the effort is everything. One had tried to give justice, in impossible conditions, but I knew I was still lacerated inside by most of the life in that wilderness which I still loved, even though one had gone nearly insane in it at times, and had done insane things, and some good things by accident. Some people like to issue justice, to sit and judge and condemn, and to feel that smug certainty, so necessary when dealing with lies and half truths and imagined happenings, all of them grouped about a mystery. But when you have condemned a killer to death, even the most ferocious human animal, you never forget that terrible moment which shows you your puny little assumption, between meals, that you can know what has brought another human into the trap. It is the very imperfection, I suppose, the very shaky machinery behind the pomp and mystery put up—the wigs, maces, woolsacks, black caps and other claptrap, which makes one pity our condition which forces pretence upon us, the pretence at making the dirty thing great and grave. The world has been a jungle since it began, no doubt of it, and The Bomb may be the one thing which has brought it to an unwilling stop, for war was man's only holiday from his poor effort at coping with the great mess which all our ancestors have left us, history which stinks of blood and lies and suffering and hunger, and which we have not even yet begun to face properly.

They may burn all the flags, the wigs, the thrones and robes and parchments and the paranoiac history books one day, may even teach real history—how one half of the human race sucked the life out of the other half and hid in stately homes, courts, gaols, barracks. August 15th may, in an ironic way, turn out to be the greatest day in history, and the burned thousands of Japan, the new heroes.

It is moving and splendid that man has at least reached a sense of nothingness, that the colossal mountain of petty certainties, smugnesses, and comic folklore about national greatnesses, and preciously protected myths, is melting away in the flood of life giving despair that we must swim in now and in which we must rescue each other, rescue all, regardless of height, colour of eyes, texture of hair, religion, skin. It is thrilling that we are faced with the choice of walking out of our history of muck and blood and lies, forever, and together, or of dragging down a flaming sky on top of us, a blazing blanket in which to wrap our ineradicable savagery, for it may prove ineradicable. After Somalia human toughness and the rest of the claptrap meant very little to me, and what little it meant was swept away by the magnificent idiocy of the Japanese troops I saw die, for nothing, in the rain and muck of Burma. One poor woman bringing up a crippled child means more in human heroism than all the billions who must have died in battle for various reasons in the last few thousand years.

It is splendid that at last the human race has run up against the wall, beyond which lies the end, a rain of ash and a silence. It is great that this tremendous revolution, so silent following the echoes of The Bombs on Japan, has poured into the works of the world like a terrifying mist, terrifying for the politicians and the Generals who no longer have their glorious way out, the battlefield and the medals and the cenotaphs.

And now Ali had a flag to die for too, a flag which would draw men's eyes away from their little tribal killings, and give them something to die as one for, and one hoped it was too late for races like the Somalis to taste the putrid springs of military glory.

Ali had talked about The Bomb several times during our three hours in Mogadishu. He wanted me to help him imagine it, this thing which the human race had learned to speak about in a very peculiar way, as if talking about a key to hell.

I tried to explain to myself, while appearing to talk to Ali how never before in man's time on earth had there been such a wish to have done with exploitation, hypocrisy, cant about justice, war, poisoned religion disguised as nationality, and never before had it been so difficult for man to understand what had happened to him and his world of habit since August 1945.

'There is no solution,' I told him. 'None. But there is a will to work the permanent mess without war and without the old cause of it, human greed, and there is such a hatred growing everywhere of petty sovereign reasons for prolonging the old mess, that the established order everywhere, including Russia, is becoming quite frightened. The Bomb has been a godsend because for the first time it has held up the usage of the ancient way out, war for a dozen splendid reasons which are forgotten six months after the war has started. The Bomb can really be the finish, not only of your enemy, but of yourself, even after you have finished him; you die too, in the ruins. If it had not been for The Bomb we would have had a world war ten years ago, for human freedom, democracy, world revolution, pick your slogan, any will do, but we would have had the war. Never before have the Generals been proved quite redundant, and all their military colleges as well. The true problem is—who will begin to tear the old fabric of political and military lies to pieces? Who will take the risk? For it is a risk, in this jungle. Can a country like Russia, or Britain, or America, really trust the rest if it gives its generals a decent suit of civilian clothes each and bulldozes all the weapons, which cost so many billions of lives in the long pedigree of war, into the sea? Can it be risked? We are on the edge of either the greatest breakout from the human mess of centuries, or we are due for the end. The Bomb is up in the air, right over our heads while we're speaking. It's the biggest thing that's ever happened to the human race in all time. And naturally we're all shaken.'

'Yes,' he said. 'But will there be war, or not?'

He was staring hard into my eyes as he asked this question, as if he thought someone from outside must know more than he knew, and it made one feel anger to think that the maniacs in Moscow and Washington and London, with their rockets and bombs, now had the whole human race in a state of fear. With the rapid spread of the radio set, and of literacy, the Alis of this world, who live on desert rims, can now wonder daily how long 'they' are going to give them to live.

As our conversation progressed it came out that he knew a lot about the gas ovens and the world-wide slaughter of the Second World War, and one could not forget that 'they' for him, 'they' who had made the two terrible world wars, were white, and that scientific war was a white occupation, and that another one, the last, now appeared to be ready for launching.

One could understand the hatred and frustration felt by the

black, brown and yellow races when, poverty stricken and yet now in tiny sight of relief, they watched final war being prepared in which they would die without having had a word to say. The mystery for them, contained in the white race which could do splendid things for human welfare, was surely in the frightening violence with which each white race dealt with each other about power and loot called principles. And all the years of preaching about Christ must have been almost as mystifying to Ali as it had been to the Kikuyu of Kenya who had watched the dozens of Christian sects quarrelling about the ownership of Christ before they, the Kikuyu, took to the despair of Mau Mau. But the white man never took time off to see himself as Ali and company saw him, especially now that the mystery of the white man had vanished— and Ali had seen white armies fight each other in his own country—a tremendous shock to the Somalis and Abyssinians who saw it. The white man now, wherever he goes, stands only for himself and represents only his personal nature, no longer for the mystery of his vanished greatness, which for Ali and company seems to have turned out to be a lie based on guns and books.

I felt despair of comforting him, and anger with the culture which had so failed him after all the arrogance and the wars and the ceremonies, and most of all the enormous vanity which had supported the hopeless arrogance.

'Let's go back to the dock,' I said. 'It's time for me to go aboard the ship.' As we walked he asked me more questions about the international situation.

'Why,' he said, 'if they know it will end us all, will destroy the world, why do they go on with it? Why will they not disarm? What is it that stops them?'

'I don't know,' I said. 'Nobody knows.'

'You don't know?' he said.

'No. I don't know.'

'Don't any white men know, the big men in the governments? Don't they know?'

'Since this great bomb has come to us,' I told him, 'the whole of history has changed, and everything in the past about war and power has become out of date. We have started a new kind of history, a new world, but not many men will accept the fact, yet. Everything is different now, but men do not want to believe it. They know it but they won't believe it. We just have to hope.'

'That is what a *mullah* from Cairo told us here,' Ali said, nodding. 'That the history of all men has now been changed. And you believe that too?'

'Yes.'

'But does nobody in this world know what is going to happen? Nobody? Isn't there anybody who can stop the war coming?'

Perhaps an assassination club could help, so that when the world is finally on the edge of the war which will annihilate it and the politicians and the generals and their scientists are about to take us all into that last manic plunge, the club assassinates a certain number of 'great men' in Moscow, London, New York, whichever of them are going through the old pathetic masculine routine of who's toughest and strongest, and then issues an ultimatum. What are a few politicians, generals and scientists compared to the human race which is in their little, stupid hands today? We can always get a few more of them to start all over again and it might be that eventually we could get actual disarmament, a world without soldiers and their dead, useless traditions. But I did not mention these wild, nihilistic anti-nihilistic thoughts to Ali.

The club would have to be quite fair, in that when it had picked its politicians and generals, it assassinated them all on the same day, on both sides of the so-called iron curtain. There must be no sovereignty or favouritism about it, just the main manic actors assassinated and then the suggestions that the new lot start negotiating again. It would need millionaires to finance it, rich men with no dividends from the arms industry, just financiers who rather like this world the way it is, ashless and non-radioactive.

The generals will never abdicate until they are sent, until their barracks and colleges are pulled down and they themselves are given their pensions and civil clothes. They have served well until now, all of them enjoying their careers under their various flags, and have fought for their little flags honestly and boyishly. When you think of the love which sprang up between some German and British officers in the Western desert of World War Two (more and more it appears as if Rommel was the commanding officer for all, the beloved knight who represented all that any general could hope to be) you realise that all that is gone now, that fine chivalry and that schoolboy honour.

'No,' I told Ali. 'Nobody in the world knows what will happen. We are stuck everywhere with the attitudes and habits of a world which vanished in 1945, and the problem is time in which to fully

156

realise it. Goodbye.' We were at the dock and the sun was blazing down, making one ache with its glaring weight.

'Goodbye,' Ali said. We shook hands, and he took the notes out of my hand with a smile and a nod.

'Take five shillings back,' he said, handing me one of the five shilling notes.

'Why?'

'I have enjoyed our talk,' he told me, 'and we are friends. This is enough.' He waved the other notes. It was a very Somali gesture, handsome and proud, and not about money at all.

CHAPTER TWENTY-FOUR

THERE was a very thin, waxen-pale Italian sailor standing in the motor boat, staring down with dark, angry eyes at the five Somali cargo workers who were lying asleep on the cases of wine, still not unloaded. He was about thirty, wearing a blue and white striped tee shirt, and sun-faded blue dungaree trousers. He had crew-cut black hair and he looked very ill.

'Look at them,' he said, 'sleeping like pigs in the sun'. He had a strong Neapolitan accent. He told me he was a seaman from one of the tramp ships in the bay. He had been dangerously ill and had just left the hospital. He was anxious to get back to his ship, 'even though it is the very worst ship I have ever sailed in', he added. We sat down and he told me how unhappy he was with this ship he had so mistakenly sailed in six months before. Bad food, no fridges, cockroaches, the kind of ship which one had come to think had vanished from the seas. And they were sailing for the Persian Gulf. I pitied him. One of the Somalis woke up, yawned, stretched, looked at us.

'When are you going to unload these cases?' I asked him. 'I am due back on board the ship.'

'When we are told,' he yawned, and went to sleep again.

'*Viva la libertà*,' the Neapolitan said bitterly, offering me a cigarette. Another Somali among the sleepers, an old man with grey bristles on his black face, opened one eye and called to me.

'Do not worry, *Effendi*,' he said. 'The ship cannot leave without you. They cannot do it. They cannot. They know we are slow here.' He closed his eyes again and dozed off in the soothing shade.

Raging, with that swift rage which the African heat and the African languor so swiftly awaken in white men who want to get things done quickly, I sat there and smoked and tried to feel glad that I had not the right any more to rouse them all up and drive them to the task until it was finished.

'We could unload this lot in five minutes, you and me, *due bianchi*,' the seaman said to me acidly, his eyes flashing, 'One white man can do twenty times the work'. Yes, but only for a little while, in that sun. It is the long, steady task of hours in the heat which makes the difference between African and white man in that climate. We sat on and waited until a Somali came staggering, yawning, his arms high in the ecstasy of his stretch, and stood staring broodily down at us from the dock. He screamed at the sleepers who opened their eyes and looked up at him, none of them moving. He was not exhorting, just cursing them, for they were part of his work, his work which he did not want to do. I had laboured in heat and I knew how he felt in that glare of sun, come out of the shade and his sleep to see these heavy cases waiting for him, this useless work which would occupy him until he died, in this backwater of Islam.

There was no shade in that big loaded barge and the Italian sea-man and I sat there in the glare and sweated, hatless, the sun hitting us like a hammer as we smoked and exchanged fragments of thoughts about our various lives. The sun struck the water and flashed off it and into the brain, through the eyes, like a white, flaring sword.

I stared along the barren coastline beyond the aching white town, and I knew I had never wanted to return here, and would never return again. I was glad I could not see Galkayu again, or Bosaso, Hafun, Filtu, Dagamedu, Golwein or Sinadogo, those aching place-names. Of all the Africas this yellow waste was a place to 'adventure' in, for there was nothing there except the sand and the nomads.

Once, in the red sand ocean of the Ogaden I had come upon a tall carved tablet of stone among the thorns. The sun-glare had lit up the carved words on it, words commemorating the long road through the bush hacked out by the Sicilian labour battalion attached to an Italian division which had invaded Abyssinia in 1935. The hot wind was scattering sand against it. The men, their tents, their empty cigarette packets, were all gone, and there was no trace of them. The Italian empire had vanished and the wilderness belonged, as it had always belonged, and will always belong, to the nomads and their camels. Forbidding and desolate, the huge desert with its towering rocks which shake in the sun, waits to turn every-thing into sand again, men, buildings, camels, even the white ants which send up their enormous towers of mystery in which they teem while they live out their imitation of the universe. I think most of all it was that realization which the four years wanderings in the interior had allowed to seep into me, that though he wrote it magnificently, Donne had it wrong. Every man *is* an island, in the desert or the city, and I can remember coming to feel certain of this one night on a high rock in fierce moonlight, looking out across Africa which stretched forever in the luminous silence. When you mingle again with people you get the impression once more that Donne is right, but it is only an impression. The longing and the effort to diminish the islandhood is everything, but it can never be dissolved.

Among our buildings we get the necessary impression that we have some kind of permanence here, but a single month in a desert, alone, is enough to allow in the echo of doubt, and it stays. Isolation in the wastes taught me to value civilization, and to get some idea of what this world owes to all the civilizers, whatever their race, or place, or time. Every time we go to a doctor it is probably in the subconscious hope that he will tell us we are going to live forever. Other people die but we don't. When we build, it is forever. Isolation makes you think of the fact of death, too much, and the city makes you think only about life, too much. And there is no in between area, and we contain it all within ourselves after we have tasted from both wells.

Any lingering ideas I had had about some races, religions, colours, or what have you, being better than others, vanished after a year in those wastes. Excellence and the lack of it are everywhere, and I knew nomads with qualities of natural intelligence and vitality far greater than hordes of white men I had known. And I have seen a white man perform acts of savagery as terrible as that performed by any tribesman. All the rules had vanished, the rules about what was supposed to be what, crumbled away by the billion thoughts sieved out in prolonged isolation, and I no longer believed in the sovereign state, the white message, or the inherent goodness, or evil, of man. For long periods I had forgotten that I was a white man at all, and had been merely a man, another flea on the desert with the nomads, and it was an experience which could not be left behind with the desert. I carried it with me, and I find when I meet friends who drank long enough at those bitter waterholes, that they too can no longer contribute to those ancient myths about the premiership of this that or the other if it has a white skin covering it. This is not to say that one did not discover how handily valuable it is to have been born with a white skin, how it helps one to share in the undeniable excellence and superiority of what Europe has defined as civilization, having clutched tightly the rope thrown out of darkness by Asia long ago.

And what did I think now, sitting in that sun-glare in the barge, about Africa, I wondered. About Africa which had stirred in its long tropical sleep and was standing up and screaming for various things lying behind a word called freedom.

No matter how much a man may try and think in the terms of the civilization to which he belongs, and thinks with its attitudes or without them, it is from his own particular heritage of myth and fact that he must stare at the scene. And I found that I, as a maverick person, was glad, but not smugly, that my ancestors had not been involved in the selling of millions of African slaves to the Americas, or in having to prove that what had been done in and to Africa had been right because my ancestors had done it. For my own ancestors had been losers too, and had been enslaved by the same force, a force which invented a mission to cover the normal human greed of the winners. And let us accept right away that the winners deserved the power, because they had won. They had conquered everywhere, the British. They had smashed Ireland first, a sort of long and obsessional battle course for the struggle to come for the ownership of Asia and Africa one day, and had then gone on to conquer all the oceans. Who can blame Englishmen for being proud of their victory in that jungle of the world in the past? It was a dangerous jungle and the British won the long, bloody day with their ships, their guns, and their money, and with their particular gift of long and carefully cherished civic patience. And now it was over.

The monarchy, the lords, the knights, the whole feudal English society, had now had to turn in on itself, following the loss of its world power and empire, and invent full employment. It was interesting to see how Gandhi had been right, how as soon as Britain lost its empire the English working class had to be given work and wages and new freedoms. Gandhi was the friend of the English working class. In freeing India he freed them too. He knew too, and said it, that once India had freed herself nothing could stop the freedom of Africa, which is why the whole European fabric of government in Africa crumbled so swiftly after 1947. Only the French went on dive bombing and fighting, from Damascus to Madagascar and from Indo China to Algeria. The British knew better than that, and went, quietly, proving that they still had the skill which had made their empire in the first place. Yet the struggle would go on in all kinds of ways, because money and power will never give justice until it is forced to. There is no escape from the nausea one feels as one surveys the world. Communism was a Godsend because it so frightened the rich and the powerful all over the earth, but that is its only virtue for me. Its presence is all, its end negative.

'I would have gone to America, if I could have got in,' the Italian seaman was saying to me. We were the same kind of people, uneducated, and hopeful, only I had had more luck than he. That means that you do not belong fully to any particular society, and can sign on in a Norwegian, Greek or Italian ship, become an American, or an Australian, and grow gradually into what appears to be your own product, instead of belonging to some strong segment with its tradition of safety and standard of achievement to look to. There is an enormous difference between the man who emerges from a safely ensconced segment of society, and the one who is flung into a world in which the shovel is waiting for him. I recommend the latter to all as a far more exciting world to be thrown into. The working class are far luckier than the monied classes, if they have a little yeast in their skulls to start with. Like the Italian beside me in the barge. He was a true man in that while he described the present misery of his condition, he did not whine about it and accuse the world of owing him a living. He still knew that he had to win the living, and enjoyed the possibilities.

It was a hell ship he was to sail in again, one of those rusting steel slums which still crawl the seas.

'You owned all that a couple of years ago,' I said, nodding at the harsh, jagged coast of Somalia, 'and now you've lost it. Does it break your heart?'

He laughed. 'What a tragedy,' he said, and laughed so loud that he woke the old Somali who had slept on among his labouring companions in the fore-peak of the barge.

In scathing and ironic Italian he described the Italian empire as a dream in Mussolini's head, for which the Italian people had paid with their blood.

'It is good that it is finished,' he said. 'What did it mean to me? Nothing. I still look for bread and peace.'

Empires were a hobby of a bored and energetic owning class, and empires made them rich, very rich, and the denizens of the empires poor, and it was good to have lived to see the end of all that. What was his dream? Everyone has a dream. His was to own a small restaurant in Naples one day—'probably when I'm about fifty, if things work out,' he said doubtfully, and then he looked across the blinding sheet of sea to the tramp ship. She was very low in the water, laden with arms and ammunition, now being unloaded, as were the other two tramps swinging at anchor nearby.

'Now I see that brute again,' he said, staring with bitter eyes at the rusty, ancient ship, 'I wish I'd died in hospital.' She was sailing next for the Persian Gulf, a suburb of hell where she would lie in the furnace heat for weeks awaiting a cargo. No fans, no ice, no cold beer. And food? Herrings, *pasta* and potatoes.

Another Italian appeared above us on the jetty and waved his hand at us, one of the last of the Italians in Mogadishu. He appeared to be made of leather, thin, dark brown skin shining from a lifetime of sun, a true *vecchio coloniale*. He began to curse the Somalis in slow, gentle Italo-Somali, insulting and friendly words, so that they all laughed. Then he jumped down into the barge and offered us cigarettes, sat down beside me and asked me if I was sailing in the liner. Yes. Ah, how he envied me. But it would not be long now before he sailed himself, for good. I laughed.

'You'll never get over Africa, though, will you?' I said. He looked at me sharply, smiled. He shook his head and looked out across the barge at the coastline.

'No,' he said. 'That's true. You hate her but you love her. You the same?'

'Yes.'

'Ah.' He knew it had nothing to do with being the big white chief, loving Africa, but had to do with the immense size and freedom of the continent, and the longing to wander from one end of it to the other. But he had stayed too long, he knew it now. It's true that there is a secret in knowing when to go, in feeling when a certain time of life somewhere is over. And yet . . .

His drinking company recently has been that of a Russian, one of the horde of Russians and Chinese who had arrived in the new Somali republic.

'He started by trying to convert me to communism,' the old Italian grinned, 'but I've just about converted him instead. "Capitalism?" I said to him. "But that's what I want to *be*. A capitalist. All my life I've tried to be a capitalist, and soon, in Italy I shall be one. I've saved up and I'm ready to invade Italy, for capitalism." I've been slowly educating him, poor fellow, and now he knows something about the world at last. He knew nothing. A real fanatic from the bookshelves. Comes along every night for a few drinks and a few more lessons in true world history. They're good fellows, these

Russians, but they've never been allowed to have any freedom, or even any real conversation. This fellow laps it up, loves it, actually talking with a capitalist foreigner.'

'With a fascist beast,' I suggested.

'Yes, yes,' he said, laughing. 'I forgot that. I'm a fascist beast, or was.' He pointed to the stack of wooden cases now piling up on the jetty, the last of which was being swung up out of our barge. 'Drink from Italy,' he said. 'The best. For the Russians, the Chinese, and—' he placed his forefinger on the side of his nose and winked, 'for some of the Somalis, Allah and the Prophet notwithstanding.'

Soon we were wallowing across the bay towards the rusty tramp, aboard which the old Italian was going to repair some electrical machinery.

'You'll get no beer aboard this scow,' the seaman told him as we came alongside the Jacob's ladder.

'No beer, no repairs,' the old man told him. He went up the Jacob's ladder, swiftly, the seaman following him. As we cast off they waved to me.

'*Ciao*. And drink a cold *Americano* for me aboard,' the old man shouted.

Africa is full of these old timers, men of many European races, and when they have gone they will be missed, when the machinery breaks down. They could fix anything. I once saw one of them, an old Sicilian diesel driver, fix a diesel engine with two pieces of tin when we were marooned hundreds of miles from any help. Another, an old South African, taught me to shoot, to skin a big beast quickly, to make rawhide ropes (a fast-dying art when he taught me), and how to seal up a leak in the radiator of a box body Model T Ford with a raw egg and a handful of maize meal. There is no better value in the world than an all night session under a thorn tree with an old timer in Africa, with a case of beer between you and a few hundred cigarettes around the place. We had one of them die on us suddenly one night in Somalia. He was too old for the game, but would not give up and had gone into that final haven, the desert locust control, and he drove three hundred miles with a case of gin for his final all night session. He had it, and sat up very suddenly about three in the morning, and died, in the right kind of country too, sunblasted, thick with hyenas, just the place he would have chosen, or perhaps chose.

Bwana Mzee, Old One, your time has gone now, for the cement mixers are massing on the horizon, and the game is finished.

CHAPTER TWENTY-FIVE

SWINGING high up over the ship again in the big canvas bag I could see Mogadishu below me, like a small blinding white wedding cake on the burned brown sand, the blue ocean lapping at its edges. I could see Wardiglei barracks where I had trained four hundred infantry and a company of medium machine gunners; the Lighthouse flats, the officers' club, and the thirteenth century mosque in which Ibn Battuta had prayed. I felt nothing for Mogadishu, no nostalgia, and I tried to feel it for the wilderness I could see stretching beyond the city, but I could feel none for that either. It was finished, and because it was finished there was an irrational sense of loss, of something unrecapturable, and of the comedy which time makes of one's solemn youth. But if I knew anything about men I had learned it out there beyond the heat haze, and what I knew about myself I had learned to learn there too, in silence. I felt a kind of gratitude to the deserts and to the nomads, or at least to life for having diced me into that world for a time.

A free Somali race will be good for Africa. Their bright intelligence, their courage and their confidence will be of value to the new Africa shaping now, if only because they never for a moment felt inferior to any white man, and were never tiresome about being black, or about you being white. They would like Emperor Haile Selassie to give them back the camel wilderness of the Ogaden, which by its very bitterness belongs to the Somali people and to their famished camels. Even if he does find oil in the Ogaden, Haile Selassie should find a way of giving that red desert back to the Somali nomads. They would feel gratitude to him, as they would to Jomo Kenyatta, if, despite his immense difficulties, he could find a way to let the Somali tribes of Kenya's northern frontier break out of the pencil lines drawn on the map years ago by careless white men, and become part of the greater free Somalia.

'What did you find to do ashore in that dump of sand, signore?' a grizzled Italian seaman asked me as I stepped out of the canvas bag on to the deck of the liner.

'It was a nostalgia,' I told him. 'I knew it once.'

'And how went it?'

'It was gone.'

He laughed, nodding. 'Yes. It is like when you see a woman you loved years ago. The fever has gone and you can look at her without trouble. Was it like that?'

'Yes. It was like that.'

'Then celebrate it, signore. The bar is open.' He jerked his thumb at his open mouth and laughed.

The ship's engines were throbbing and she began to swing slowly on the blue silken water, and as I watched Mogadishu disappear behind the slowly swinging prow of the ship I felt sure I would never see it again, and felt no pang, no regret.

I went in off the roasting heat of the deck into the air-conditioned bar and felt the immediate response of gratitude from the tortured skin and eyes as the fresh, cool air enveloped me.

'How are you, signore?' the barman asked me.

'Madly in love with civilization,' I told him, 'especially air-conditioned civilization. Long live engineering and science.'

He laughed. 'I told you not to go ashore,' he said.

'But I'm glad I went,' I told him.

'Why?' he asked while he mixed the Campari and the crushed ice and lemon.

'Because I had experienced so many things in that country,' I said, 'important things that greatly affected me, I had a moment this morning when I decided not to go ashore at all. I felt I should remember it as it was, years ago, which was ridiculous, so I went.'

'And what did you feel, seeing it all again?'

'Older.'

We laughed and he handed me the drink, and it tasted good after the sweat I had shed during the morning.

The South African passengers were gathering in the bar now, all healthy, well heeled, well travelled, many of them with over a hundred years of family behind them in that lush paradise of gold and diamonds in the far south. All about their comfortable world a new muscular Africa was gathering in what might become a vengeful freedom if these white men did not change things in South Africa.

They had been on holiday in Europe, some of them for pleasure and others for business, and now they were going home, to a country for which they might have to fight one of these days. I met no fire eaters among them. They were solemn when they talked about the problem facing them. 'We let it go by, day by day, and hope for the best,' one of them told me. 'Whatever that may be.' The Dutchmen among them were bitter about the British South Africans, who, they claimed, liked apartheid and hid behind it, while professing to feel more liberal about it all than the Dutch, etcetera.

In Jomo Kenyatta's hands lies the only real pilot scheme for a multi-racial society in Africa, in which Africans, Indians, Europeans and Arabs have now begun to live together as people, instead of a set of separated societies. If he can get it to work it will prevent much bloody bitterness, perhaps even in South Africa eventually.

Racing through those warm tropic seas in the darkness, the ship shuddering softly with her own power, I could see the lightning exploding again over the dark hulk of Africa on our beam. She did not look threatening in the livid light breaking across her vastness, and she never has threatened anybody yet. She has been sold, underpaid, used, but always loved by those strangers who have got to know her.

I could see the lights of the tiny town of Merca far across the rustling sea speeding past us. Now I knew a fellow there once who . . .

Part Two

CHAPTER TWENTY-SIX

WHATEVER the Mau Mau war in Kenya did or did not do it did shatter the sealed compartments in which Europeans, Africans, and Indians, all lived for years.

In Mombasa I watched the young Indian girls walking in groups, their old time shut-in solemnity gone now, and dressed in blue jeans and shirts, their saris thrown away. They were talking loudly and laughing openly, something surprising to someone who had not been in Kenya for nearly eight years. Indians in Kenya had always been so solemn, so self-suppressed, so mutely clenched looking.

Like all emigrants in a new country where a certain hostility surrounds them the Indians had tenaciously preserved the customs of their ancestors, a sort of protective shield of customs which had begun to wither away in the land of their origin. And suddenly, in Kenya, when the dam broke, the younger Indians joined that new mass world-culture which some very sensitive people seem to hate and fear so much.

The Indians were nervous, though, in this new post-Mau Mau Kenya, so soon to be free of British rule. They knew that many Europeans, and most Africans, disliked and even hated them. The Europeans said that the Indians were unscrupulous and 'bred like rabbits' while being able to 'live off the smell of an oil rag'. The Africans said they cheated the simple Africans in the stores and markets and that Indian artisans took all the jobs which Africans should be doing.

'I'm tired of it all,' a young Indian told me in a late night bar in Mombasa. 'Sick and tired of hate and misunderstanding and politics and colour and the whole bloody mess. They can come and burn my house over my head when Kenya's freedom comes. They can kill me, too, but I'm not moving. I'm not going to be a refugee again, for anyone or anything. I'd sooner bloody well die and get it over if that's what they want.'

He was about thirty and worked in an insurance business. He had had a few drinks, but it was the tension of the subject itself which made his handsome face become pallid while the sweat came out in beads on his forehead. He gripped the sleeve of my shirt and stared into my eyes.

'I walked from Lahore to Delhi in 1947,' he said, 'with the other millions, and I saw thousands die on the way, and I swore then that I never wanted to hear again about religions or politics or colour or caste, or any other damn nonsense which wrecked my family's life fifteen years ago.' He said he felt ill and he gripped the edge of the bar. 'My name is not Paul,' he said. He had told me it was Paul. 'It is Pyare.' He smiled sadly. 'It's not the drink,' he said. 'I've only had three whiskies.' He swayed there for a few seconds, his eyes closed, the jazz from the juke box slamming against the walls while Swahili prostitutes danced nearby with some Swedish and English seamen. 'I'll be back in a minute,' he whispered, his face quite white now. 'I'm going to be sick. I'm sorry.' I patted his arm and he smiled. He walked unsteadily away towards the toilets.

Really, I thought while the big Swahili barman poured me another bottle of Tusker beer, it could have been much worse, the breakup of an empire as enormous as the British. The British rearguard actions all over the earth had been small and half hearted compared with the vast bloodlettings in the French retreat from their colonial possessions. Though here in Kenya over nine thousand Kikuyu had died during the Mau Mau war. About thirty Europeans died.

'I'm sorry,' Pyare said when he came back. 'I think it's because I'm frightened of what may happen here in Kenya.'

'It's emotion, you mean,' I suggested.

'Partly,' he said. 'Mostly fear, and not talking about it much.' He meant the door being smashed down in the early hours of the morning, the rushing Africans with their big, sharp, whizzing pangas come to chop him to pieces because he was an Indian. I said I did not think it would happen.

'You don't know how much we are hated here, we Indians,' he said. 'I think I'll go on to beer.' He started on a Tusker.

'Yes, I do,' I assured him. 'I got tired hearing about it here years ago. But maybe we all have to pay now for what our grandfathers everywhere did to each other for cash and land and medals and power and religion and so on.'

'But do the African politicians know that?' he said excitedly. I said I thought Jomo Kenyatta certainly would know, and possibly many

172

of his colleagues. But Pyare was not convinced, and neither was I in my heart. I had seen the mangy dogs snuffling among the shallow graves of the thousands who died in the upheaval in the Punjab in 1947 and I knew by Pyare's eyes when he spoke of that time that he did mean he would rather die than become a beggar again in a desert with even farther to go this time to safety. And I did want to believe that Jomo Kenyatta knew enough about the history of how men had looted other men in the past, leaving us all now with the screaming and frustrated children of their greed. Not to be too wide-eyed about it, I told Pyare, I believed there was more goodwill and knowledge and understanding alive nowadays, trying to find its voice, than ever before in the world's stinking history.

'They can burn the roof over me,' he said, 'but I won't move. I *won't*. This is my home now and I love this country, and I want the right to go on living in it and loving it. Or is that too much to ask?' He looked as if he might weep just then, and had forgotten where he was, his eyes staring past me into the Punjab of 1947. He told me about some of the terrible things he had seen, and a hatred of India came out of his words, a hatred of its ignorance and poverty, and the enormous trap its millions stood in, a trap of caste and disease and mangled history laced with rancid religion raped by politics. His hatred covered his deep love for India, because he was ashamed of India, ashamed of the giant frenzy he had seen when the British police lid was wrenched off the Raj and the *goondas* swarmed up with their grins and their knives.

I said I thought that that shame might come because of the frustrated hopes of Gandhi, who had tried so hard to bring Hindus and Muslims together, and was finally slain for it by a fanatic of the highest Hindu caste. Pyare said he did not feel bitter about the way Gandhi had been killed, following the million or so innocent people slain in the Punjab, and the pleasure it must have given India's enemies. Yet Gandhi meant nothing to him as a leader or saint or politician now. 'That time is all gone now,' he said. 'I am just me, or someone trying to be me, a person, in Africa, but I have to remember I am an Indian and hated for it, and may be killed or uprooted for it soon. When will we all leave each other alone and become just people?' Probably never, I said.

'Though we may stop killing or torturing each other about it, I doubt if we will ever stop watching each other, the various races, and looking for failings to hate. It seems to be a human hobby.'

Would he go back to India if the situation in Kenya did become dangerous for Indians? 'I've told you,' he said, grim now. 'I'll die here first. I mean it. India? I'm finished with India.' He began a tirade about the repressed family relationships of India, about the power of the father there, about the destruction of character caused by the imprisonment of dead and useless customs and rituals. But he could not hide the love and hope he felt for India. He had the same feelings for her that some Irish people have for Ireland, knee deep in a puddle of pride and shame for an ancient society which lay prostrate in a museum of historic nightmare, the recent owners gone back to their factory base to find a new way of making money and finding comfort.

'Perhaps the British should have found some way to destroy Hinduism,' he said. 'It is Hinduism which has poisoned us all in India, Hinduism which is only a set of dead customs now. I'd better not say anymore.'

'Why?'

'I'll be sick again.' He smiled tiredly. 'I hate it all.'

CHAPTER TWENTY-SEVEN

THE first Indian I ever got to know in my life I met in Kenya long before the war, and in a piece of silent far off Kenya where we had plenty of time to talk and work together. He was a Sikh carpenter called Gulab Singh, a kind, benign, elderly man in a pink turban who happened to be sitting beside my camp bed when I went down for the first time with malaria, and, who strangely appeared several times again years later during other malarial deliriums, thousands of miles away, and always wearing the same pink turban.

The Sikhs have no colour bar, though they are not averse to advertising for wives with 'wheat coloured complexions'. The *langar* or community table of the Sikh temple is open to all, and in India I have seen Tibetans, black Tamils, and Europeans, sitting at the table in the *langar*. They are a fine and healthy community, warm hearted, passionate, generous and hard working. Gulab Singh worked hour after hour, singing to himself, one eye always open for the wandering rhinoceros from the forest who frequented that plain on which we were building the big sheep-shearing shed. We spoke Swahili, though sometimes he would work on his English, and I learned Urdu words from him too.

At night when the lions roared Gulab Singh would sing loudly, not because he was afraid, he told me, but so as to shut out the sound of the lions for his wife. They lived in a hut near the working site and his wife was an African whom he had wooed into Sikhism. She was of the Wakamba tribe and wore a gold ring in her nose and the finest saris Gulab Singh could afford for her. She looked far more graceful than she would have done in a cheap European print dress and those high heeled white shoes which are so hard on the graceful walk of an African woman.

It was from Gulab Singh that I first heard something of the complexity and variety of society in India, and years later in India when I heard old British diehards telling of the differences of races and language and custom in India, which somehow was supposed to prove how hopeless Indians were, and how hard to rule, I realized that these various Indian races in their sub-continent had made a far better job of living together through the centuries than had the many races in that other continent, Europe. As Pyare said during that emotional tirade in the Mombasa bar, although he was deeply ashamed of what had happened in India in 1947, he had to remember the gas ovens of Europe and the two world wars started there in order to find some doubtful comfort for his shame.

I used to go up into the deep lush elephant forests of Mount Kenya to fell the timber which Gulab Singh would use for the shearing shed.

It was the time of the Box Body Model T Ford, that marvellous car for Africa, of ox wagons, sea mail, hurricane lamps, and I was twenty and I thought that no matter what else ever happened to me in life I would never love any place as much as I loved that Kenya of forest and bush and game, and I was right. No matter how you may disagree with the Kenya diehard European, or he with you, one thing you do have in deep common is a love for that unique and beautiful country with its red deserts and nomads, its forests and its varied Bantu peoples, and even its film set called Nairobi . . . as long as you only have to stay for a few days, for the drinks and the meeting of friends. There was nothing 'paternal' about that love for Kenya, for in the bush the Africans with you enjoyed its marvellous freedom as much as you did yourself, especially the meat feasts over the fires of olive logs at the end of a long day in the sun with the breeze whistling in the ant-eaten bulbs of the thorn trees overhead.

The forest was vast, the home of happy elephant herds who used to come down and reap our wheat when it was fit to eat, and of rhinoceros and buffalo, and of the beautiful colobus monkeys who watched us slyly when we plodded into the silent trees behind the oxen dragging their heavy chains and tackle. The monkeys heard the cross-cut saws striking into the big cedars and would gather a safe distance away in the high branches and watch us with their sad eyes.

The forest rose up all about Mount Kenya, impassable barricades of high tangled and smashed bamboos laced through it, dangerous to be caught in by the suddenly awakened or wounded rhinoceros. Many of the towering trees were polished to black mirror smoothness at elephant height and it was curious to pass one's hand over these black glass-like surfaces and to think of the elephants whom one wished so well, and who only brought danger to themselves unknowingly when they rolled in ecstasy through the wheat crop far below on those forays in darkness. I always felt that these silent forests belonged by right to the elephant herds, but even then, without hindsight from this time, I knew that that Kenya was doomed and that we white men always destroyed what we claimed to love. We were shooting it, felling it, making way for farms. And now that we have slain so much, mown down so many millions of head of game over the years, we start societies for the preservation of the remaining relics, because the Africans, free now, feel it is their turn, and want to shoot what has been left to them.

Working in Africa, amidst all that game, for the plains swarmed with it, with lions raiding, you do not look on the game with the eye of the man who has come to Africa for a quick hunting safari. You come to accept the game as part of the silence like yourself, shooting it to eat, or to stop the lions killing your cattle, always hoping that the lions will be sensible and go back to their real prey, the game. If the game left you alone you seldom bothered them, and the early bloodlust of your first days in Africa soon faded when you had begun to wonder what you were doing one day with your rifle in your hand and something uselessly dead at your feet.

On the edge of the high forest you could look down from Mount Kenya on to the red floor of Africa stretching into blue mists beyond which lay Abyssinia, Sudan, and Somalia, long dust plumes trailing on it from invisible game herds, at night long bush fires burning on it like glowing necklaces of phosphorescent gold, and always the marvellous silence and the many scents of Africa, sharp, acrid, fragrant, bitter, and the smoky scent of sweating, grinning Africans when we had dragged the fallen cedars into the clearings for splitting.

We lived in the forest at that time, the Africans and myself, working hard and long, and I have never been so happy before or since, and the Africans were happy too. They hated going down to the ranch again to the routine of dipping cattle, digging channels for water, though there was always hope of adventure down there too, lion or leopard, or even raiding Wandarobo nomads come to plunder the sheep flocks and then escape back with their loot to the red floor and thorn trees of the plains below.

The Africans with me in the forest were Kikuyu and Meru tribesmen, all of them wearing cloaks of monkey or calf skin, or a single ochre reddened blanket slung over one shoulder. I was lucky enough to know I was enjoying something which would not last many more years, and was sentimental only about the strange breaking mystery of the tribesmen with whom I worked so closely.

You could not live out in the East African bush for long without learning to admire the patience, the stoicism, and the good nature of the Africans who seemed to have no past and no future, only a silent, sun-glowing now of forest and plain in which I lived as a pale stranger with them. They could be cruel, as cruel as any white man, though the white man always liked to think that the African was crueller. The rules were as usual when made by men who can get away with it—pay as little as possible until there is an explosion, an explosion which is always a very long way off in a doubtful future. The Africans did not complain about their low wages but they did not dream at that time that they could get more by striking. They lived in a sort of in-between time, a dreaming halt between their old pre-white man tribal world, and that of the cement mixer waiting behind a future world war.

CHAPTER TWENTY-EIGHT

ICHORO was the best and steadiest of the three Africans I worked with on the big cross-cut saw, and I had to learn to take it slow and steady in order to last out with Ichoro, who would glance up with his dark eyes and grin, watching to see how I was taking it. Inch by inch the big steel teeth ground their slow way into the enormous girth of the cedar tree. The other cedars we had felled had torn down lesser trees in their long fall and lay all about us in the forest, Africans already splitting them open with the sharp steel wedges. When they finally struck the earth these great cedars made a thunderous sound, heard and felt by the elephants and the other startled game farther into the forest. The two old, grey-haired Africans in charge of the oxen trotted far into the forest sometimes to listen, for they forecast anger from the elephants, and they were right.

'What about this Indian *fundi*, Bwana? This carpenter making the big shed?' Ichoro said to me one day as we swung our arms in the steady rhythm of the rasping saw blade. 'Could one of us black ones learn to do that work? Why is it that only Indians are allowed to do this work?' Other young Africans nearby working on the wedges turned to hear my reply. It was a good excuse for Ichoro and me to have a sly rest from each other's will. The Africans squatted to take *tumbaku*, their powerful brown snuff made of raw tobacco and soda while I lit a cigarette. Complete silence in the dark green forest, the sun glaring down on the distant plains far below us seen through an archway on the edge of the forest. How good a cigarette tasted then. How real the friendship we had in that work with its question and answer during the rest breaks. I was *kijana*, a youngster like the warriors become labourers around me, and the two old men sat a little behind them, sieving all the words they heard through the framework of good manners and wisdom imparted to them by elders long dead. Old men of a time before the tribal world began to dissolve for wages paid by pale-eyed strangers, they carried no resentment. What was happening to their world was *Shauri ya Mungu*, the will of God.

'It is not easy to learn that work and do it properly,' I told Ichoro. 'It takes long training and practice. I cannot do that work of the *fundi*. If I could I would be doing it and not Gulab Singh. Think of the measuring, the reading of the plan off the paper. If he does anything wrong the building will collapse. You could learn to do it, if you had the patience. I have not that kind of patience.' Ichoro laughed and the others grinned.

'*You* cannot do that *fundi*'s work, Bwana?' Ichoro said. I shook my head. None of them had ever thought of that before. They had assumed that a white man knew everything about his own toys, cars, guns, tools, radios, electric lights. Just as the newcomer imagines every African knows about tracking and hunting, the poisoning of arrows, the weather, where to find water, all the African lore, so did many Africans feel then that any white man must know all of his own world and how it worked. And there were plenty of white men who wanted them to keep thinking that way.

I cannot help laughing right now when I think of the white man away up country who had just received his copy from South Africa of a monthly magazine for farmers. In it there was an advertisement for a certain kind of cattle food, announced as so excellent, so nutritious, that milking a cow fed on it was like milking a cow with six huge udders. There was the big drawing showing the monstrous cow with six full udders and six white men milking the cow, one at each udder. 'That's the kind of cow we have down in my country,' this exiled South African rancher said to his cook and houseboy, showing them the drawing of the astonishing cow. The news travelled fast.

'You have no land and no cattle, Bwana,' one of the old men said to me in the thoughtful pause that followed Ichoro's surprised question about carpentry. 'When will you get land and cattle of your own?'

It was hard to answer that one truthfully, without revealing the already begun process of wondering who really owned Kenya, and what was conquest and what right had white men to be here in this paradise one loved already so deeply. The first small seed of what Africans felt secretly had been revealed to me quite innocently only a few weeks before while hunting a leopard with a Meru called Muntu Mareti carrying a spear beside me. The leopard had killed over twenty sheep the night before. They kill for pleasure.

'I was born right here, Bwana,' he said, grinning, stabbing his spear butt into the ground where we were walking. Looking round I could see at once that it was the site of what looked like an old Masai *manyatta* or homestead. We were on a high hill in the middle of a vast European owned ranch, wild uncivilized country all about us, only about fifteen or sixteen years since the first real European settlement in Kenya had begun. I sat down with Muntu Mareti and asked him to tell me about his relationship with the Masai, and he told me of things which I only had clarified for me twenty-six years later by the old senior chief of the Masai himself.

'The Masai owned all this, Bwana,' Muntu Mareti told me, sweeping his arm to show me all of North Kenya's grazing plains, 'when they wanted to use it it was theirs'. He shook his spear and grinned, meaning that all this immense ocean of grass and bush had belonged to the Masai by right of the spear. 'We Wa'Meru were beholden to the Masai by right of agreement and by mixture of blood. It was to us they came when the cattle and human diseases struck them so hard in the times of my father.' Twenty-six years later I was able to unravel the meaning of this statement by Muntu Mareti who could not answer all my questions.

Muntu Mareti was too well bred and too knowing to tell me, a white man, that he regarded this land on which we sat as more his than any white man's possession, and for reasons selfish and personal I did not pursue that subject with him. I was certain, though, that he remembered this place we sat on with the nostalgia of a man who recalls his original freedom of ownership, even though it be by permission of the warlike and proud Masai. I rush to add that I have never been a worshipper at the shrine of the noble savage Masai legend, a legend which helped the Masai to live on in their tribal museum until yesterday. Now they have suddenly discovered that the Kikuyu politicians in far Nairobi represent an imaginative and forward looking Kikuyu people who have gone the white man's way and have been schooled, and now were to have the main say in the running of free Kenya. The Masai today are tragic, a noble people who have suddenly agreed to learn how to read the time and have found it is too late for them.

So Kenya was like what Ireland had been under the alien land-lords, the original owners become helots and never forgetting that even though a thousand years may pass this land somehow still belongs to them and not to those who wrote out their own title deeds and had them stamped by legal Druids in London with red seals. The Africans, though, were not sure then what they had a right to feel. There had been no war to conquer Kenya. The Masai fell back before the white man for their own reasons which I shall explain in another place.

'I shall never own land in Kenya,' I told the old man who had questioned me during our rest break up in that rain forest on Mount Kenya. 'I shall always work for another white man as a manager or a helper.'

He nodded sagely, too wise and good mannered to say, 'Because you have no money, I understand.'

We used to drive four long steel wedges into the fallen cedar tree, hammering them until the tree split open with a sharp crack and fell apart to reveal the red gold shining timber within, a rush of golden cedar oil in its long narrow heart filling the warm air with its magical fragrance. I used to dip my hands in this oil and breathe it up, a sort of sensual ritual learned from the Africans who enjoyed it too.

I was learning to speak Swahili fluently then, the bastard Swahili of the bush, and the elegant (and, unusable, except on the coast) true Swahili from Bishop Steer's friendly manual, and, although I did not realize it then so far up country and isolated, I was being taught a good deal of Kikuyu and Meru as well by the Africans with me, for when I pointed at something and asked what was its name, they would hasten to tell me its name in their own tribal language rather than in Swahili.

When we sat down round the big fire under the trees to cook our meal they would answer my questions about their tribal customs, the old men acting as judges over the sometimes uncertain knowledge of the younger men. Fine points were weighed by the old men and a decision given, often to harsh and jeering laughter by the young men who already had begun to despise some of the old customs of their people.

I used to eat sourdough rye bread, cold venison or cheese, and potatoes baked in the ashes, and we all drank black tea with sugar in it, a taste passed to me by the Africans. They ate maize meal with beans, and sometimes a little meat, and always thick milk if they had it.

One day the rains broke over us, lashing down in blinding silver sheets into Mount Kenya's thick glistening green hair under which we crouched, my box of matches sodden and burst in the pocket of my bush shirt. It was then I saw the old men have their triumph over the young men who had already fallen easy victim to the white man's packaged magic, my small piece of it now useless in my pocket, and we badly needed a roaring fire. I had the luck to see the use of *gesi-gesi* because of that downpour and my ruined matches, and so did the young men who had never seen it before.

CHAPTER TWENTY-NINE

OLD men of any not too urbanized race are far more interesting to sit and listen to than any of the other age groups. Old Indians, old Africans, old Arabs, and old Irishmen are the best I have ever listened to for knowing how to throw the salt of necessary doubt into any bowl of wisdom they may serve up for you. Men who have travelled far, and worked while doing it, are the men who know it is wise to retain belief in what, before they travelled, they would have regarded as impossible travellers' tales. Old Indians and old Irishmen who have kept their roots tight in their hands, whether they be cutting down sugar in Fiji or shovelling grain in Chicago, seem to keep the same sense of reverence for the possibly impossible and the fabulous as the old Africans I used to like to listen to when they told me of some legendary warrior who had beaten down all in the battle, an eye and a star painted on his shield to show that he intended to die in the battle, and longing for the warrior to come who could defeat him. Tragedy if he never found that warrior and had to return to the women when he had said his farewells to them before battle.

Old Kimondo, a toothless grizzled naked elder, laden with copper and bone bangles, a monkey skin cloak about his shoulders, who stepped forward that day in the rain to warm us with a piece of wisdom the young ones did not know, was that kind of tale teller who appeared to be brooding aloud to himself when, hunched over the fire, he answered your questions about *zamani*, the times that were gone.

He grinned with his blue gums at the circle of young men shivering with cold under the rain, as he unslung the square satchel of hyrax skin slung about his shoulder on a piece of rawhide strap.

'You have laughed many times at the old and withered,' he told them severely, 'but now you are cold and you need fire, and I shall give you fire with the *gesi-gesi*.' He took a buck horn of snuff out of the pouch and sprinkled some on to the back of each of our hands as we proffered them to him. We sniffed it up and it tingled in our noses.

Then Kimondo gave orders in Kikuyu to one of the young men,

but all got up to obey. They rushed off into the trees to get something for him.

I wiped the rain off my rifle and oiled it while Kimondo hunched over the coals and sharpened a small skinning knife on one of the big stones ringing the dead fireplace.

'You are going to rub two sticks together, old one?' I suggested. He looked at me sharply.

'Different kinds of sticks,' he said. 'How do you know about this?'

'I have read about it in books.'

'So they have written about it in books, have they?'

'They have.'

'But you do not know how to do it?'

'I do not know.'

'I shall show you. You will see it with your own eyes, not in the books. You cannot get a fire from reading a book. All these young ones, they want to write in books and to wear glasses and sit at tables writing for wages. But they have not the brains for that either.' He sighed and looked hard at me with his aged, milky blue-brown eyes. 'If ever you have time, Bwana, I will teach you all, customs and language. You listen to old men and that is a good thing. These young ones—' he gestured to the forest where we could hear the young men calling to each other as they foraged, 'they sneer at the old men. The customs are broken.'

'Yes. The customs are broken,' I said, 'and nothing can change it now'. He nodded and got up to meet the young men who were rushing back to us with their finds. What they brought satisfied Kimondo for he nodded approvingly as he examined the wood they brought him. 'You have not forgotten the names and shape and colour of things, at least,' he said grudgingly. The young men sat in a circle about Kimondo and we watched him work with his hard old black hands and his quick, cunning knife.

Kimondo had two pieces of wood in his hands, one a thin hard branch and the other a branch of smooth grey wood as thick as a man's wrist. The thin branch he peeled halfway up its stem and then he sharpened the end to a pencil point. The thick one he split in two with his sharp knife and then he scooped out its soft pith until the piece of wood resembled a canoe. He cut a deep notch into it half-way along its length, a sort of channel leading to the centre. Next he drilled a hole with the point of his knife into the bottom of the canoe shape beside the end of the notch.

We all crouched and watched this careful, patient labour, the young men grinning at each other in between watching their withered elder about his curious doings, but when they caught my eyes they looked proud and nodded approvingly towards Kimondo. They wanted him to succeed, while reserving the right to laugh at him, if he failed. Kimondo worked on with a calm dignity. When he was ready he twirled the hard, pencil-sharp branch between the palms of his hands and then ordered one of the young men to take some of the dried leaves they had brought and crush them into a heap of powder, and he supervised as this was done and the powdered leaves heaped up in the hollow of the canoe shaped branch.

Kimondo softly pushed his pencil shaped branch down through the leaves until the point fitted into the small hole he had drilled. 'Now for the firemaking,' he said, the branch held between his palms. He glanced at us all with his weak and aged eyes. 'Remember this,' he warned us, 'for a time may come again when you may need to remember it.' We all nodded solemnly and then Kimondo bent over to work the magic which had been handed down for nobody will ever know how many generations.

He began to revolve the drill at high speed between his palms, pressing down on the point, yet never letting his palms slip down the revolving branch (very difficult to do as I found later when he let me try it). He twirled it back and forth, breathing hard, total silence all round him as we watched for the first sign of an answer to his magic. Then there was the faintest wisp of blue smoke creeping up through the heap of powdered leaves. Exclamations on all sides, and one of the young men, obedient to a sudden command from Kimondo, began pouring more crushed leaves on to the heap from which the smoke was coming. There was a dark red glow as Kimondo revolved the drill back and forth at greater speed, and we all shouted with pleasure as the heap of leaf dust burst into flame. '*Monno! Monno!*' we cried, 'Fine. Great.' We began throwing heaps of dry leaves on to the flames and one of the young men heaped some broken dry bamboo on to it and the fire began to answer with cracklings, and then sharp reports as bigger pieces of bamboo caught fire. In five minutes we had a big fire blazing and then we all stood back as Kimondo stood up and grinned at us with his empty blue gums, his eyes unusually merry, an old out of date elder who had created a moment to be remembered and recalled by all of us, for as he said himself, 'I told you no lie. Tell that to others.'

To the young men of his own tribe he was stern, and they did not smile as he lectured them in the traditional way. '*Moigwa*,' he said, using the ancient rhetorical beginning, 'now hear this. You are all young and I ask you what is the use of the book and the writing pen, and the impudence, and the breaking of old rules, if you do not know how to warm yourselves when your stupid matches are wet? I say what is the use of the new ways in the wet forest?' He went on for a long time and everybody listened patiently and then applauded. It was hard seeing him so right, but they had to take it.

We all ate potatoes baked on the edges of the huge fire and afterwards we went with old Kimondo, carrying firebrands, to a tree he knew of on the edge of the forest where the wild bees had a cache of good honey. Kimondo smoked them out of their hollow tree in clouds of buzzing black fury, and they stung him all over, but he was immune, as so many of his tribe prove to be when handling wild bees, the stings showing only as small grey dots on his old, brown hide, and he felt no pain. He handed out the pieces of dripping comb to us all and we feasted on it, looking out over the hundreds of miles of East Africa below us as the glowing sun burned up the recent rain in soft clouds of golden steam. Kimondo had forbidden the complete looting of the honey in the hollow tree. He said it was a sin to steal all from the bees, and once again the young men felt free to laugh at him, but they obeyed him.

After that rainy day in the forest, watching Kimondo so closely as he went through his ritual, I began to take a deeper interest in the world represented by old men like Kimondo, for they were the last survivors of a world which had no written records of their experiences. It was all in their heads, remembered perfectly as handed down to them, and it would vanish into the grave with them. I began to keep a diary and I wrote down in it many legends and customs told me by old men of various tribes. The diary became something to talk to in the evenings, but after what happened to it, when it was an extensive record, I was never able to keep another one.

CHAPTER THIRTY

In the warehouses by the Mombasa dockside were mounds of new packing cases, their European owners living in nearby hotels while they waited for sea passages. Hundreds of Europeans were leaving Kenya, many of them to be welcomed in South Africa. One elderly man told me he would rather die than live under an African government, for Kenya was soon to be free. No, he had no colour bar, he claimed, but he did believe in 'the culture bar'. It was an interesting scene in which I met this interesting and embittered old man.

I had been walking about Mombasa, revisiting well remembered places, and found it far more attractive even than it had been in the past, for nowadays your conversation in dining rooms and bars was not confined to people of your own colour, as in the past, when only 'safe' views had been the usual currency of talk. Now you could meet Indians, Arabs, Africans, Somalis, Greeks, all mingled with Europeans, so that there was livelier talk on more varied subjects. It was obvious that many Europeans had practised the colour bar only because it was there, and because it was the easiest thing to do. The old diehards had always set the pace and the others who liked a quiet life had followed their lead. Another good thing for East Africa had been the influx of Italians after the war, and it was in one of their new restaurants in Mombasa that I began to meet some of the Europeans who were leaving Kenya.

The first one I met was slightly drunk and was having a not too playful argument with the Italian barman about whether he had had the five whiskies he was being charged for, or had had only four. He was trying to annoy the Italian, but the Italian had obviously got to know this particular type of humour and was playing it cool and smilingly, so that it was the Briton who began to lose his temper because the Italian refused to lose his. He finally paid for his drinks by slamming down shilling after shilling on the bar and calling out the score each time, his eyes flashing angrily at the Italian, until the bill was paid. Then the Italian said, with a smile, 'And now will you have one on me?' Everybody at the bar laughed.

'Never mind, Jim,' a European nearby called to the frustrated man, 'get yourself pissed into a good mood. You're sailing tomorrow, aren't you?' Jim accepted the drink from the Italian and started to explain how it had only been a joke anyway. The Italian said what he felt was expected of him, something about how interesting English type humour could be sometimes. Jim said how sad he was to be leaving Kenya, and how glad, and how much he hated the British government which had lured him to Kenya after the Second World War, how he had made a farm, and how now the British were throwing him, and many more like him, 'to the bloody wolves'. Argument started then. There were some there who agreed with Jim and one of them, one of those solid 'brass tacks' types from Yorkshire, who was so anti-British that even Jim had to protest.

'Brass Tacks' went right back to the American War of Independence then, saying how at last he understood what those Americans had put up with, until, driven too far by the bastards in London, they had resorted to arms. Which was why he was never setting foot in Britain ever again, and why he was going to South Africa where he would fight on the side of Verwoerd when the showdown came, as come it certainly bloody well would in the not so distant bloody future.

They were all men who had never been trained for retreat, but who had lived to take part in one, a massive retreat from Asia and Africa, and having committed their capital and a certain number of their valuable years to post-war Kenya, they had now been told that in the event of 'trouble' the British Government could not guarantee British troops to protect them. It was nobody's fault at all, in actual fact. It was just one more permutation of the history of colonialism, but it was a fact that any European farmer with children in up country Kenya, remembering the Mau Mau war, felt he could not farm any more in peace of mind. Nobody knew what might happen in Kenya after Independence.

There was only one old time settler there, that is to say a European who had lived in the 'old Kenya' before post-war settlement. He was silent while he listened to the newer men, who like himself, were waiting to leave the country. He stood and watched his beer, sombre and nodding occasionally if he agreed with something said, or looking irritated, shaking his head angrily if he disagreed with something. Every so often he took his passport out of his hip pocket and checked the mass of papers in it. He was about sixty and was wearing khaki drill trousers and a short sleeved khaki shirt, unlike the newer men who wore white shirts and flannel trousers. His arms were sunburned red brown and one imagined that the big strong hands had castrated many a thousand sheep or calves, mixed much cattle dip, lowered a rifle after many a shot long ago, and clutched the driving wheel of the old pre-war Box Body Model T Ford in many a sea of red mud before the asphalt came.

Had anybody, he wanted to know, heard about this settlement of Kenya types going on in Perth in Australia? It was even said that they had a pub going there called 'The Simba Arms'. He himself was going to South Africa. Australia was too far away at his age. And it wasn't Africa either, which was another thing.

Yes, it was true about 'The Simba Arms' in Perth and that plenty of Kenya types were settling there, somebody replied. But you had to work like hell. No labour. (No labour in that sense meant no cheap African labour.)

Just as well, the old timer said bitterly. He was finished with Africans after his experiences here in Kenya. Once they had been fine, difficult, lazy, but fine, until the war came, which ruined them, which gave them ideas they were not able to digest, and which finally drove them into Mau Mau.

He lowered his voice to talk about the colour problem, for there were Africans and Indians sitting at tables nearby. He *had* tried, he said. He had tried to accept what he now saw about him, the mixing of all the colours socially, but he could not, and would not, take it—not after Mau Mau, not after what had been done during the Mau Mau period.

For him, the Kikuyu were like the Germans for a lot of Europeans—they had all been in Mau Mau as all the Germans had worked in the gas chambers of the Second World War.

What was needed was a culture-bar, a system which would ensure that only coloured people who could pass an examination, to prove their right to have free use of the civilized amenities invented by the whites, should be allowed to mix on equal terms with Europeans. That was why he was going to South Africa where there was not even a culture bar, but where each race was segregated so as to be able to live its own life in its own culture. But if the culture bar had to come there one day, it would be after his time anyway. You can't teach an old dog new tricks.

It was the Kikuyu he had come to detest, not the other tribes, though they too were pretty far gone now since the Mau Mau period. You were never really able to trust a Kikuyu, even in the past long before Mau Mau, and after Mau Mau it was impossible. And so on . . .

CHAPTER THIRTY-ONE

BACK in the hotel I oiled my rusty Swahili again with three tall, gangling and good natured African servants who dragged my kit up the stairs. I had always stayed in this old hotel in the past and I could recall sitting late in the bar here one night years ago with an old man who, when young, had been left to die in the bush, at the bottom of a twenty-foot deep, dried-up waterhole, by his African gunbearer, but he had got out of it and he followed the African right into the Congo until he caught him. He got him put into a Belgian chain gang, for revenge. 'He had guts,' the old man told me. 'Plenty of guts, but he stole everything I possessed and left me to die. But I had even more guts. It was a fair deal and he knew it.' He would be long dead now, that leathery old timer, vanished into the everlasting silence.

Life, the hotel servants told me, was very worrying just now, and everything depended on what 'those talking politicians' in Nairobi were going to do when independence came. What did I think about *Uhuru*? Was it really true that self government was coming for Kenya? I told them it was true but I did not know exactly when, for I was a *mgeni* now, a stranger remembering his Swahili. What did they think about *Uhuru* themselves?

'We are not ready to rule, Bwana,' the oldest of them told me. I looked into his eyes to see if he was sucking up, to see if he was trying to please the *Mzungu*, the European who might rave if the wrong thing was said to him about politics and *Uhuru*. He really believed, though, that Africans were not ready to rule themselves.

'No one was ever ready to rule themselves,' I told him. 'They all had to learn. You have to start sometime, and you can't stop it now. It's almost here.'

'But will all the Europeans leave us?' he asked me, and the other two watched me intently with their dark, trusting African eyes. It is that look of trust in the eye of Africa, that look of a people who long to believe and to be assured of something, which so easily made Europeans feel like Gods. But underneath that dark, trusting look is a most observant eye, and many resentments which are never spoken directly to a white man. At times they reveal them in a frenzy, after too many servile silences.

'The Europeans will go if life is made too difficult for them,' I said. 'If you don't want them to stay here then they will go. Do you want them to stay?'

'We want the good ones to stay,' the older man said. 'We don't want them to leave us.'

'What are the bad ones like? What do they do?' There was a strained silence, and the older man saw that he had opened his defences without thinking. 'It's all right, tell me,' I went on. 'Don't be afraid. I'm not in the government. I'm a *mgeni*, a traveller who lived here once come back on a visit.'

'To me, a bad European is one who shouts at me, who does not like me, and who calls me names,' the older man said hesitantly. 'It is men like that who cause trouble.'

'They will be going,' I told him. 'They will not want to live here in *Uhuru*. But the good ones will stay if they are wanted.'

'They will be wanted,' a younger man said. 'We have a lot to learn.'

'We do not want to be ruled by the Kikuyu,' another one said. This was the first of many times that I was to hear this said.

'Who do you want to rule you?' I asked.

'A mixed government,' the older man said. 'Not Kikuyu.' They resented the Kikuyu for the Kikuyu assumption of superiority, as much as they feared them for the ferocity of the Mau Mau time. But I think they knew as well as I that it was the Kikuyu who had most to do with the white man in the sixty years the white man had come to Kenya, who had learned all they could, who had shown a thirst for schools and for all the responsibility they could get.

I asked these three hotel servants their tribes and all of them were from up country tribes, one a Jaluo, one a Meru, and the other a Kipsigis. They feared upheaval, tribal warfare, domination by the Kikuyu, but most of all they feared for their jobs, for their wives and children. They did not believe that black men could have that cool assumption, that casual confidence in government which every white man seemed to possess. They did not believe in themselves, which is not surprising when one remembers that they have never been taught to. So they were afraid of the future.

The bar was empty, the barman, an old wizened African reciting the week's accounts to an African youth who was writing them down for him on a piece of paper.

'Jambo, Bwana,' he said to me. 'You want drink?'

'Beer, but finish your accounts.' He smiled and the youth laughed, saying, 'He is an old one and has never been to school.'

'That's right,' the old man told me, 'I am illiterate, but I have a memory which never makes a mistake. Isn't that true?' he said sharply to the youth.

'All illiterates have better memories than literates,' I assured the old man.

'*Kweli?*' he exclaimed, staring at me, as if I had given him support in a long losing battle with all other opinion. 'Is that true? Is that what white men say?' He was delighted and slapped the youth on the shoulder, growling, 'There, you see, the pencil and paper isn't everything.' He turned to me and while he poured the beer said, 'Even now when I am old, Bwana, my memory is as good as ever. Now is that because I cannot read and write? Do you mean that if a man can read and write his memory loses its power?'

'I can assure you that in my experience an intelligent man who is illiterate remembers nearly everything he hears and does,' I told him. 'Perhaps he has to, or how would he remember anything if he cannot write it down?'

'That's it,' he said, nodding, satisfied. 'That's it. *Kweli*. I knew it. And these young men laugh at me and call me stupid because I never went to school, yet it is to me they come when they want to know what happened a few days ago. I forget nothing.'

'What is your tribe, old one?' I asked him.

'I am a Kamba,' he said proudly.

'You are a long way from home here.'

'Yes, Bwana, a long way, and I am glad. Down here in Mombasa there is not the same amount of trouble and worry that there is up country. What do you think is going to happen to us all?'

'I don't know. I have only just arrived on a visit. It is a few years since I was last here, so now I have to learn all over again.'

'But you have not forgotten your Swahili.'

'It is coming back, more and more words all the time, even while we are talking now it is coming back.'

'That's good,' he said.

'How are things here in Kenya?'

'*Mzuri kidogo,*' he said, gloom coming down on him suddenly. '*Mzuri kidogo tu.* Only a little good. Not really good at all.'

'What is it only a little good?'

'No one knows what is going to happen here in this country,' he

said. 'We don't know what the big-mouths up in Nairobi are going
to say or do next. We are all waiting on them. We are waiting to
hear what is going to happen to us all. And that is no good. *Mzuri
kidogo tu.*'

'Who are the big-mouths?'

'The men of politics, the people who are telling us all that a new
life is beginning. I don't want a new life. I want this one I have. I
have work and a family. What will happen to my work if things
change? Will I be called a friend of the white men and be driven
out of my job?' The old man had got it into his head that all those
who worked for white people would be in some way victimized when
Uhuru came. 'What if the Mau Mau starts again?' he asked me.
'What if all the tribes start fighting each other? We don't know
what's going to happen.' The old man was no 'Uncle Tom' who
saw everything through European eyes, far from it. As the conversation went on he said that because the black man in Kenya had begun
to feel that he was 'losing his country, his tribe, his customs', and
yet could not advance in his new life, Mau Mau had come, and that
Mau Mau 'was like when a prisoner goes mad'.

You can have some surprising conversations with Africans who
were born in the old tribal world and have come, scarred and
bewildered, into this new one which seems to be full of unknown
terrors. When all the polite chatter has come to an end they often
reveal aches, rages, fears, unsuspected by many of the whites who
cannot or will not find the time to converse with the Africans. The
Africans do not dislike white people, but many of them hate those
whites who show their hatred and contempt for Africans. Some
whites just cannot come to any kind of terms with Africans, as if
they were born with a congenital inability to have patience with or
affection for them as a people, and nowadays there are many
Africans who are willing to return the coin.

Late that night I went into an African bar from which the throb
and jangle of jazz was sounding and found a quartette of Africans
with a guitar, a tenor saxophone, drums and maracas, in that shining,
sweaty ecstasy that comes over African jazz players when they are
sending each other well and unmistakably. Three Swahili girls,
their whiskies standing on a table nearby, were doing the Twist in
an effortless African way while the African barman served drinks
to two haggard, pink-lipsticked African whores who sat on their
stools and uttered little dry screams at the right ecstatic time in the
music.

193

'*Habari gani?*' I asked the barman when he had given me a drink, and again it was the answer given by the old man at the hotel, '*Mzuri Kidogo*.' The way of things was only a little good, not really good at all. And again it was because no one knew what was going to happen in Kenya.

'What would you like to happen in Kenya?' I asked him.

'Nothing,' he said sadly. He was a big, fat, greying Swahili with *bhang*-reddened eyes. 'Nothing. I want nothing to happen. I want it just like this, but with more people drinking here. It's been bad lately. No money around. Everyone is frightened.'

CHAPTER THIRTY-TWO

IN the soft, hot evening with the sky slowly reddening beyond the palm trees I sat drinking iced gin. The verandah of the hotel on which I was sitting looked out over the shabby garden where rickety sun-scorched green tables ached for new paint. A small African boy with a big shaven ebony head, beautifully balanced on his very thin neck was sitting on the parched grey grass while he picked swollen ticks off a snoring dog. When one of the ticks, with its fangs buried deep in the dog's skin, was hard to extract, the boy would pick up a cigarette and hold the glowing end close to the tick, and the dog, still snoring, would agitatedly kick its left hind leg until the tick came away. The boy would look at me with his big dark eyes and grin conspiratorially. This boy was somebody's dog *toto*. There were all kinds of *totos* and everybody had one, the dog *toto*, the car *toto*, the gramophone *toto*, the *toto* who looked after the water drums on a long safari, and a *toto* attached himself to all kind of men, African, Indian and European.

'Where are you from, *toto*?' I asked the boy. He said he was from near Lake Victoria Nyanza, and he named his place, his tribe and his village. Did I know that place, he asked me. I did, I told him. I did not tell him that I never wanted to see it again because I had once nearly died there of malaria, and of weariness of its sickly shabby jungle, its steamy heat, its hot rain, its single monotonous bird call clanging in the heavy, panting dusk, and its swarms of big ugly grey speckled tsetse flies, which, when they alighted softly on you, their glistening wings crossed, pierced you so deeply and painfully with their bayonet stings that you bled. The only insects you could compare with the tsetse for ferocity were the camel flies of Somalia, which, when caught, you have to roll between your pressed palms, and even then they could still live, so tough were they with their brown leathery hide.

'What are you doing in Mombasa?' I asked the *toto* while he gently turned the sleeping dog over on to its other side and began to probe for more ticks.

He was down here with his Bwana who was about to sail away from

Kenya forever, and he was sorry this Bwana was going because with him he had travelled far and had had many adventures and learned many things. His Bwana had let him come down to the coast with him to see Mombasa and had bought him a rail ticket back to Kisumu. Perhaps I would like to employ him?

No, I told him, I am only here for a short stay. It didn't matter, he said, he would come with me and do this and that job for me. *Mzuri?*

He had no idea where I might be going but it could be a new adventure. He had no idea if I was cruel, or kind, or mean, or rich or a drunk. He had no knowledge of my character, but if I said I was driving in a truck to a place he had never heard of, say Lagos on the West coast, he would come, would collect firewood in the evening, light the fire, make the tea, wash and iron clothes, sew on buttons, and appear unexpectedly with fresh maize cobs from some village nearby, grinning, in a time of hunger.

There was the gramophone *toto* who had worked for a run down remittance man on a plantation I knew before the war. The Bwana was a two bottle a day man, and in the evening he would sit on the verandah while the gramophone *toto* went through the nightly routine of playing every single record in the dusty collection, one after the other, in the same order, while the Bwana drank. From where I lived I could hear the *toto* winding up the tired portable gramophone between each record ('Thora', 'What Are The Wild Waves Saying?' 'The Snowy Breasted Pearl', 'St. Louis Blues', 'Gas Shell Bombardment at Loos, 1915', 'Funiculi Funicula', 'Making Whoopee',—) and every month when we drove through the dustclouds, the white men of the plantation, to the far off town for 'a party', the gramophone *toto* would load the records and gramophone into the back of his Bwana's truck and leap up after them. He would play them throughout the night's uproar in the stinking heat of the bar overlooking the vast moonlit lake.

His Bwana was a real remittance man, paid by his family in England to stay away from them, to stay where he was in this leprous piece of Africa, and if he left that place, his money would stop. He committed suicide one night, in the middle of the suicide season, and the European who arrived on the verandah to super-intend the brief check up—no farewell note, no will—bequeathed the gramophone and records, on his own responsibility, and with the urgent and hasty agreement of us all, to the gramophone *toto*. The *toto* vanished to Nairobi on a trade truck with the intention of setting himself up there in a bar or brothel as music master of entertainment, but not having forgotten to get a letter first from the generous European to say that he was the legal and rightful possessor of the gramophone and records. I wonder how 'Gas Shell Bombardment at Loos, 1915' went down with the detribalized crowd in the sleazy bars and knocking shops down on River Road, Nairobi? Or, another favourite of the dead Bwana, which I knew by weary heart, 'Light Cavalry' played by a banjo and harmonica group.

An old Englishwoman came into the hotel garden and sat down at one of the shaky tables. The dog *toto* greeted her and she told him she was glad to see him taking care of the dog. She ordered a large whisky from the African servant who came to her silently on his long, flat, dusty bare feet. She was very old, and eccentrically dressed, having on her head a strange floppy hat made of soft and shiny buckskin from under which her snow white hair straggled. She wore a long, loose, shapeless dress of heavy brown silk, and when she kicked off her pointed Punjabi sandals sewn with old and faded gold wirework, I could see her small, bare, delicately shaped feet. They were sun-dried and fine-boned. She was marvellously beautiful and a lot of men long ago must have moved in and out of her life. She smoked a cigarette and watched the *toto*.

The evening was ready to die now, and I could hear from a house nearby the beat of Indian film *geet* and the thin, erotic chirrupping of the inevitable Indian film beauty who had starred in the Bombay 'quicky'.

The fine looking old woman took the big whisky from the African servant in his long grubby white gown, thanked him and paid him and then asked how was his wife? He said she was better today, and how was the memsahib herself? The old woman looked at him with her big blue magnificent eyes and smiled. She was well, but watching the *toto* there with the dog, how she wished her own dog was still alive. She took a big photograph out of her handbag and showed it to the African. Somehow I knew he had seen it many times before, by the way he smiled and studied the picture, and the way the woman watched him study it.

'He was a fine dog, wasn't he, Mulei?' she said.

'He was, Memsahib,' the African said, and he sighed for her, deeply, in the African way which is at once heartfelt and exaggerated. The old woman drank the whisky down, neat, in one graceful movement, and, a familiar drill, the African took it from her and hurried off to get her another.

Mulei, a Kamba tribesman judging by his name, grinned at me as he passed. When he came back he gave the old woman a saucer of cashew nuts, saying, 'Something for you to eat, Memsahib.' They smiled at each other, obviously old friends. You could tell that she was never going to leave Kenya, but would die there. It was a pleasure to watch her, even the way she smoked, the cigarette gripped lightly between the very tips of the long time-yellowed fingers of her right hand, and the way she held her beautiful head back to watch the dog *toto*, who had finished now, and she smiled at him with her good white teeth, nodding to him.

The blue dusk was coming down swiftly now and lights were going on in the yellow and white buildings beyond the palm trees, and I wished while I sat there that I could explain to myself what it was about evening and dusk in the tropics that makes one feel so haunted by the special and peculiar silence which lasts some moments before the darkness comes. There is a piece of Indian music composed for, and meant to be played, only at that particular part of the day, a special and haunting *raga*, and this music evokes all of the mysterious essence of those moments. There is a sadness in the tropical dusk, yet the sadness can be almost a pleasure, if you are alone and let it come right in to you.

CHAPTER THIRTY-THREE

I had not seen Nairobi since Mau Mau time, and now, sitting behind the Kikuyu taxi driver coming from the railway station I stared about me. I knew the road but I could not recognize the buildings, and when we came to a tall new hotel I was lost. I would surely recognize the old New Stanley hotel when we got to it, with its verandah on the first storey.

'There's the New Stanley, Bwana,' the taxi driver said to me. '*Huku!*' He pointed in the old way, with his chin, and there it was, a towering new building with a wide stretch of cement in front sprinkled with tables, a tall thorn tree growing in the middle of it. Everything was built up and the old Wild West looking Nairobi had vanished in the glittering steel and concrete. The place had been given a charter as a city so they thought they ought to build a city on top of Nairobi.

I never liked Nairobi, but I liked the old New Stanley and I sullenly resented that they had jazzed it up into a super hotel, though they left the old bar as it was. I wanted to get in there and look for faces of old friends. The best friends you ever made were in East Africa, people of a certain kind, who knew wilderness and how to enjoy it, who were generous and with whom you would go anywhere, and through anything. Yes, something to splurge about, that particular world, something to feel emotion about. Many good things had happened to me in this country, and many good people were still there and I was excited at the thought of coming across them again after so long. I could not wait to sit out at a table under that unhappy thorn tree, so lonely looking in the middle of its sea of cement, and watch for old friends. 'People sit round the thorn tree at this time,' the woman behind the desk had told me. 'They go into the bar later.'

I sat down at a table, ordered a coffee, and had a look round. Delamere was still sitting on his block of stone in the middle of the traffic. They would have that removed as soon as self government came. I later suggested to a European with influence that Delamere's statue would be far happier sitting on a hill somewhere below Narok looking out over the Masai country, and to put it there now, before it was removed—the old Masai would remember Delamere, who had liked them and got on with them. It was a harmless statue, not at all like the nauseating one put up in the last century in Lahore, of a British general standing amongst a welter of cannon and other weapons, with an inscription asking the Indian people to make up their minds if they wished to be ruled by the pen or by the sword. They sensibly settled for the pen, after 1857. I wonder what Delamere would mean to educated Kikuyu? Chief Bwana of the old time settlers who had, in the late twenties, looked on Harry Thuku as a demonic force, not dreaming of the Mau Mau, waiting far off in the future, a force which, as one old settler told me, made him realize, too late, that Harry Thuku had been a good and reasonable man. Or would some Africans see Delamere as the romantic he was, a man who had loved Kenya, but who, naturally, never dreamed of it as a place Africans would want to own and govern one day. Delamere was an unusual man, but not as unusual as Kenya itself.

Africans and Europeans and Indians, some of them in groups of the three races, came and sat down for coffee and to watch the passers by. It was very strange to see this in Nairobi, and it was good to see friendships among these three races laughing together as they talked over their coffee. Yes, if a multi-racial society would not work here in Kenya then it could not work anywhere in Africa. You cannot make people like each other by law, but you can certainly arrange a society in which they can mix together if they want to, and avoid each other if they wish. Kenya seemed to be working it that way.

About ten minutes after I sat down a voice said, 'Well, it's been a long time, hasn't it, chum?'

It was Dougy and I had not seen him for years. We had been desiccated together in odd places in Somalia. After some ironic exchanges in Somali we sat down and he gave me news of each friend as I reeled off the names. Dead. Hunting. Somewhere in the wilds of Tanganyika, it was rumoured. Gone to Australia. Dead. Remarried. Divorced. Don't know. Broke. Said to be running a bar somewhere in the Mediterranean. In New York lecturing on game migration. Don't know. Then Dougy reeled off his own list and I gave him this or that bit of news of this or that shagbag if I knew.

Dougy, a white hunter now, was about to leave for safari after buffalo with an American client. We would meet later. I watched him stride off. There is no doubt about it, I thought, that the people you like are the people with whom you have been able to enjoy lousy and depressing places in wilderness, perhaps more than with friends with whom you have other kinds of accord far from wilderness. Dougy was witty and emotional and sensitive, and he liked to laugh, and in sad places he never whined or complained. It was a tonic to see him again.

Five minutes later another voice said, 'Drinks are being served at the earliest possible moment. But at the *very very* earliest.' Yes, I knew that dialogue at once. It was Tony, one of the best friends I ever made, and he was grinning at me when I looked up. A twenty-four hour party followed, out near Karen on the Ngong road, and I knew I was back in Kenya when Tony put on the music we had played so often during the Mau Mau evenings when his children were asleep and loaded pistols lay nearby on the chairs.

One night we had driven an old Kikuyu back into his village, right into the middle of the Mau Mau country, wilting banana palms everywhere around the straw conical roofs of the Kikuyu huts, and the castor oil plants, so much a part of the old Kikuyu life, growing everywhere. It was that dusk time again when we got out of the car and said good-night to the old Kikuyu. It was silent, and in the forests the hunted Mau Mau would be squatting under the rain-dripping trees, red mud everywhere, waiting for darkness.

The silence in that village seemed more eerie than the usual silence of an African dusk, if only because the whole atmosphere of Kenya then, especially at night, was soaked with the tragedy which was happening to the Kikuyu people. It was despair which had caused Mau Mau, despair of a special kind, for they could not break out fully from their decaying tribal world with its dying code of extremely strict rules for living, its oaths and secrets and traditions, though they longed so much to break with it—and even if they succeeded they still could not enter the new society around them in the cities, which still belonged to the white men whose world they had schooled themselves to enter. It was as if they had decided to drive themselves back into a new kind of tribal world, darkened with a perversion of all that had been strict in their own tribal code—the oaths which Kikuyu had always taken were now redesigned to shatter all the old oaths, to break them as Kikuyu and make them Mau Mau fighters in the forest.

The hundred and two odd versions of Christianity preaching the messages all around them for years, about Christ's message of brotherhood, were publicly denied by the white society which would not let Africans, no matter how educated, into hotels, into restaurants, into ordinary friendships with white men. The African who had been to school felt trapped when he sat at his clerk's desk in Nairobi—he had lost his tribe and he could find no new one with the white men, who did not want him except as docile labour.

Tony and I had watched the darkness come while we stood in the village and the old Kikuyu made his way to his hut among the banana groves. He would lock himself in there for the night, would lie there listening for the Mau Mau group which might suddenly arrive, smash down his door, and force him to take the Mau Mau oath—the oath to hate white men, to deny their rule, to die denying that rule, if necessary. (Or had he already taken the oath, voluntarily, long ago?)

The old man looked after Tony's small children. He was a man of the old times, stooped, grey stubble on his cheeks, gentle, and bewildered by the bloody shadow which had fallen across his life and his tribe.

A Kikuyu's life then was not worth a light; anyone might kill him, black or white, for the fear was everywhere, and fear has a sudden and enormous voltage. This old man, one night, asked me why the white men did not wipe out the whole Kikuyu tribe. He asked me because he did not want to live any more, and he meant that if the white men were fighting the Kikuyu, and people were being killed in large numbers, why did not the white men bring his machines and finish it all and have done with it?

'Tell them to bring the bombers, Bwana, and finish us all off now, for it is finished anyway, our old life, and we do not know where to turn, and it has gone on too long.'

'What will you do if they come one night and force you to take the oath?'

We looked into each other's eyes, and his were blurred and aged, and utterly pathetic. He folded his withered brown hands and looked at the children playing on the carpet nearby, and at the pistol on the chair, and then at me.

'I would tell Bwana Tony at once,' he said. 'I would tell him at once if I took the oath.' He could go then, could vanish, or be locked up, but probably he would silently vanish, this sad old man who had lived to see this explosion of despair.

'You can feel it in the air, can't you?' Tony said while we stood in the village that dusk. We could hear the old man locking the door of his hut, the only sound, iron, and sad. Yes, you could feel the demonic despair in the air, in that strange silence, not just because you were a white man who might get panga-chopped at any time, but everybody could feel it, black, brown and white, that ferocity which powered the Mau Mau, as well as much of its opposition.

When hatred and distrust for the Kikuyu was at its peak during the Mau Mau war, many Europeans refused to sack their Kikuyu labourers and clerks, and their trust was returned, though a few paid for it too. Yet you could not deny, watching the Kenya of that time, that, if you were a Kikuyu, you knew the time had come to challenge the white men, for the right to aspire to equality in your own land, no matter how much you might deplore the terrible killing-oaths taken in the forest. It will be a long time before we hear the real story of the Mau Mau war. Only one side of it has been heard so far, the 'official' side.

Mau Mau was an eruption which nothing could have stopped, given the frustration and the dilemma in which Africans of the post-war period lived. So many thousand things produced that frustration. You have to imagine yourself an African in ragged shorts, standing on the red dusty road near Nairobi, and having a sudden flash of recognition of the situation, while watching the European cars (they got bigger and bigger and more numerous every year), whizzing by on the roads into and out of a growing Nairobi. Truly another self contained race lived in Kenya, on top, the white men, who lived an enormously full life twenty-four hours of the day, while more and more Africans were being born to enter frustration. And what colour was God? White? And which God was the best one? God was owned by so very many Christian churches, and however different he was according to each church, he must be white and rich, with a special feeling for the owners of big cars, who seemed not to need God anyway.

How much frustration and hatred must have lain behind the decision to slay a goat on the altar of a Christian church and leave it there? The very contempt behind the gesture showed that the Africans had been ready for an Ecumenical year a long time before Pope John arrived at the throne. Even though they knew of the very many good things done by the varied sects of Christian missionaries, the Africans had had enough of being on the sidelines and watching the ridiculous Christian quarrel which had been dragged into their lives. And God was a white man, apparently.

So let God be black instead. Not only were they ahead of the ecumenical year which lay far off in the future, but the Africans were even ahead of the Black Muslim sect which was to grow in North America—if you are not allowed to love, then hate, and with all your might. At least hatred was an aspect of love, denied love, its other face after the quiet kick in the teeth. American negroes feel belittled, in their own trap in America, by seeing the new free Africans arrive in America, Africans who cannot be slapped any more if they are impudent.

The Mau Mau convulsion was as if the Africans had said, 'Let's smash everything up. We are not much good, according to the white men, so let's prove it by going right down the line with knife and torch and the blackest mumbo jumbo we can invent.'

A hint of the size of that despair can be found in one of the letters sent into Nairobi by the forest leader of a Mau Mau gang, Dedan Kimathi.

BAMBOO No. 6
Kenya.
20/12/53.
(A drawing of a star here)

The Star is the Light of the
whole country of Kenya.

First I greet the Government of Kenya. I am very very happy. Broadcast this letter to all races, black and white everywhere.

COME. COME YOU ALL TO KENYA.

This letter has been written after the meeting held after 8/12/52 in Nyeri, in Embu and in Meru.

(1) Kenya aims that it will never be ruled by another nation until the end of the world, though we are under British rule this long time past.
(2) These three meetings decided that Indians will be prosecuted because they take the lead in spoiling Kenya. Indians in Kenya are to be reared by the people and by their wealth, but my soldiers will now fight as hard as possible, for I had warned them not to give Indians any sort of suffering, but now it has been found out that the Indians are the sole spoilers of Kenya.
(3) Cast your eyes on India and see what happened there. Never say you are to be protected by government forces. All these are mine. Think and see that even in India they were there.

(4) Her Majesty the Queen, her kingdom is cursed, for it was cursed when she was here in Kenya. She left here with tears when her father died. It is really cursed.

(a) British Government, though you rule over Kenya 100 or 150 years, no longer shall we be in good terms. Just pray to God to maintain your rule to the end of the world.

(b) Because the British Government intends to make the peoples of Kenya its slaves.

(c) They never regard them as human beings. What is going to happen in Kenya has never happened in any other country, just sadness and tears throughout Kenya.

(5) Mr. Oliver Lyttelton, together with Her Majesty and the Governor of Kenya, should be told to record the loss incurred by the dropping of bombs over Kenya, and the loss of people accounted for by government. Africans should take these into account. The bombs are merely spoiling the land. There is no cause for dropping them.

(a) The bombs and ammunition you are using should be spared for next year's use, 1954, because of the fight that is to take place within that period, whose end is not known.

(b) African Government Kenya Voice has the power to do what it can these days.

(c) Government, do not suppress women and children and invalids and homes, then afterwards to deceive the community that it is the gangsters you have arrested or killed— just come over to Bamboo No. 6. 6/Kenya. You will find me there, for I am already back from my three months journey which I had been making.

(6) This is what I wish to say, and it is important to all races in Kenya.

(a) How foolish is the Government to decide that it will be confiscating people's lands. Is there anybody in Kenya who is good? Probably soldiers and H.G. and some Chiefs, together with some other people.

(b) Try to reach me where I stay to confiscate lands there.

(c) Again, hypocrites, enough, for you have cunningly approached Kikuyu old men, telling them to accept this measure as it is the only way to end the present troubles, and they agreed, they being God's fools.

(d) Murders are what has been done, by people of all races— had you to win, could you win by killing people—it is better all people in Kenya to finish then to get troubles and tears.

(e) Had you to win or if you like doing justice, you ought to have tried to reduce troubles, but because you use Colour-bar in Kenya, that is why trouble will remain even more than it has been in the past.

(7) The last point is that Houses or colour discrimination or wages will never solve the problems that exist presently in Kenya. Kenya needs nothing else other than lands and freedom itself.

Remain in God's peace.
I am,
D. Kimanthi.
Mt. Kenya.

P.S.

It is I who made my presence in Nairobi on Monday 21/12/53. The Star you see there is my light wherever I go in the country.

Government, you will exhaust your stores searching for me. Our co-operation with you need only be sought by clever people, for it shall never come again though you ride a ladder to the skies. You troubled India for 60 years, and when you got what you wanted, you left the country in 1947, completely.

Come, Come, Come you to Kenya. It is a good country. Justice is necessary to all races other than colour-bar in a country, for colour-bar will never be solved by bombs or ammunition. Justice alone will do it, together with mutual understanding—beyond that there is no solution, sooner or later.

Before he was caught and hanged Kimathi had killed many of his own men in the forest. A messianic madness overcame him, but what he had said in his letter about the colour-bar was true. It ended in Kenya, after Mau Mau. It had to.

Mau Mau cannot be defended. It was too vile for that. But it can be explained, by anthropologists and psychologists who understand Kikuyu and the smashing effect European civilization with its greed had upon people like the Kikuyu.

It is laughable to hear people talk about the 'savagery' in which they found Africa, when one thinks of the savage slums of Europe, the crucifying poverty in which its people lived, the long murder of its wars and its diseases, and most of all its jungle attitude to riches and power. And finally its gas ovens, its mass bombings, its torture chambers.

In old times no Kikuyu with a wife and children was allowed to be without land, even if it was only a maize patch. Nobody 'owned' land among the Kikuyu. It belonged to the Kikuyu people as a whole. Idyllic? Not really, but it gives an idea of something other than the ferocious savagery and anarchy from which they were told they were to be saved.

CHAPTER THIRTY-FOUR

THE rains were lashing down. It was the wrong time of the year for the rains, as so often in Africa, and they came down in teeming silver stair rods, which broke across the ground in a hissing, sparkling carpet. The rain diminished and eruptions of grasshoppers swirled into the air like thickening green smoke clouds, and, as they must have done for a thousand generations, old men of the Kavirondo tribe, lost here in Nairobi so far from their lakeside home, scooped them up—though time had brought a change—they were packing them into big plastic bags thrown away by careless memsahibs.

I stood in a doorway in Nairobi and watched one old Kavirondo in a cast off army greatcoat patiently filling his plastic bags. Years ago I had seen them squatting over holes in the earth from which the insects swarmed, and packing them by the handful into rusty petrol tins, but now, with the advances made in civilization, a man could wander in the city with a dozen plastic bags folded up in his pocket and be always ready to add to his larder.

'When will you eat them, old one?' I asked the old man when he paused before me with his right hand full of the big insects. He came into the doorway for a cigarette and we talked while we watched the rain coming down again, the heavy highland chill seeping in the night air.

While he talked he stripped the creatures down with his swift fingers, detaching the wings, legs, and head. Later he would fry them all gently and then pack them in fat. He reached out occasionally and snapped up a fresh handful of the ecstatic insects, blowing wheezily into the plastic bag to open it afresh.

'How would you say life is for you now, old one?' I asked him.

'For us old ones now, hunting the money is very hard. Our time is finished, and the young push us aside. It is getting hard to find enough to eat, especially when you are old.'

He was a watchman for some city firm, but about him still clung all the old attitudes and sentiments of the far off bush village. He asked me for another cigarette and when I enquired if he was finished with the old time pipe and the snuff, he shook his grizzled head. 'All that is of another time,' he said. 'In the city here it is the cigarette a man hunts. The time of the little pipe is gone.' He laughed to think of it, in the African way, high and innocent laughter with his head going from side to side. The Kavirondo used to smoke tiny metal pipes which hung round their necks on strings.

'Goodbye, Bwana,' he said.

'Goodbye, old one.' He stepped out of my life as fast as he had stepped in, trotting off into the rain, his right hand flailing among the whirling insects which he rammed into his bulging plastic bag. Other Africans ran up and down the streets with their plastic bags. There were more insects flying about in clouds than they could ever catch in a lifetime. They piled up their filled plastic bags in shop doorways. Later they would trot off down to the rusty tin shacks they lived in on the edge of the city—the sad casualties of the broken tribal life.

The white men had been here only about sixty years, far less than that in any numbers, and now it was all finished and the few educated Africans would soon inherit the strange mess made by the collision of two totally different worlds which hardly understood each other.

Standing in the doorway watching the rain, I remembered driving down this street only a few years ago in a dusty battered Ford, twenty years old, and dressed in khaki shorts, bush shirt and hand made leather veldschoen, in a time when you could dress like that for about three pounds, and the war had still not given Africa that savage and bewildering kick in the guts which felled it to its knees.

That war had come into quiet sleepy Africa like a mad giant, tearing up tribal society, bringing once and for all the enormous change that had lain for so long on the horizon, like a promise, a threat.

In pre-war Kenya the Africans, when they met a white man, met only one kind of white man, and never met them in swarms, dressed as soldiers, who, bored, womenless, soon sought all the drink and women they could find—and unlike the Middle and Far East which had known soldiery for generations—East Africa was not rigged for the big garrison life—brothels, pubs, soldiers' quarters in the local town.

It had been strange too for the Africans to see the enormous barbed-wire encampments in which the thousands of Italian prisoners were kept—white men locked up by other white men, the strangest situation.

Years later the Kikuyu whores, working for the cause down River Road during Mau Mau, used to prefer, rather than money, a clip of rifle ammunition, five rounds, and when they got it they sent it to the gangs in the forests. By Mau Mau time Kenya was well rigged for garrison life—but a garrison life which would not last very long.

When the rain stopped I walked through the whirring mists of grasshoppers and a hunched old African stopped me outside Lavarini's, one of the new Italian restaurants. He was wearing ragged khaki shorts and a torn grey-blue shirt of the kind once worn by the Somaliland Camel Corps. He had a look of hopelessness in his eyes as he spoke to me in a low voice. He was telling me apologetically that he had never begged before, and that he was only begging now because he had just arrived from his tribal country, knew nobody, was puzzled, and was starving. When he had finished he looked at me fearfully, as if about to run off, as if he wished he had not after all brought this information into this pale stranger's busy life. Then he looked at the ground and, uselessly, I wished that European civilization had never been allowed to come here into Africa, and that Africa had had the time to make its own arrangements with Europe, but which it had never done until the Europeans finally walked up from the coast through a silence which had lasted, on the edge of Europe, since the beginning of time.

The Arabs had made a thin trail into East Africa from the coast. While the white men had worked the West African coast for slaves for about four centuries, the Arabs ran the slave trade in East Africa, when they were not fighting the Portuguese down on the coast. Small blessing it is true, but at least in the Arab world an African slave could become a Muslim, and Islam had no colour bar, and he was not chained up in stud breeding stalls as his West African brother was in the Americas—if he survived the terrible Middle Passage in the slave ships. But the Arab was as merciless as the white man in many ways. The slave trade belonged to all of them in the end, European, African and Arab, for many of the African chiefs worked wholeheartedly to rope in slaves for the visiting traders. And I wondered, looking at the old man hanging his head after begging, if there was much difference for this African in the two systems, the old slave trade and the new big, civilized machine in which he was lost tonight in the rain.

He told me he was from beyond Machakos, a Kamba, and he had walked all the way, to find work, perhaps the work of a watchman, but there was no work to be had, they had told him among the rusty tin shacks where the poor and the detribalized lived.

'Why come here?' I asked him. 'You are an old man now and should be sitting in the village in peace, like an elder.'

'That time has gone,' he said. 'It is finished. It does not matter now if you are an elder. There is no money. Without money now you die. The village is finished. No one in my village wants to look after old men now.' He could not fully explain what he meant, but he meant that a man was now worth what he had in his pocket, or could sell, and all he had to sell now was his age, and nobody wanted that in this new time of new values.

In the time of *zamani*, the old times, you would never see an African beggar. His tribe would not have allowed it. Now, Nairobi was full of beggars, nearly all of them casualties in the upheaval of their dissolving tribal world. The unemployed swarmed by the thousand in Nairobi, and were turning to crime in order to live. Unemployment was the biggest single problem that the new government in Kenya would have to face, and it was growing all the time. The proletariat had been created but it had no work to do.

I gave the old man some money and I could see that, glad though he was to have it, he regretted having had to ask me for it. He stood there with the money in his hand, looking at me with his sad old eyes while he said, 'Let me work for you and pay for this money. Let me clean your motor car.' I told him I had no car, and had no work for him, and to forget it and to go and eat.

'*Mungu na saidia wewe*,' he told me, God would help me. He shuffled off into the darkness and I could see that his feet were hurting him, the way he put them tenderly down and lifted them again. Perhaps Tom Mboya, who felt about these things, would find some solution to all this mess when *Uhuru* came, I thought. But perhaps it was going to be too big to solve, like those endless waves of beggars which broke, whimpering at your feet wherever you stopped in an Indian city. Or was it Communism . . . when its contemptible political contempt for human fallibility had been finally buried. . . . which would give millions the work they wanted?

CHAPTER THIRTY-FIVE

THE more I saw of the new Nairobi with its cafés and restaurants where Indians and Africans and Europeans mingled together without any self-conscious effort towards One World stuff, the more I felt that all East Africa needed now was good Brazilian music, or at least an exotic national music of her own. Britain had no national form of typical music to export, like Portugal and Spain had, and it is an important lack. Britain abroad is very dull, almost as dull as London for the London masses—everyone wants to slam the door of the café or shut the bar at the drop of a policeman's helmet. Men have worked hard to spread the grey London Sunday all over the British Empire—and it never really suited the African temperament, though they tried, because they had to, to adapt to it. In Nairobi, though, as in London, the Italians brought some life into the public greyness. It was obvious that Nairobi would develop into a brighter and gayer city eventually, and that the Europeans who stayed on would enjoy it too. The British upper class who always behave so stiffly and correctly for their masses, have always been able to have a ball privately—in their clubs, night and day clubs. Late night entertainment, at prices they can afford, has never been available for the British people—which might be why the younger generation in Britain, not so docile as their fathers, want to smash everything up these days when they take a look around at the load of bye-laws surrounding them. There certainly is, or was, something forbidding in British rectitude which frustrated Africans and Indians in the past. Africans in Nairobi told me how much more refreshing to be with they found the younger generation of Englishmen.

More at ease, because not so privately scared and hence publicly arrogant, as the deep-frozen public school type, the new ones *looked* easy to get on with, for a start. They had not the old built-in hood-eyed contempt for non-British people (though it could be a terribly friendly contempt in its way), and did not seem to assume that anyone non-British hadn't really *lived* yet. Just as they were beginning to work out the ending of the long preserved class structure in England, so were they bringing a new attitude abroad in their relationships with those who had been even farther down the ladder than the English working class, the 'coloured races,' or the wogs and nigs as they were called in the days before Empire Day discreetly became Commonwealth Day. The British Commonwealth might really work if Britain can send more of her new young people abroad. No African or Indian or Arab I have ever met denied that the British had great and unusual qualities as administrators, but they never felt wanted or accepted, and their resentment was all in the painful area of the most important territory, human relationship.

During the war I wrote a story about how we buried, on an air-dropping zone in Burma, an American pilot who had just been shot down while dropping food and ammunition to us. The burial party was made up of African infantry who had been collecting the air-drop. They had never seen an American before and they talked to me about how they appreciated the bravery of the American airmen who fed them from the air in the jungle. They were not singling the Americans out as compared with the British airmen who flew the same sorties. I described in my story what the Africans had said about the Americans. The story when it reached England found its way to a desk in some branch of the Colonial service. On the side of the MSS was then pencilled—'It is not the business of this department to tell the Americans how much our Colonial troops like them.'

Only the opinion of one sun-dried personality, true, but it encapsulates the whole attitude which Asia and Africa felt they must drive out, so that they could breathe any kind of air they wished.

When I read that pencilled comment I began to look forward to the day when that kind of tiny, frightened personality would have no more say in what Africans were to feel about Americans, or about anyone else, including the Chinese. The fear of the Americans and their power and influence was already keeping the older sahibs awake at that period of the war. Their jealousy of America, a pitiful jealousy, will die with them, no doubt.

There were plenty of Americans about in Nairobi in 1962, and soon, there would be plenty of Russians and Czechs and Chinese, but I doubted if the Africans would feel they must choose one or the other. It felt as if Africa wanted to make its own decisions.

'We're not very interested in what the West or the East think is good for Africa,' an African trade union leader told me in a Nairobi bar. 'We've got to find ourselves first, and that'll take time.' He had no 'chip' on his shoulder about white men—he had accepted long ago, as he put it, that 'there are good ones and there are bastards, and you have to learn to see them like you see other people, just as men with good and bad personalities'. He was unusual in that he was an African first and a man of a certain tribe second, and he knew that this attitude would have to spread in East Africa as fast as possible. Like many other non-Kikuyu he worried about the Kikuyu love of being Kikuyu first—being African for them came a long way behind, he said.

This tall, powerful and witty African was a truly *good* man. It shone in his face, the goodness and the honesty, and he already had a touch of the *mzee* about him, the fatherly African who would wear his grey hair well and with dignity, who would be able to give good advice. His personality had had a chance to get out of its colonial prison early in youth, and had been able to make mistakes and make discoveries about itself. He had done all kinds of jobs in his life, from labourer to journalist, and had always studied the trade union principle as the only platform from which the working man could squeeze a few more rights from the employer. He knew the one about how the working man has his duties as well as his rights. He knew that one backwards, as does any labourer who has slung a sixteen-pound sledge-hammer for too little money, while having a headful of small dreams as well. He hoped that a day would come when the employer *would* be good, because it could be good to be good, and would give justice along with just wages, instead of waiting for the strike which would force them from him, and create bitterness with it. Unusual too, he knew there was no real solution, only a continuation of hope for a better world, while trying in his personal life to make it one. MRA material? He said he had no time for MRA, but he was a religious man. He had been brought up a Catholic, but had left it—in order to have a full life—he laughed sadly at me—remembering things, I suppose—but now, at thirty-five, with three children and a wife, he had gone back to Catholicism, in order to live a good life. He had found that Catholicism was necessary for him. 'For *me*, I mean,' he said. 'I discovered it was necessary for *me*, if I was to live any kind of good and useful life. I'm happy now inside. Let's have some more beer. *Mbili mkubwa*, eh?'

He talked about the white men he knew. There seemed to be only two kinds. Those an African *knew* had no prejudice, hidden or otherwise, about Africans, and those who had. You could tell

214

at once, and you got tired, long ago you had got tired, of trying to pretend you didn't mind a white man putting up with you even though you were only a nigger.

'*They*'ll have to go,' he said. 'It's no use their staying here. They can't hide it, even if they live in the dark they can't hide it. So this place is no use to them anymore. We all know the white men we want to keep here.' He turned round at the table and looked at the crowd of white men at the bar nearby. '*He*'s a good one. And *he*'s a good one. That's a bastard over there. He'll have to go. And that one too. *There* is a really fine one, that one there.' He laughed. 'We know them *all*.'

He was not a sentimentalist about Africa, had none of the sentimental feeling that there was some dark mysterious African strength, some natural elemental force in Africa which had a message for the world, and therefore that any old African custom must be preserved because it was African. He knew that the Western way of life had come to stay, everywhere, and would be adapted now, not destroyed, or replaced, but lived with and made better and better. That went for the Russians too. We were all involved right now in digesting one enormous way of life which was spreading into every culture. He kept reading in the Western press that the greatest single world problem now was the colour problem. He did not agree. He thought the biggest problem of today was how to get disarmament. Somehow, he felt, we were not going to be allowed to have it—too many billions were invested all over the world in the arms industry. And it was so dangerous now that Africans like himself, well back on the sidelines still, felt they might be extinguished just as they were about to emerge into recognition as a free people. How could men, ordinary men, find a way to sweep all these militarists and their arms factories out of the way forever? There must be some way as yet untried, something other than the insincere disarmament conferences that went on for years? We could find no solution, even after six more beers.

CHAPTER THIRTY-SIX

'EVEN now,' the small handsome jet-black African with me said, as we entered a restaurant and the European heads turned to stare at him. 'They still look at you in one of these places as if you had just fallen down through the roof. It'll take some years, I suppose.' He was laughing as he said it, genuinely amused. We sat down at a table and ordered food. We had met to talk about the Masai, but the conversation had turned to the Kikuyu, to Mau Mau, and to East Africa's waiting period for self government.

It was a curious time, this waiting period. The British were still governing Kenya and the Africans were waiting to take over. The atmosphere was tense but controlled, but no one could guess what might happen when freedom came. There might be tribal warfare, there might be a massacre of Indians, with fleeing Europeans piling onto the train for Mombasa, or there might be a multi-racial society which buried the past.

'For my part,' J., this small African told me, staring hard into my eyes, looking for something there—might I not be just a very good white actor playing it liberal?—'I will draw a line across the past on the day we get freedom. I begin again there, and I hope everyone else will, black, brown and white. But after that my attitude to any European who insults me will be very different from the past. I will react strongly. But the past will be dead for me on the day *Uhuru* comes, as long as it is dead for everyone else.' He had had his experiences of being kicked around by a certain kind of white man, and while he was bitter, he had a sardonic humour which had protected him from blind rage. He had never wanted to panga-chop a European, though he understood why some did, which brought him back to the Kikuyu.

He was anxious for me to know that he was not anti-Kikuyu. He was detached in what he said, but he wanted me to know that he, like so many non-Kikuyu, was watching the Kikuyu more closely just now than they had ever watched anything in their lives. He was not anti-Kikuyu, but he did not like them, as a tribe. They were greedy, hungry for power, too proud altogether of being Kikuyu.

Too self-satisfied. He laughed. 'I want to say something to you,' he said. 'I'm serious about it too. If ever you *should* discover what is the matter with the Kikuyu as a tribe—why they are rotting away as a tribe, and they are—please don't print it—in case the Kikuyu should read it and find out what is the matter with them, and then cure themselves.' He paused. 'We *want* them to rot away as a tribe. We want them to fall apart as a tribe. Then their secrecy and their fondness for intrigue and oaths will vanish with their tribalism. And Kenya can be then glad of their individual abilities as Kikuyu. But as a tribe we are sick of them, all of us.' It was a very surprising thing to hear this put so quietly and vehemently by this small, quiet, reasonable man. Not that one did not know this opinion was held by many non-Kikuyu, but it was never said like this.

He was not exultant as he went on to say, 'We are even glad to see how their sixteen-year-old girls are pouring into the city to become prostitutes—it means that the tribe is breaking up at last. It is finishing—' I had seen these girls. When you drove out on the strip of asphalt running through the bush in the darkness, heading for Ngong, say, you saw lines of these girls along the road, holding their dresses up for you as the bright headlights licked across their brown loins. It was enough to astound you when you remembered the strict moral code of the Kikuyu before Mau Mau.

'Yes,' said J., 'they are finishing as a tribe at last. Although they are intelligent and hardworking, they stand, as a tribe, in the way of Kenya's progress, and they have got it into their heads that they are better than all the rest of us. We don't want anything to stop this rotting away of their tribe. We want it to go faster and faster. We need the end of them as a tribe if we are to make a new Kenya.' He smiled. 'Some of us are weary of tribalism, especially Kikuyu tribalism.' He laughed. 'So, if you *should* discover what is ruining the Kikuyu tribe—' his underlining *should* intimated that I would know how maniacally secretive the Kikuyu were as a people— 'don't print it, and you will help Kenya.'

He talked about the new African politicians in Nairobi, and here again his views were unexpectedly novel.

'They don't mean much,' he said. 'Except for two or three of them, they're just a bunch of good time boys, but I *like* to see them driving around in their cars and spending money on parties and so on. It is good. It is good that they do this and let the people see them doing it. When the people have seen enough of it and get tired of it they will push them out of the way and get real people, the people to lead us who will teach us to work, without big cars and parties. But it is very important that the present bunch reveal themselves to the people.' He burst out laughing. 'Several of them are idiots,' he said. 'But they won't last. The power will go to their heads and the people will see it. The people watch hard. You would be surprised how hard the people watch them all.'

I asked him what he thought of Jomo Kenyatta and Tom Mboya. 'We're not sure yet,' he said, smiling. 'We're too happy just now, with them and with everything, because freedom is coming and this feeling makes everyone happy, but we will know better when this feeling wears off, after *Uhuru*, and then we will see what Jomo is really like. But I think he will be all right—he's too wise to let the Kikuyu think that they are going to be top dogs and rule over us all. And that's what most of the Kikuyu think, that they're going to rule us all.' He smiled. 'But they're not. No more than my tribe will, or any other tribe. We'll get rid of tribes here, all of them. They're a curse. You see—' he tapped my wrist—'the more the Kikuyu stay Kikuyu as a tribe the more it makes the rest of us become more tribal too—in fear and self defence—and that's why I'm happy that the Kikuyu tribe is rotting away. It frees me too.' All my conversation with small, jet-black, bright-eyed J. gave me more to think about than any other talks I had in this new Kenya.

He was going to help me to get copies of the agreements made between the Masai and the British before the First World War, when the British moved into Kenya. They were saying, in the Foreign Office in London, said J., that they could not find the originals of these agreements—but, he grinned—'We've got copies of them here and I'll help you to get them.'

The Masai were feeling very hurt by the swift way the British were leaving East Africa, and 'giving it to the Kikuyu,' when '*we*, the Masai, gave Kenya to the British, a Kenya never owned by the Kikuyu.'

J's hatred for the Kikuyu, as a tribe, did not prevent him having many personal friends who were Kikuyu, but, and he smiled slowly at me, 'They are usually people like myself, tribal purely in name, by parentage, *but Africans first*.' He came back to that theme again and again, the necessity of being African first, for the tribe was a curse now in the kind of world they would have to make.

His hatred for the Kikuyu tribe was, in an odd way, a tribute to the almost Masonic togetherness of the Kikuyu, their secret solidarity and their sense of destiny which seems intact despite the signs of breakdown in the tribe which gave J. so much hope.

It is a bromide in East Africa that the Kikuyu trembled before the Masai in the old days, only sixty years ago. But the fact is that the Kikuyu, inside their own forest territory, gave Masai raiding bands many a severe defeat. On the open plains the Masai were supreme, but against the ambush in the trees the long spear was helpless, defeated by the poisoned arrows and the concealed pit with its impaling spikes. The Kikuyu of those times never bothered anybody very much. They were rich and they worked hard at their agriculture. Their military organization was defensive, and efficient. They were on their way to civilization even then, and the Masai were not interested in the patient toil required by agriculture.

CHAPTER THIRTY-SEVEN

THE Masai have a nobility of character and an openness which is striking. When you meet them, no matter how much you have hardened your heart to accept every form of change and progress, you cannot help sighing for the old East Africa of silence where men like the Masai mattered more in that vast waste of bush than a thousand technicians. The emergence of the Kikuyu as a power, the sudden withdrawal of the British, who protected the old Masai way of living, has left the Masai stunned. Suddenly he is under a new government, a government of Africans over whom he once lorded it by right of his long slender spears and his war-pride. And the Masai has no education, no leaders; they are suddenly a museum piece, dressed as they were a thousand years ago, plastered with red ochre, tall and leanly handsome with ancient Egyptian features, standing in the hot silence, their long spears in their hands, wondering what has happened so suddenly. It is tragic.

With their nobility goes a simple and trusting nature, which says, 'A word is a word, and a bond is a bond, and so is an agreement. The British have betrayed us.'

The last time I had spoken to a Masai was on a high ridge in Burma which stank of high explosive. The Masai was an N.C.O., lying on a bloody stretcher with several holes punched through his body by a Japanese machine gunner, dead now over his Nambu machine-gun, while not far off were a couple more Japanese slain by this Masai, one of them an officer whose long Samurai sword was now clutched in the Masai's hand.

The Japanese officer had come for him in the hand to hand fighting, swinging his sword, and the Masai—they love to fight even as much as the Japanese do—killed him and, taking his sword, went in and fought with it until he was shot down. The Brigadier, knowing how generous the Masai could be, had written a little note and attached it to the wound tag round the Masai's neck. 'Please do not take this sword from this soldier. He is a Masai.' The Masai reached East Africa with his sword, and he has it now where he lives, far down in Masai-land. The Masai did not join the army in any numbers—though those who did were highly valued.

I wanted to go down into Masailand but first I wanted to make a sentimental journey into North Kenya, where once the game had swarmed, where I had once been very happy, and where for me, the real Africa began, the descent to the floor of East Africa which sweeps on through red sands and mirages into the wastes of Somalia and to the rain mountains of Abyssinia. I wanted to see it once more, for I felt that this was the last time I should come to East Africa. I must get it out of my system forever. But already I knew I would never rid myself of it. It was in too deep. Love of that enormous country gives all kinds of people a bond, people who know that country and cannot even agree with each other about what has happened or what should happen to East Africa, can all agree that they can never feel anything but love and nostalgia for it.

While preparing to leave for the safari northwards I was meeting many Europeans and was finding that some hated the thought of the new Kenya and were going to leave, while others loved it too much to be able to think of leaving, but they worried about what might happen to them. Most of them were convinced that Jomo Kenyatta was their enemy. It was strange this obsession they had about Kenyatta—and it was there long before Mau Mau. I had even found it in London years before Mau Mau, in a nineteen-year-old who had never seen Kenya but was training to go there as a cadet. He had been well grounded, I found, in all the 'correct' attitudes. The occasion on which I met him was interesting too for another reason.

I was to do a series of short programmes for broadcasting, about East African students in London. I wanted to meet some students and I applied to a branch of the Colonial Office for information. I went to meet a retired officer there. He handled 'The student problem'. In the ante-room was this bright-faced keen cadet, fresh and sparkling with freedom after his public school, and waiting to go out and give his all in East Africa. He told me about the great problem facing him out there, the chief one of which was Jomo Kenyatta, who, unfortunately, had 'been allowed to go back there'.

'But he's drinking himself to death, of course,' the cadet told me. 'He's at it all day, bottle after bottle, which is probably the solution to the problem, I suppose.' One felt it would be all rather jolly with Jomo out of the way. That was in 1949. I didn't tell the cadet that two years before that I had been in Nairobi when Kenyatta arrived there, after years away from Kenya, and he couldn't go into a hotel anywhere to buy a drink like an ordinary Kenyan, and it might have been a great help later on if he had been allowed to live like a normal being in his own country. Kenyatta liked a drink as much as any white man, but he was no lush.

Then I met the retired army officer who was going to arrange for me to meet African students in England.

Yes, there were East African students I could meet. Letters to the students, and letters from the students to me, should pass through him, opened, and everything would be fine. Why? They were being got at by the Communists. It was useless to say that to treat grown men like this was the simplest way to interest them in Communism, or indeed in anything that was opposed to what this elderly monitor thought he stood for. I left it there and dropped the programmes, which was probably what the retired officer wanted anyway. It reminds me of an Indian friend, who, after studying at Oxford, and falling in love with England and with John Stuart Mill and company, sailed for India with his chests of books. When he landed in Bombay the police arrived. Books eh? They went through them all and found the revolutionary writings of the student's favourite Englishmen, and confiscated them. He was under suspicion. He went straight off and joined the Communist party, and stayed in it for as long as he could stand it, which was for some years. As Nehru often said, the Indians had no quarrel with the British people—only with their government. I think Africans who have got to know the English people feel pretty much the same. The old gang who have called the score for about three hundred years had just about reached the end of the game, in England as well. But you had to admire their tenacity, their skill, and their good humour, and especially the way they could cynically ennoble the poor man's radical and thus tame him.

Jomo Kenyatta had done the usual amount of gaol service and therefore seemed fairly certain to be Prime Minister. I was to meet him and I wondered what he would be like. I admired the way he had handled himself during the Kapenguria trial. For me they had not proved that he had led Mau Mau. He may have led it, but I did not think they had proved it. I found even one or two diehard settlers, who, with an awkward love of justice, could not convince themselves that the case against Kenyatta had been made. They were, of course, discreet about where and when they voiced such opinions. Public climate could be severe. In 1947 I knew a European who lost many friends, and was miserable, because he had sold his house to an Indian—something unheard of then. They were talking about throwing him out of The Club.

If Kenyatta was to become Prime Minister I hoped he would keep some of the old British administrators who had spent half a lifetime out in the bush patiently weaving, out of very little, the fabric for a just administration. Some of these remarkable men had lived in what in Europe would be considered hard conditions for most of their service, but, despite the public relations officers who dreamed up the stuff about how these men had given up everything 'to serve the native races', they did it because they loved the free and easy life. In years spent wandering in Africa and Asia I never met a European who had gone out there 'to serve the native races', with a 'mission' or merely, as one elderly General once said during a radio interview when asked what was the finest thing a man could do with his life, answered 'to serve'. Everybody went out to the tropics for adventure, colour, money, pleasure, experience, and plenty performed great labours in isolated places, and they usually enjoyed it. You often heard Europeans, usually a certain kind of Memsahib, complaining that the 'natives had no gratitude', but the natives knew that the Bwana or the Sahib was pulling down a fairly good salary, lived far better than the natives did, and would retire on a pension. Anyone who knew 'the natives' never bothered to expect gratitude, and the natives certainly never expected gratitude from the white man who had been supplied with an interesting life and a certain amount of power, and with a pension at the end for enjoying it.

I saw one of them get out of his heavily laden truck and walk up the steps of the Norfolk Hotel on the edge of the town. It was all there, the badge of the old timer, stained bush hat, khaki shorts and shirt, battered crepe-soled suede boots so quiet and squeakless that there was no sound as he strode up the long verandah to where the cold beer waited. There is a certain look in the eyes of a man who has lived in the isolation of the bush for a long time. It is almost a bleakness on surface appearance, but it is a sort of raptness, an inner and outer awareness working at the same time. It is an absent sort of look.

Downstairs on the road the old routine was being gone through as the Bwana's Africans, dusty from the safari, jumped down from the truck and lit cigarettes while exchanging news about who they were, their tribes, where they had come from and what they did for

223

a living, with the bored hotel servant in his long white gown who leaned against a pillar and watched them, these men who had this free life of continual riding about in a white man's truck. In the front of the truck, standing in its grips, was the usual rifle, and outside the truck hung the usual green canvas camp bucket and an Indian *chargul* or water container.

The administrator took off his bush hat and wiped his red-dusted face as the barman pushed the tall, chill-misted glass of beer across the bar to him. The white man's hair was grey, close cropped, and his face was deeply sunburned. His lean throat worked as his head went back and he let the cold beer down into his thirsty centre. A grateful gasping exhalation as he put the glass down and said 'moja ingini', and the barman poured him another cream foamed half pint of Tusker. He lit a cigarette and looked out of the bar across the verandah with his lonely blue eyes, at the rearing white cement buildings going up across the waste land. Where would he go when his time was up here? Majorca, the Seychelles, Madeira, or would he settle for Suburbiton outside London, and clipping those soot choked little hedges into animal shapes outside the red roofed box house? One thing was sure; he would never get over the years he had spent in this wide country, and he would find it hard to talk to people who had never been on a safari beyond Brighton or Blackpool, for what was normal to him, lions killing nearby, elephants walking through the starved garden, suicides during the rains, and the strange stories he could tell of Africa, would be fabulous and unbelievable to his new neighbours in Suburbiton. Only with his own kind could he talk of these things for what they were, ordinary daily things in the distant Africas he had wandered in.

Living as they had done, for years out in the bush, dealing directly with unsophisticated Africans, these administrators had gone well beyond the daily round of the Europeans who dwelt in Nairobi, had moved their lives into an area where they were no longer Europeans worrying about the telephone bill or about whether the rubbish collecting facilities of the city's municipality would improve, nor were they Africans. They were somewhere in between and the life they had lived could not be replaced, and it was a way of living that was about to vanish. They knew the customs and the problems, and often the tribal languages, of the Africans who were still way out on the edge of the convulsion which had moved into Africa and built cities and headquarters and government buildings. Some of these administrators had tried to slow up the speed and force of the Western machine, while others had tried to hasten it. Whatever you did it was a matter of grave decision. The nomad, naked except for a strip of dusty cloth and a dagger, standing behind his camels and listening to music and news from a transistor radio set hung on the point of his spear, stuck hard in the throat of many an old time European bush hand who had discovered that really what he wanted was the tribesman to stay as he was, a way he could never be himself, free, in danger from dagger and disease, but free. And it was a dream, something impossible to protect or keep. In a way the African in the bush lived a life for us that we could never have, and were glad we did not have, but wanted to share, as long as one could get a reasonable supply of whisky and a number of good books.

The old timer at the bar finished his beer now and bought three large bottles of Tusker. He went along the verandah and down the steps to his truck. He handed a bottle of beer to each of the Africans waiting for him. They grinned. They looked like Samburu tribesmen, lean, hawk faced, uncomplicated. One of them handed round a paper packet of Crown Bird cigarettes and the European took one. They lit them and puffed smoke into the hard sunlight. Then they got back into the truck, the European turning to shout, 'Don't forget to remind me about buying kerosene and matches,' and as the truck drove away the Africans shouted to him that they would not forget. I wished, for a minute, that I too was in Nairobi for a little shopping and then would drive away up into the Northern Frontier for a year of silence. I was going to the edge of that frontier but this time for a last look.

CHAPTER THIRTY-EIGHT

THIS place was called Enai-uruur when the Masai owned all these rolling cattle ranges which stretched to the Maranya river on the border of the Meru country. It had not changed at all since I had last seen it in 1947, and the small hotel above the rumbling waterfall still had its tiny bar with the record of the best rifle shot for each year hanging above the bottles.

'Does Bwana Soandso still come in here?' I asked the African barman. It was twenty years since I had seen Bwana Soandso.

'There he is now,' the barman said, pointing out to where a station wagon was just drawing up in a cloud of yellow dust. Yes, it was him all right, no doubt about it. He grinned when he saw me and said, 'Hello, you bastard, how's it going?' We had last met at a place called Dolo in Abyssinia in 1942. That was about ten minutes ago in his book.

'It's going fine,' I told him. 'Beer? And how's it with you?'

'It's O.K. with me,' he said, 'but it's not quite the same with Kenya, as you've probably noticed.'

Yes, he was going, not sure where, maybe Australia, though if old Jomo wasn't going to be bloodyminded about things he might cancel Australia and stay in Kenya. It was no good, one could be happy nowhere else, could one? No, not really. Jomo *might* want everyone to live together in a new Kenya. There was no knowing. But after those nine years externment down in the Northern Frontier he might want to make it tough for whites. There was no knowing.

We had a couple of beers while he told me who was dead up here since last time, and who was gone, and so on. He was off to Nairobi himself, for shopping. We shook hands and said goodbye. We'd meet again in a few years somewhere, probably—maybe in Australia. His car churned away in the dust.

I looked out across the country as the blue dusk began to come down like fine warm smoke, and that silence which was greater up here, and unforgettable, stronger than the rumble of the waterfall, began to give things a lostness and a feeling of eternity. Down below was Olomuruti as the Masai had called it in their time, near, yet far off in the thorn bush, and beyond it was Laikipia, also of the Masai, and Samburu, and away out to the North East beyond the quickening dusk were the Jombeni hills and Meru. Some small African boys ran down to the waterfall to wash and I could hear their voices echoing in the silence of which this waterfall was a permanent and unchanging part.

Far out beyond the Jombeni hills was the desert, the red desert I loved more than anything in Africa, with its grudging, scattered waterholes and its nomads stupefied with centuries of sun and silence. Night would be falling on the desert now and the nomads would light their fires and crouch over them, the camels sitting nearby. They would talk poetry, genealogy, raids, scandal, and God. It was too far for me to go this trip, and maybe it was a good thing. From where I stood, to Addis Ababa, there stretched a great ocean of wilderness, across which you could drive in your truck for day after burning day, only a small stretch of the giant African continent. I had once driven for twelve days across it and could recall the increasing awareness for the first time of the many Africas I would never see, the continent was so huge. The truck was like a tiny insect on the body of Africa.

The barman came out to tell me there was a phone call for me. A phone call, in this piece of outback. Now who could it be?

'Father Jim here,' the voice said. 'You may not remember me, son, but I heard you were here and I *must* speak to you about some of the grave theological errors you made in your novel *Without Love*. I must speak to you about them before you leave here.'

Father Jim? That Dublin tinged voice at the other end was certainly a sacerdotal voice, but I could not recall a Father Jim. 'I knew you years ago,' Father Jim said. Father Jim . . . Could he be one of the mission priests I had met years ago? 'Well, Father,' I said, 'it's good of you to ring out of the blue like this—'

'But you can't remember me, you stupid bastard, is that it?' the sacerdotal voice said in the same warm gentle tone. 'Well, I'll clue you up, my child. We were on the Foreign Mission together in a number of muddy foxholes in Burma.'

It was Jim all right. He was laughing at the other end. 'Come up to the club,' he said. 'A spy in Nairobi phoned me you were heading this way.' I was delighted. I had not seen or heard of Jim since the end of the war. He was a mile away.

I remembered his description of how he had known 'it was time

227

to go', when, overrun by a Japanese Banzai attack on a position he was helping to defend, he had been lying in a muddy ricefield, a hot rifle in his hands, and had seen a badly wounded British officer running past him to the rear. 'When I saw this bugger wearing two Thomson splints on his legs, and going faster than I'd been going, then I knew it was really time to go.' He shot the Japanese major leading the attack, but it was too late. The Japanese, ecstatic with Banzai, were everywhere, and Jim had dodged about for days in the burning paddy fields, finally making his way back with his feet in bloody rags.

He looked even more like a small edition of my father when I met him that night in the club, for he was grey now. The same pale skin and large blue eyes, the same grey moustache and small handsome head, and the same Dublin voice. He was holding court at the end of the bar. He was very neatly made, a handsome and cultivated man, witty and kind, the most delightful of companions anywhere anytime, and it was a landmark in this trip to meet him again. We talked right through the night, until long past dawn, and we began at the bar in the club, a bar which had many more bullet holes in it nowadays. Jim took me on a tour of the bullet holes. The most interesting set of bullet holes was in the wooden wall at the end of the bar and was in the shape of a small man, a man not more than five feet four inches tall. You could see how the bullets had made the outline of his head and shoulders, and how the artist firing the pistol had briefly sketched in the outline of the legs of whoever had had the insanity to stand there while the markmanship was performed.

'A little drunken bugger from a Scots regiment,' Jim explained, laughing. 'He stood there and let this character shoot all round him, and the character doing the shooting had had a few too. That's what I call real trust, don't you?'

Back at the bar Jim took me over his life during the years since the war. A few weeks ago he had been attacked on his farm during the night, by Kikuyu from the forest. They had knocked out a couple of his teeth and broken his arm. He had always got on well with Africans, and it was typical of him to say, when I asked him why they had attacked him in this way, 'Unemployment. They're starving. They're being sacked right and left on the farms. No one knows what's going to happen, and the unemployment's becoming terrible. They're all hungry. That's why they came for me.' He pulled at his moustache. 'We never paid them enough when we

228

should have done, when we were able to,' he went on. 'It's got to be said, but it's too late to say it now.'

It was true, and it was only an old timer of Jim's particular kind who would have said it, and he said another thing about Kenya which only he would have thought of. 'What's ending now in Kenya,' he said, 'is the last piece of the Edwardian age, the last Edwardian backwater'. He laughed. 'A place where the day seemed to be forty-eight hours long, and the sun always shining.' He did not know what to do with his farm—it hardly mattered anymore. He had written it off in his head, devalued it long ago, and would not miss it. The Africans could have it. He thought he would go down and live with the Masai—he had plenty of friends down there among the tribe, and he could live the old way in silence and solitude, for his needs were few.

We took a bottle of whisky over to my room and we sat on the beds and drank it slowly while we talked.

Once, during the Mau Mau war, he had had to officiate at a burial service over a dead askari, a Christian, and the askari's family had come for the funeral. There was no bible (not that Jim knew the funeral service anyway—but he was empowered to act as padre in this emergency). He had taken a good thick dictionary and had scratched a big, neat cross in the cover—'Mind you, it was a lovely *limp* leather cover and looked the part when I'd finished'—whitened the cross, etcetera, and then had gone out and held the service, inventing it as he went along, the 'bible' there in his hands for all to see. The funeral was a success. Jim smiled sadly while I laughed. 'I suppose there's a meaning somewhere in that story,' he said.

CHAPTER THIRTY-NINE

WE went down to Isiolo after a couple of days.

In Nairobi an acquaintance we met at a party shot himself over a woman the next day, and another acquaintance went over a cliff while driving at seventy miles an hour and died—Kenya had lost none of its electric violence and low flashpoint.

I had a last look out over the glowing red desert from Isiolo far down below the foot of Mount Kenya. On the way down we had picked up a Somali *wadad*, a holy man with his big *mal-mal* rosary wrapped round his wrist. He let me have the loan of it for a few minutes for good luck and then wrapped it round his wrist again. He was going down to Isiolo and then on foot to the pagan tribes beyond it, looking for converts. He had the burning black fanatical eyes of the bush *wadad*, and when we dropped him at Isiolo he blessed us and strode off in his worn sandals to spread a little more Islam, and with the blessings of a fellow Muslim far to the north, General Nasser. There was a big drive going on all over Africa for Islam—the religion which made all men one regardless of colour. Christianity had harmed itself by standing too close to the flags of the colonialist rulers, and had seemed to make God look too white, too much a part of protocol, too like an old time Bwana high up in the sky. And the hurrying nowadays to make black bishops and hand over cherished forward positions to Africans, perhaps too late, was not too pleasant to see, as if God might be right after all about all men being His children—but only after bitter political struggle. Yet there were Africans who had stuck to their Christianity while in danger for it, and while jeered at by those who saw it all as just one more white trick to keep Africa in subjection. There was no open and shut answer to any of the mess caused by the so recent meeting of the black and white races in Africa—what is amazing is that there has been so little blood spilt when we think of the oceans of it which have drenched Europe for centuries.

The game was all gone. For hundreds of miles we drove where once there had run herds of eland, kongoni, Tommy, impala, all the antelope, and thousands upon thousands of zebra, and with the necessary lion numbers to keep them swift and watchful. They were all gone now, shot out or driven away in their scattered few to drier country where it was safer, where men with spears were less dangerous than those with the ready rifle.

In Isiolo, still a huddle of low stores with corrugated iron roofs, the sun burned fiercely, and ahead was the great silence of the deserts, deserts of various coloured sands.

Two Turkana tribesmen talked to us outside one of the stores. One was a hard looking man of about forty, black, hawk faced, and the other was a youth of about eighteen.

How was the tribe? It was well, the older man said. How are the cattle of the Turkans these days? They were doing well, and were increasing. The older man kept the talk going, telling me about why he was here in Isiolo to buy cloth.

And how is it with your branch of the Turkana, I asked the youth.

'How would he know when he is a creature of this town here and has never seen our country?' the older man said, laughing sardonically. 'He has spent his life here among the Indian huts eating bananas. If I were to take him out there—' he pointed to the desert—'he would kneel down and cry. Wouldn't you, son?' The youth laughed, ashamed, and walked away. 'Yes,' the hard nomad said. 'Just a banana eater with water to drink at hand every minute. What would *he* know about how things are with the Turkans? Farewell.' He grinned and waved his hand to us as he walked away to his desert. That jealousy about being virile, about being tough and hard and able to suffer more than anyone else, which goes with the warrior culture everywhere, how interesting it is, how necessary, and how boring in the end, when you remember the torn corpses it has produced for your inspection near far waterholes.

Well, goodbye, Isiolo, and everything beyond in the hot silence, and goodbye the hawk eye and the hawk face and the dagger and the spear and the slow burning wheel of sun and moon on the bitter desert.

Up on the lush mountain, under the forests, I went to where Davey used to keep the little pub before the war, on the bar of which I had discovered that I was not a gold hunter, had not the necessary inner feel for it which drove you after gold from one end of the continent to the other, if once you got that fever in you. And there *is* a gold fever, a real driving mania which can send you

231

through swamps, survive all kinds of suffering and disease and danger if the hope of a big strike lies at the end of it, if you only have that inner feeling for it.

Davey was long dead, the new owner of the little pub told me. No, he had never met him. The new owner was clearing the place up, 'doing it up', and was getting rid of a lot of stuff.

The bar had not changed at all after twenty-odd years, just the way Davey liked to keep it. 'That's Davey up there,' I told the new owner, pointing to a small photograph framed in passe-partout. 'Why, yes, I suppose it is,' he said. 'Would you like it?' I said I would and he gave me the photograph of the tiny man in the slouch hat standing exactly as I had known him in the past. He had loved this place, and so had we who had occasionally made our way to it round the mountain when things became too lonely out on the scattered ranches. There was a company of African infantry based here in those days. They used to fight off the Abyssinian raiders far north near Moyale and then come down here to rest on the green, forested mountain among the Meru tribesmen in their beads and ochre.

'You can't mistake gold when you see it,' Davey told me one night at the bar. 'You *know* it when you see it. You can't be fooled by iron pyrites which looks like gold. You know the gold as soon as you see it.'

'Yes,' two old timers leaning on the bar assured me. Like Davey they were gold-lovers and we had just been talking about two Indian transport drivers who, coming up from Lamu on the coast to Isiolo, had found precious stones and were now packing up to race back and live in the wilderness while they made their fortune.

'I'll show you,' Davey said. 'You'll see how you can't mistake gold when you see it.' He took two pieces of quartz from the drawer behind the bar. 'One's got gold in it and the other's got iron pyrites. You can't go wrong!' He threw them on the bar. 'Pick up the gold,' he said, while they all watched me. I picked up the iron pyrites to a burst of laughter. 'You stick to those bloody sheep and cattle of yours, son,' Davey told me, handing me a drink. 'You haven't got the eye for gold.' I could not understand how I had not 'the eye for gold', and when I examined the two pieces of quartz again the pyrites and the gold looked exactly the same to me. I was sorry I could not have that fever, even though I had seen the results of a bad case of it in an old timer I had lived with in the bush, who taught me to shoot and to skin and to walk far. He had several times

232

given up home and wife for the gold hunt, and when he came back from the last gold hunt his wife had gone and he never saw her again, and all he had for his trouble was a small pill bottle with a little gold dust in it. It was his African servant who had got him away on that last ruinous gold hunt, for when coming back after leave in his tribal reserve the African, a gold lover like his master, had panned some specks of gold in an obscure stream, and his master had gone with him to make their fortunes.

I had once filled half a diary with the stories told me by a few ageing gold lovers on a plantation before the war. It was the only diary I ever kept and one day it vanished, with all the photographs I had pasted into it. I knew that the small Kavirondo boy working as my servant had taken it, for he loved to stare at the pictures in it, pictures of games and tribesmen of a kind he had never seen. I tried everything to get it back from him, trying to explain to him how valuable were the words written in it to me, telling him he could keep the photographs if he would only give me the diary back. But he denied taking it, even though he knew I knew he knew I knew and so on. I offered him money, but he had gone too far with his denials to come back, to risk admitting his lies. He was a happy little savage who had not meant any harm in stealing the diary, but had only realized the size of the crime when he saw how much I wanted it back. He was a good, honest boy, appalled by what he had done once he saw my concern to have it back, but he could not back down, even though he knew I longed to force him to give it up. I paid him off, and wondered if he would leave the diary behind him when he went, but he didn't, and often I have wished to read that diary again. In the diary were about ten pages describing every trick of 'salting' a mine with phoney gold, as detailed to me by a hard, leathery old man with white hair who had ransacked many wildernesses for a fortune he was never to find. One of the most ingenious was what he had called 'the cigarette come on.'

You had the greenhorn with the money squatting beside you when you began to pan the stream in the piece of dead country you hoped to sell him. You had already searched every inch of it and knew there was no gold there, but watch—the cigarette burned between your lips as you panned and the ash of the cigarette, into which you had sprinkled plenty of gold dust before you rolled it, fell, as it lengthened, into the pan, and the greenhorn saw the gold shining in the bottom of the pan, and wrote out his cheque on the

233

spot, freeing you to wander on to the next piece of wilderness. 'They come in all sorts and shapes, the greenhorns,' this old man told me, 'bastards who won't do the hard work, in need of a fortune.' Another good one was to put gold dust into pistol cartridges and then blast the stuff into the rocks, ready for the visit of the greenhorn with the cheque book.

This side of the Jombeni hills in the low rolling dry country in which the lions used to hide after killing the cattle further up, the Wandarobo lived, swift, cute men who used to come up into the hills and steal sheep, sending one of their number to make plenty of tracks for us up the mountain to the forest, while the rest went down again to their trackless bush with the trussed sheep. Here was Saboiga hill on which I had come on to my first lion, and how unbelievingly I had stared at the big, haggard swift creature who raced out of the bush, so unlike the King of Beasts I had been expecting, rakish, no fat on him at all as I raised that big double barrelled I had hated so much because of its weight, and because it fired black powder ammunition. You had to step aside after firing it to see—

All this country down here had been a lion playground, and I had celebrated one of them by writing a novel about him, and had him shot in the book, which was more than we could do about him in life, he was so cute, so able and so thoughtful. About a mile over there was where he had walked round and round a specially designed trap I had spent two days building for him—putting *two* doorways in it so that he could look through and see the moon or the stars and—come on to the trip wire which would fire the rifle, I hoped. But he was much too cute for that, and with his spiked teeth he had snapped off large flakes of red rock nearby, in his temper. The tough, laconic South African Dutchmen who trudged so many hot miles with me after him for months, swore this lion was crippled, which was why he sometimes missed when he wanted to kill. One night this lion missed twice and ripped open the two cows he tried, and killed a third one. I shot the two cows he left and then a day or two later noticed another cow in that herd was ailing and had stopped grazing. She went to skin and bone and I shot her. But, while skinning her, the Meru herdsman called me and showed me the long thin slash above her udder, the udder which had so mysteriously swollen before she died and had leaked pus. Here was another one that lion had missed, and all he had done to her was inflict one deep, fine slash with one of his filthy razor claws. This

234

lion went miles to kill, sometimes as far as beyond Timau on the plain and then he would come back with his friends for some of our succulent and easy Aberdeen Angus Native Grade steak.

There was an old Meru herdsman who grazed some of the steers near Saboiga who had twice seen this lion in moonlight. He was an amusing and witty old man who had once looked after a couple of thousand sheep during the shearing period, and was visited one night by the Wandarobo raiders who went off with five sheep. When he described the incidents to me he said, 'The leader of the Wandarobo is a tall man who was wearing a monkey skin cape, and one of his front teeth is missing. He said, "Don't move, old one, and there will be no trouble." '

'And you didn't move?' I said scornfully to him. 'I thought you were a warrior.'

'Well, I am,' the old man said, deadpan, 'but you don't feel like one with a spear blade stuck in the ground between your legs, do you? So I didn't move. He had me there, Bwana.'

He had been sitting in the doorway of his hut, nodding over the ashes, when a long spearblade hissed down between his legs, right under his groin, and he was advised not to move, while the Wandarobo watched him and the other thieves moved into the sheep, no doubt feeling swiftly and expertly, like good sheepmen, for the thickness of fat over the sheeps' tails before they made their choice. We ran the leader of that Wandarobo band into the ground one night after the rains, and he finished up lying on his back in the rocks, completely done in, as we, his pursuers were done in when we reached him. We had followed him for two days, down past Aranjiju waterhole which had been cursed once because a menstruating woman had drawn water there. One of the Kikuyu with us, a cute hard tracker, kicked the exhausted Wandarobo and said to him, 'You see, you're too fat. You've eaten too much of the white man's mutton,' and they had all pealed with that high African exaggerated laughter.

'We will never get that lion, Bwana,' this old man who had twice seen it, told me. 'Not now. He knows you and all the tricks, but you'll never learn all his.' We never did get him.

Maurice stopped the truck near Saboiga for an old bent man with a Kikuyu face who raised his hand to us for a lift. He was carrying the usual bundle of sticks and he said he lived in a hut a few miles ahead. He got into the back of the truck and we talked about the usual polite things, his age and the cattle and the rains to come.

When we stopped to let him out near his hut he grinned toothlessly and looked at me with twinkling eyes.

'You don't remember me, Bwana?' he said. 'But I remember you, when you were a youth, up there.' He pointed to the far forests up on Mount Kenya about twenty miles ahead of us, the snow on its peak glistening against the hard blue sky.

'That was a long time ago, then,' I said, staring at him, but excited that we had known each other in this country I had loved so much in that silent Kenya before the war. 'And you remember. *Monno! Monno!*' How pleasing to one's vanity to be remembered after so long, but apart from that, how good it felt to me that here was an African who had enjoyed what I had so much enjoyed in that marvellous time before the machine had really got into Kenya's guts.

'Yes,' he said, and recalled for me how we had cut down so many trees in the high forests altogether. He had been one of that carefree band. 'Ah, and where is Kimondo, who was old then?' I asked him, knowing. 'Gone,' he said, waving his hand. 'Long dead. I was young then too.' He must have been forty when we worked the forest, and now he was bent and withered.

'The game is all dead,' I said. 'Do you remember all our lions here?' I waved to the country around us, which was unchanged, unfenced, but the game gone from it. He laughed and pointed down towards Isiolo and Engare Ndarei. 'The lions haven't gone,' he said, 'They have only moved down into the bush beyond Engare Darei because there is game there.' He grinned at me. 'We went many times after their fathers, didn't we, in these hills?' When he told me his name, Murangi, I remembered him. He said he knew me at once by my eyes, because there were specks of yellow round the pupils, and then he had remembered my way of walking.

'There is a lot we could talk about, isn't there?' I said.

'There is. Here, have this.' He pulled an olive wood *rungu* out of the bundle of throwing sticks he had in his hand.

'I will remember you when I see this,' I said, taking it. 'All I can give you back is this.' I gave him a few shillings and he took it and laughed.

'I will spend it on tobacco,' he said. We shook hands and said goodbye. Corny it is, but I felt I was really saying goodbye to my youth right there, in that country I had enjoyed so much, and I knew I would never come back to see it again, and there was something lucky in meeting Murangi again in that empty country, after

236

twenty-six years, I watched Murangi lope away towards his grass hut near the maize patch so bright green against the dry grey of the Saboiga grass and the pale poisonous strength of the splendid candelabra trees nearby from which the Wandarobo used to take the blinding white milky sap for their arrow poison.

'Well, that's the end of my crying jag through the old territory,' I said to Maurice as I got back into the truck. 'Back to Nairobi and the cement culture.'

'Well, you had a nice end to it meeting that old fellow anyway,' he said. Yes. I felt almost overpowering nostalgia as we drove away, a longing for that good time again when Africa had seemed more carefree, more wild, and when there had been a lot more Murangis about, old men who still wanted the young ones to respect the past. Murangi, going to his hut in that wild country just now was going back into that marvellous silence, with that splendid view of the Northern Frontier, while I was going back towards the machine age.

I turned for a last look, for a long stare down on to that baking red floor of Africa with its thorn trees shimmering dots in the heat, where the Rendille, the Boran, the Samburu and the Turkans lived, and beyond them the Degodiya and the Aulihan and the Omar Mohamed and the Dolbohanta, all the nomads who were locked in the trinity of the spear, the camel and the waterhole. Would they one day queue up outside an air-conditioned Odeon to see the latest film feature, popcorn on sale in the foyer? Certainly they would, if they could get it, and I'm sorry to have to say that I think it would be a very good thing if they could, while secretly glad that it can never be. The nomads will always own that limitless desert, I think. I hope they will anyway. Every white man wants to keep Africa the way he enjoyed it most, while hoping it will change and become a more comfortable place to live in—and while he changed it, year by year, he wondered why it was not like it was in the good old times.

There is no one so puzzled as the pioneer who has lost his frontier, who has dissolved what challenged him, the wilderness. Maybe that's why some people want to go to Mars so badly now—they've tangled it all so neatly down here.

CHAPTER FORTY

I T was an ugly little scene in the Indian store down in Masailand, and the old Indian behind the counter was not able for the shouting, gesticulating, detribalized Masai who was threatening him. The Masai was very handsome, but his face had that peculiarly savage and brutal expression in it which many of the detribalized Africans wear, like a looseness, a ruthlessness, the face of the thug prowling among the rusty tin shacks on the edge of the town, lost. And he was shouting too loud to convince himself. His Swahili was not good enough to contain all his rage against the Indians.

'We smash you,' he shouted. 'You not take money from Masai no more. We smash you. You old and I young. I smash this store up with one hand when time comes. You have no voice now. You small and old. You rob African. We smash you.'

This Masai was wearing an extraordinarily ragged European sports jacket and torn shorts, and his teeth and eyeballs were yellow. He rolled his eyes as he shouted, watching me swiftly because he saw I was listening, and was his audience. He shouted so loud and long that I wanted to kick him down the steps off the verandah. The other Masai in the store ignored him while they fingered the cloth they had come to buy. The old Indian was scared but tried to hide it as he stood there behind his counter, wondering, no doubt, if it was not time to return to Gujarat after a lifetime spent down here in the red dust and thorns of Masailand. A beautiful Indian girl haunted the background of the store, her dark eyes steady as she listened to the shouts of the Masai. One of the old Masai nearby, tired of the noise now, turned and said something sharp in a low voice to the detribalized one, who jerked his head up and down uncertainly while he eyed the Indian, for it was time to go now, he had been told, and he wanted to go with some dignity, but he could not do it well. He shouted again from the road and then drifted, mumbling, away. The Indian wiped the sweat off his face with a silk handkerchief, and smiled wanly at me.

'A bullshitter,' I suggested to him. 'A big mouth. Do you have many?'

'Not many here,' he said. 'But it is getting dangerous in Kenya now, with Africans like that one.' It was too big a subject for us to go into, and we seemed to know it without saying so, this matter of how many Africans wanted to have revenge on the Indians, for making money, for working too hard, for 'cheating', for—being Indians.

One of the Masai, dressed like the others, in striped blankets slung over their shoulders, was wearing a most complicated re-conditioned shoulder holster under his left arm, various straps buckled about his shoulders and waist, and the holster, converted into a wallet, had a padlock on it. He unlocked it and took a big roll of hundred shilling notes out of it. With one of these he paid for his purchase. They all carried the long, shining Masai spears, copper and beads round their necks, goodwill and contentment on their proud and handsome red-brown faces. They smiled when they looked at you, no chip, no load on their backs about history, though they had a bigger grudge than all the other tribes in Kenya, I was finding.

They cannot understand how the British Government can 'go back on their solemn promises' as they have done, in giving Kenya 'to the Kikuyu', 'who never owned it anyway'.

While the Indian poured me a beer in the back of the store—he wasn't allowed to give it to me at the counter because open drinking had been forbidden since a drunken tribesman had killed another recently—I watched the Masai in the store. Very little had happened to them since that day when their chief druid, the Laibon, had told them not to fight the new white men, but to accept them and work with them, for God had ordained that these white men should come to East Africa.

Driving south from Narok towards Morijo in the Loita hills, well down into Masailand now, I thought again of how the white man had appeared in so many places just as one dying culture was about to be killed by another, in India, South America, and in Africa. For years before the white man appeared in East Africa the Somalis had been driving south towards Kenya, wiping out the Galla and moving across the Juba river, while down south they had been pushing back the Boran, both Galla and Boran falling back against the spears of the Masai. In the eighties and nineties of the last century the Masai were enfeebled by smallpox, by the new disease, pleuro-pneumonia, so virulent to an unaccustomed host, and their inter-tribal wars had weakened them further. Even so they were still formidable, yet from years spent among the warrior tribes of the Somalis I doubted if the Masai, even at their best, could have withstood the Somali warriors for long. It would have been a *jihad* for the Somalis, as it was against the pagan Galla and Boran, a holy war of the believers against the *kafirs*, the infidels, than which there is nothing more headlong, not even the prize of thousands of cattle. This war of the Masai and Somalis would certainly have taken place had the white man not appeared, so that by accident the white man saved the Masai, and the Kikuyu, the Nandi, the Wakamba, the . . . No matter how well organized in their regiments, and they organized well, I could not see the Masai standing up against Somali warriors, such as the Degodiya and the Marehan.

A chief of the Marehan boasted to me in the mid forties that he could put ten thousand spearmen (*Gashankad*, shield carriers) into the field. He was giving me a hint, of course, while he eyed my slender force camped under the thorn trees as to how I ought to feel about the coming negotiations between us. It was the same with the Degodiya Somalis whose past raids on the Galla and other peoples had set them astride the pencil lines dividing Somalia and the northern frontier of Kenya. They had had their history frozen, their drive south halted, by the appearance on the scene of the white man, like Moghuls and Mahrattas in eighteenth-century India.

Thinking it over, nearing Morijo and seeing Masai warriors waving their spears in friendly greeting, I wondered though, wondered if the Masai might not have held Kenya against the Somali hosts, for the Masai fear death as little as the Somalis, and love war as much. But I decided that the *jihad*, in which every Somali warrior is a *mujahid*, a warrior of God's will, would have been too much for these splendid looking lanky warriors of Masailand, themselves invaders from the north beyond Baringo and Mandera so long ago. Hamites, Bantu, and Nilo-Hamites, all had been in warlike motion only sixty–seventy years ago when that thin police cement was laid down by the white men. You can see how different these races are by considering their languages, which are as different as their physiques, as different even as their skin colourings. Take the way they count up to five, for instance.

The Luo-Kavirondo count up to five as follows—*Gachel, Gario, Gadek, Ongwen, Gabich*. The Kikuyu say—*Kemwe, Iggiri, Ithatu, Inye, Ithano*. The tribal languages identify the race, Negro, Bantu, Hamite, Nilo-Hamite. The Somalis count—*Ku, Labba, Sada, Afar, Shan*. Some of the tribal languages sing sweet, others sound hard

240

and brittle, like stones falling on rock. But Swahili is spreading and one hopes it will one day be spoken as the *lingua franca* of all Africa, the language of the *Suahel*, as the Arabs called the coast people of East Africa, a mélange of Arabic and Bantu, which counts, *Moja*, *Bili*, *Tatu*, *Nne*, *Tano*.

Yes, I thought, nearing Morijo with the Kanunga hills out on the left, you will never get over this mighty country, no matter how long you stay away, even if you never come back here again. From the plains round Kilimanjaro to the bitter rock of Gardafui, and from there to Filtu and Mandera, I loved it all and if I could would spend the rest of my life there, with a truck and a tape recorder, taking down a thousand tales, recipes, cures, legends, so many wisdoms painfully won and which would soon vanish, unrecorded. Placenames ring in your head no matter how far and how long you stay away, and each placename evokes faces, hawk faces, flat faces, red, black and brown, placenames like Skushuban, Laitokitok, El Wak, Sinadogo, Muddo Gashi, Wal-Wal and Aranjiju and Garisa, and the hunt for meat, *nyama*, or *hilib*, and grilling it over the ashes on the red sand turned fiercely pink in the moonlight, all squatting round the coals, unaware that we are supposed to be different, strangers.

Yes, the best friends you ever made, black and white, were in these lands, and the face of *Bwana Katinga*, but known as *Guswein* to the Somalis he ranged with, (a complimentary nickname, as some *Gal* Somali speakers will guess) came into my mind, and the memory of how well the Somalis looked after his soul, when he died on them in about as murderous a piece of country as you would find between Las Anod and Zeila. Somalis, as more than usually pious Muslims, abhor liquor, but *Guswein* drank hard, when he could get it in those wastes. And they knew how much he loved his gin at night under the thorn trees (before they cut them down in the morning for the goats and camels to eat) and when he died they took him to the coast, near Las Khorei, where they buried him. It may sound hard to believe of people so Muslim, but a group of these Somalis got together and they sank a length of three inch steel piping down into *Guswein*'s truly 'lonely grave' in the sand, and very covertly, each night for a month, three of them came with a bottle of gin, part of a supply they had got from an Arab trader on the coast, and poured a shot down the pipe, and always round the time they remembered he liked to have his gin. They had enjoyed his company for years across thousands of miles of bush, and they missed him as much as they guessed he missed his nightly gin. I could imagine them flitting across that grey shale in the moonlight, silently, nothing solemn about them but grinning as if they knew that *Guswein* was waiting. Where else on earth would you get such friendship after death? They gave him a month of nightly gin shots, then they removed the steel pipe, and left for Berbera, one of the stronger claimants for that much disputed title, 'The Arsehole of Africa'. My choice would be Massawa, with Berbera about fourth. If ever you are trapped on that Christless coast, where you can whimper in the end with your prickly heat, a hellish affliction when the pores of the skin, exhausted with sweating and raw with salt from the sweat, swell up into millions of itching pimples, I recommend the following treatment. Get an ordinary anti-mosquito spray, fill it with gin, if you have any, and spray your naked companion with it, who then sprays you. If the gin is of the cheaper kind so much the better, as this is even faster in effect. The swollen pores shrink, faster if you can find even a thin breeze to stand in, and failing a breeze you can fan your companion, and you have about an hour or two of relief. I have tried all kinds of remedies in temperatures over one hundred and ten, when prickly heat affects me—people get it at different temperatures, some getting it by merely being shown a photograph of Berbera or Bosaso, but the gin spray is infallible. Prickly heat suffered for a long period without relief can drive you mad. It can certainly affect your judgment, and I have seen a man quite crazy from its effects, scratched raw and suppurating. Africans and Indians get it too, and badly, contrary to popular belief. I have seen an African soldier in Burma rubbing himself against a tree with it, like an animal.

Morijo at last. Ol Morijoi, a tree from which the Darobo hunters take an extract for use in their arrow poison, but also the name for a fully fledged Masai warrior, a senior spear carrier.

Morijo is a beautiful place, high up out of the scorching heat, green and fresh, wide rolling grazing, and you can see right across East Africa, down into Tanganyika, in the clear light, and we pulled the truck up near the few wooden huts. A few Masai elders were sitting under a tree and playing that game you can play from Alexandria to Cape Town, three rows of small holes in the soil, and a few small stones, or pellets of goat dung, the game that goes by a hundred names across Africa.

Ole Senteu, Masai chief of the Morijo area, has been expecting us. He is at a Manyatta a couple of miles out of Morijo. He is on his way in. So we rest under a tree, smoking, enjoying the peace, the silence. If they only knew it they have not done too badly, the Masai, despite the pencil lines, the swift history of the past sixty years which has made them a museum piece. Two generations of peace anyway, and in what superb country, though the Masai stockman looks at the grazing, not the scenery. If only they knew, these Masai, how millions live in other countries, in hutches huddled together, in buildings so high the mothers watch in fear as their children play, or in sleazy slums with the grey rain falling on it, with hired television to watch and the continuing illusion that they are involved with what they are watching, even with the eternally firing pistol of the endless gangster serial from the cans on the serried shelves. The Masai want none of it, that plastic world, but I have the feeling they are going to get it, whether they want it or not. They will have to become consumers.

I remembered a fellow I met near Kajiado before the war. He worked for a tobacco company and the back of his box car was full of cartons of cigarettes. His job was to 'give them the habit'. He would drive for thousands of miles through the bush, handing out cigarettes, lighting them up and getting the tribesmen started on inhaling the smoke. 'Once they've smoked thirty or forty,' he told me, wry with his blunted sensitivities got from a good education, 'they want more, which means they trek in to civilization looking for work to get the money to buy some more cigarettes. Bloody sad, isn't, I suppose?' Inevitable though.

Ole Senteu, the Morijo chief, was a handsome man, humorous, sensitive, with quiet steady black eyes. Slim and muscular, he had enormous vitality. He was about fifty. He wore a tight, black woollen skull cap, brass ear rings, and he carried the short black club (*rukumá*) of his chiefly authority. The people seemed to revere him. There seemed to be more than respect for him, which the Masai are punctilious in giving, and receiving; there seemed to be real love for him. And he gave it back to them. The women rushed to him, to kiss him, and those who could not get through the crowd, to kiss him and be kissed, had his kiss passed on to them by those who had been kissed. Beautiful to see, the way the Masai hug and kiss, touch, hold hands, smiling and laughing. The children came running forward, boys and girls, and bent their heads for us to touch black and white, which is custom and good manners, and then they rushed back to play.

While the chief discussed a problem with some of his elders I sat under a tree again and tall beautiful Masai girls wearing tanned leather cloaks, their breasts bare and their skins glowing with red ochre, came and shook and twitched and jumped up and down for me, and for everybody else, for these were *Olamal*, a singing bouncing ecstatic group wanting blessing, for luck, or to be fertile, or loved. They were in such a condition of physical and mental bliss, as they shook and undulated for me, that it was almost comforting to know they had never read Jean-Paul Sartre, had no idea that a white woman had thrown herself under a racehorse fifty years ago, for their liberation from male oppression, and were never going to hear that Lenin had written 'What Is To Be Done?', or that there has been no reply to his question, not even by Bwana Stalin.

Later, sitting with Ole Senteu and planning our trip, we were surrounded by these girls, by children and old men, all happy to watch Ole Senteu's face. One of the girls was so very beautiful that I could hardly take my eyes off her, and in an aside, the chief said to me, 'She is watching you too. She likes you. Do you want her?'

'What about the trip south?'

'When you come back then,' he said. There was nothing lecherous, no leer here, just Masai facts. He was not giving her away. He was telling me that he noticed things were going well for me. We passed on to plans for the safari.

Again I decided that a good definition of the ridiculous, or the impossible, would be a Masai on a psychiatrist's couch talking about his sex problems, or any other problems.

Masai warriors, nearly naked, painted with red ochre, their hair plaited and shining with ochred mud, bangled and ear ringed, stood by, leaning on their long slender shining spears, looking exactly as they had looked when they made the caravans of two generations ago stop and pay *hongo*, permission to travel on into Masai country. The lions they used to kill with spears as part of their initiation into warriorhood, now run to the tourist trucks in the hope of a few cold zebra sandwiches and the thrill of being photographed by the tourists. They too miss the old days, I think.

The last time the Masai killed a white man was just after the last war, a fellow I had known in the army. He did not know Masai customs and he did something wrong, well meaningly, of course, and made the mistake so easy to make, of standing by the mistake made. The Masai who killed him gave him three warnings. When he killed him he hurled the spear so hard that it went right through the white man. So it is still there, under the lanky, gangling nonchalance of sixty years of peace, that warlike will to have amends made. Yet nowhere in the world will you find a more relaxed, well mannered and good natured man than the Masai, with none of that nervous wariness which so often goes with vanity.

When the Masai decided early on that they wanted no part in the white man's world, wished for no progress such as education, the British government agreed, though as time passed some administrative officers were pressed to at least *try* and get even a handful of Masai pupils for a school. When this request was tactfully passed on to the Masai chiefs it was considered, and the officer's position understood, so the Masai solved it by buying a few Kikuyu children, giving them Masai names and handing them over for schooling.

Some of them are sorry now for that attitude, for the Kikuyu loved education and progress, and now the Masai burn a little to see Kenya in the hands of those who went to school and got ready for these strange days of *Uhuru*. But I met only one well educated Masai, who really cared about it. He felt it was shameful, this situation of his once powerful tribe, still equipped only to live the life of pastoral nomads.

'We never copied or aped the white man, you know that,' one elder said to me. 'We never went as servants to the white man's house in Nairobi, or tried to imitate him in schools. A Masai could never do that, could he? And now all these tribes, like the Kikuyu, who have imitated the white man like slaves, they are going to rule us, the Masai.' But I could see how lost he felt. 'I do not have to read a book to know what is good and what is bad,' he said to me pathetically, defiantly. 'Tell everybody I said it too.'

So it was quite an important experience for me that day, to watch Ole Senteu, the chief among the adoring women and the glad, respectful warriors, the hot sun gilding their red shining flesh. I felt I was seeing the last of something very ancient, for they had looked exactly like this far up in the Sudan somewhere in their past, a thousand years ago, before they came and fell on the tribes of Kenya in their regimented thousands, for it is their handy belief that once upon a time the Masai owned all the cattle on earth. So that whenever and wherever they raided and took cattle, they were not stealing. They were only taking back what was once their own.

Some of them spoke of 'taking Kenya back' with the spear. They gave Kenya to the British by agreement, or rather 'loaned' it to them on condition it was never to be given to any other tribe, they said. Dreams, old dreams, but the agreements are there to read.*

They remember every place-name across Kenya where their cattle once grazed, from Isiolo north of Mount Kenya to Kiliman-jaro, and now, they told me, some of them wished to send women with donkeys to occupy every place once owned by the Masai, in what had become known as the White Highlands, and should one woman be touched, or her right to the place be disputed, then the warriors would form in their regiments again and move to take Kenya back. All the way up the Rift Valley the women would go with their donkeys, and occupy beloved Naivasha and Elementaita again, and Nakuru, and the sacred circumcision area of Kinangop, and on to Laikipia in the North East where they would join up with their cut-off Masai group, the Samburu, and right up the Maranya river to the edge of the great forest on Mount Kenya. Could I see all that? I knew those places, didn't I? I knew they had all been Masai, didn't I? Well, what had I to say to that idea? These were old men, who had been born in those far places, who had fought battles there, had grazed their cattle there far and wide, hemming in the Kikuyu and the Wakamba, and their eyes yearned for those places again. If anyone was to have those rich highland pastures again now the whites were leaving, should it not be the old owners who had handed it all to the white man?

I knew that in eighteenth-century Ireland, when Irish tribe-family tradition was still alive, and when ancient Gaelic genealogies were still remembered in Irish, old men before they died sometimes had themselves carried to where they could look for a last time at the old tribal lands, now owned by Englishmen. Every place-name carries a tribal history in it, and it was like that for these old Masai, the cattle people, the warriors, when they spoke of place-names like Laikipia, Samburu, Naivasha, Elgon, and of the waterholes where the Meru country touches Isiolo. They had lived to be mystified by names like KADU and KANU and Mau Mau, and they could not understand it because they did not wish to.

The Laibons, or druids, of the Masai, when they struggled for the place of chief laibon, one laibon only to rule, caused the Masai to make war on each other, one war group for this laibon, that war group for the other, both laibons being brothers, sons of the last

* See Appendices 2 and 3.

Laibon called Mbatian. And it was Mbatian who had forecast the coming of the white man, and said he should not be opposed.

'Forget your donkeys and women and the place-names,' I told the old men. 'Those times are gone now. You will have to see that the younger generation goes to school—or, stay like this.' They said they would 'stay like this', rather than imitate foreign ways.

CHAPTER FORTY-ONE

OLE Senteu's brother, Simel, was the present chief laibon of the Masai, and both were direct descendants of the last Laibon to rule before the white man came, Mbatian.

Ole Senteu agreed to take me to see Simel who lived down near the Tanganyika border at Entisekera. I was grateful because I had so many questions I wanted to ask the laibon, about the past, about his ancestor, Mbatian, and about the struggle between Mbatian's sons which, with the smallpox, had all but shattered the Masai as a people who might have resisted the white man's entrance to East Africa.

It was late afternoon when we reached Entisekera and Ole Senteu went off to find his brother and the elders.

Thick elephant forest stretched away beneath the rest house where we put up our camp beds, Maurice Brown of the B.B.C., a wizard with the tape recorder, and Ole Kipoin, a charming and travelled Masai who worked in Kenya Radio. There was an Indian *duka* down on the edge of the forest, standing on the place-name called Entiskera, a tiny shack of a store where we heard we could get beer.

We went down there and walked into one of the oddest parties I have ever been to.

It didn't matter what the climate or the desolation, between the Tana river and the Ruvuma, an Indian trader would try and put a store up there if he could.

The floor of this store at Entisekera was of stamped earth and round a forty-four gallon drum standing in the middle of the floor were half a dozen Masai elders of the old school, laden with copper, wearing skin cloaks, and on top of the forty-four gallon drum each one of them had his bottle of Bristol Cream sherry standing before him. And they were quite high on this latest discovery, this Cream from Bristol.

The shagged out malarial looking Indian behind the battered wooden counter with the slit in it, the biggest moneybox in that part of Africa, told me that the Bristol Cream passion was quite new.

Resignedly he waved his hand at the many dozens of *fiashchi* of Chianti hanging on the walls about us. That was their favourite drink until recently, he explained, until one elder had come stumbling in with the news of his discovery of Bristol Cream. Before he could try and sell us some of the Chianti he was now burdened with —one felt the Masai had been fickle, unsteady, wayward—we ordered bottles of beer, and as we drank we watched the happy elders getting drunk.

It was quite a thing to see, in that *duka* in the forest country, these nobles, these representatives of a great fighting race of aristocrats, pouring the Bristol Cream down their throats and exchanging slurred and smiling chat about the state of their world. These elders would be at the *shauri* we were having tomorrow with their laibon, and cold beer, by the look of things, would go down well with the hangovers they would have, for they were slopping the sherry into their tin mugs faster now. And, we had been told, the laibon, Simel, was a beer man anyway, so we ordered a few dozen beers to be sent up to the rest house that night.

I watched the Indian watching the Masai drinking. His time was nearly up in East Africa and I wondered if he had made his fortune with that splendid patience of his, that readiness to trade at the ends of the earth, for they have a sense of adventure, these merchants. They were trading with East Africa long long before even the Portuguese saw Mombasa for the first time in the fifteenth century. The Arab and Indian history of East Africa has not yet been written. It will be full of surprises.

The Africans hate the Indians and there is no arguing about it, no explaining, no grey anywhere, just black resentment. Many whites hated them too, even a white I knew who had been loaned thousands of pounds by an Indian merchant. There may be a clue about the African attitude in what was said to a friend of mine by an African chief. 'The white man brought us knowledge,' he said. 'He brought us schools, and religion, and all kinds of medicine and lamps and so many other things we take for granted now, and true it is that many of the white men exploited us and treated us badly, but they did give all those things to us. But the Indian gave us nothing. He merely took.' It seemed a hard saying, that, but one must speak as one finds. For my own part I never had any reason to resent Indians in East Africa, but I know they took advantage of Africans when they were less sophisticated then now, but who didn't? Maybe there *is* something in caste, something real, *Vaisya*

249

being *Vaisya*, worshippers of money, and *Kshatriya*, the warrior with the sword who borrows spending money every so often from the *Vaisya*, the merchant.

It was sentimental to wish Africans liked Indians more than they did. There are immutable laws—the worker bees are never loved for storing up their honey so tirelessly. Envied, admired, but never loved, and yet it made good trader's sense, this Indian standing over that slit in the counter as the drunken money fell into it again and again, and the elders staggered back to their forty-four gallon drum with another bottle of the magical Bristol Cream. The thing about being a publican surely, must be to watch the customers working for you hour after hour, until they reel off into the moonlight for a rest, until tomorrow.

The next day we set up a table and chairs on the verandah of the resthouse, and it was well that we had laid in so much beer, for the laibon, Simel, and his elders, brought a great thirst with them. The elders carried their sherry hangovers with dignity, only a sigh from one or two of them as they watched the unopened bottles of beer on on the table.

Simel was quite different from his brother, the chief. He was a big heavy man in a blue-beaded robe of fine monkey skins, and unlike most Masai, truly vain, with big staring swollen eyes with which he sought to dominate the listener. He had shining black-red skin. He was very impressive and he took the place of honour at the table, Ole Senteu on his left, and two venerable elders on his right, Ole Seronei and Ole Kaiyet.

Ole Kaiyet was a bald clean-plucked old man with a face which could have presided over the embalming of some Ancient Egyptian king. He had more dignity than even Ole Senteu, and he had a fabulous memory of times long gone. The other elder, Ole Seronei, was the oldest man present, a man so withered, so laden with living, that he seemed about to slide down, any time now, into the mindless death which great age in health must finally choose. He was wonderfully intelligent, a mine of tribal lore with whom I wished I could have worked for a whole year, he had so much to tell. And he knew what he possessed, a fund of poems, genealogies, clan histories, all about to vanish. He had too the most important thing in a keeper of tribal lore, a sense of drama, as well as the great respect for what had been handed down to him. I could see that his sense of truth would not allow him to alter anything for any stranger's ear, and most Masai are like that. 'Ask me,' they will say to you, 'and if I don't know it I will tell you so. If I have merely heard it I will tell you that too.'

For a long time we let the laibon hold the floor, while we dealt with beer after beer. Ranged round the room were many other elders who listened in silence as the laibon performed for us, for me, for himself, as he told me again and again of his great powers, so that I had to remind myself that it is the tradition that counts, not the temporary owners of it.

The laibon is the seer. Surely this laibon, presiding over the tribe when the white men are going, at a time more perplexing and worrying than it had been even for his ancestor, Mbatian, who saw the white men come, surely he must be plagued by the Masai for a description of what is to come? I had not the heart to ask him. I felt too much for them all to do it. I asked Simel to give us a short history of the *loibonuk* family from the time of the first laibon.

Kidongoi, he said, was the first laibon of the Masai, and then he gave his own descent from Kidongoi, and there was something fine in hearing his genealogy, the chief druid of the great Masai who are now like a pool in the rocks, left by the wave of conquest which has gone back to the ocean.

'Tisikiriashi son of Kidongoi, then Parayombe son of Lesikiriashi, then Kipepete son of Parayombe, and then Kenka, Muja, Sitonik, Supeet, Mbatian who had two sons called Olonana and Senteu, and then I, Simel, son of Senteu,' he intoned.

Yes, that was where it went wrong, with the two sons of Mbatian, whom the Masai destroyed themselves over. But it was not said that way, not here by Simel anyway.

'Tell me of Mbatian, father,' I said. 'What was he like?'

It must have been a worrying time for Mbatian, when the white men with their powerful weapons began to appear on the coast in numbers, demanding trading rights, and penetrating inland.

'Mbatian was born in Kisongo,' Simel said. 'It is known that he was not a tall man, and he was not heavily built. And he was one eyed. His position in Masailand was that of ruler. He ruled over all clans, all sections. He ruled the country with the help of four elders who acted as his advisers, and with the help of the chiefs, and then of the *Moran* (the warriors).'

He gave me the names of Mbatian's elders. 'First in importance was Ole Murera, then came Ole Moiyae, and after them Ole Leposo and Panying Ole Kaiyet.' Then Simel turned his powerful eyes on our companion from Nairobi, Ole Kipoin, who was asking him to which sections of the Masai the four elders of Mbatian had belonged. Ole Kipoin had a vague idea that he himself was related to one of them, but he had not said so to Simel. Ole Kipoin was very pleased when Simel said to him, sardonically, 'Do you not know that Ole Moiyae was of the Kaputie section? Or are you telling me that you don't know your own great-grandfather's name?' So Simel had made his own enquiries about Ole Kipoin the night before, and had traced his genealogy correctly. We were very impressed. Simel said then that Ole Leposo was of the Purko section, and Ole Murera of the Loita section.

'The elders used to live with the laibon, and it was from the laibon's home that the warriors were directed as to where and when to engage their enemies.'

'At that time, all the clans and sections of the Masai were united as one people, only the Laikipiak section in the north being separate. The Laikipiak were very brave and they defeated all the rest of the Masai who united against them, but eventually, because they thought the Laikipiak were becoming a menace, the rest of the Masai sections made a special effort and overcame them and took all their land.'

That land is still called Laikipia today but there are no Masai left in it.

'Is it true that Mbatian prophesied the coming of the white men?' I asked Simel. 'Did he really make that prediction?'

'It is true,' said Simel gravely. 'Mbatian called the elders together and told them that the white man would come, and that the white people would put an iron rope or snake across the country, and that this iron snake would run from East to West. Then he told the elders, "I cannot find the head of this snake"'.

The chief, Ole Senteu, cut in here to say, 'When Mbatian called the elders to him he told them that something white (*Olkelerua*) was coming, and would bring with it a long snake. That is the railway which was built from Mombasa to Uganda.' Then Mbatian said 'I have tried to stop these people in the sea, but I have failed.'

'But the Moran (warriors) feared nothing,' Ole Senteu went on, 'And they refused, saying, "Let them come and we shall face them." But Mbatian told them they could not fight the white men. The Moran insisted that the white men should be allowed to come, so they could be defeated in battle.

'Mbatian said, "Very well, I will allow them to come, and they are coming."'

Mbatian lived until about 1885 and he did not need to be a seer to know the power of firearms, and what they could do to the Masai when they came to Masailand in force. In Mbatian's time the Masai had reached the peak of their conquests. They had been killing the Galla up on the Tana river, where they were beginning to meet Somalis, and had raided as far south as Vanga and Bagamoyo. In Mbatian's time only a couple of white men had passed through Masailand, but the Masai had had a taste of what firearms could do in a place called Sadaani on the coast. The Arabs and Africans of that town, hearing that Masai warbands were coming, moved the women and children out of the town in dhows and then fortified the houses. They left the town gate open for the Masai, who poured in. The gate was then closed and every Masai in the town was killed by riflefire.

Not that the Masai warriors had any fear of death, by rifle or spear, but Mbatian and the elders had the task of collecting intelligence and of making all decisions about war. They knew too that the Masai were already weakened by the fierce inter-tribal warfare which was increasing among them, and then came the rinderpest which slaughtered the enormous Masai herds.

Looking at the laibon before me, Simel, who probably had old men urging him to send donkeys and women up to occupy the old Masai lands all over Kenya, I felt sorry for him. In a way his problem was not unlike that of Mbatian's, what to say about the inevitable to the warriors, only now the white man was going. The white man had come and gone, all in seventy years. It seemed incredible, thinking about that now, sitting with the stoical and dignified elders of this great tribe.

'The white men cannot come in my lifetime,' Mbatian had told them. 'They cannot come while I am head of the Masai. If they want to come during the lifetime of Olonana and Senteu (Mbatian's sons) then that is their affair.' Then he picked up a stick and waved it as if hitting out at people, and said, 'Go back. I cannot have you here during my reign. Go, and come back during the time when Senteu or Olonana will reign.'

'Mbatian died at Enosamburubur in Oldionyo Orok (nowadays called Namanga Hill).'

We asked if Mbatian made any other predictions.

Simel said that Mbatian had foreseen the great epidemics of smallpox among the Masai, as well as the rinderpest which would almost wipe out their cattle herds. He also predicted the wars among the Masai. He said, 'I see a lot of Masai blood being spilled and I hate what I see. If what I see happens I will bring white men who will stop it. So when these white people come receive them and live with them. Because they will stop the fighting I foresee, and they will bring law and order to the country.'

'And later the Masai realized that Mbatian had spoken the truth,' Ole Senteu went on, 'because if the white men had not come the tribal wars among the Masai would have continued for a very long time; in other words, right up to this moment.'

Ole Senteu was not telling me this to please me because I had a white skin. Masai do not indulge in the servile approach. He was only telling me what all Masai know. They are such ferocious fighters that they would certainly have destroyed their tribe, if the white men had not come.

'When Mbatian died, or before he died, which son took his place?' I asked Ole Senteu,' 'Olonana or Senteu?'

I had heard many stories of how Olonana had cheated his brother Senteu who was the son of Mbatian's favourite wife. The dying Mbatian asked Senteu to come and see him on the following day. But Senteu's brother, Olonana, came instead and received the blessing and patrimony of his father (who thought him to be Senteu), so that when Senteu did come he was too late. But Mbatian gave Senteu the original calabash of medicines which had belonged to Kidongoi, the first Laibon, and Simel has it to this day.

'How did Olonana know that Senteu had been called by his father for the following day?' we asked Ole Senteu.

'Olonana, it is said, was hiding in Mbatian's hut,' the chief continued, 'because he knew that Senteu was a son of the favourite wife and that Mbatian liked him. That is why Olonana hid so that he could hear what Mbatian said to Senteu, and he came the following day, very early, and before his brother, who he pretended to be.'

Olonana became an important man, and his decisions were to have great consequence for the Masai, and the British.

'How was Olonana physically?' I asked Simel, who described him as tall, and bald-headed.

'He wore an *enkaranda*' (a tight skull cap of beaded leather), said Simel. 'He was tall and slim.'

'And how was his brother, Senteu?'

'He was the same height as Olonana, but more heavily built than Olonana. And both of them had very long ear-lobes.' (The Masai, like many East African tribes, stretch their ear lobes by insertion of

254

bigger and bigger plugs over the years. Very long ear lobes were much approved of.)

Olonana, as chief Laibon, had obeyed the British and told the Masai that he had agreed they were to leave the highlands and go south of the 'iron snake', the railway which had been built through Kenya. It is possible that the Masai might have fought had they not been disorganized by their civil war, and had their herds not been so shattered by the rinderpest. Even so, Olonana must have been a man of great personality to be obeyed in such a strange decision as to agree to give up their lands and power.

I asked Simel how Olonana had announced the decision to the Masai.

'He told the Masai that the railway was to be our boundary,' said Simel, 'and that north of it will belong to the Government' (the white settlement).

I had heard that Olonana had been cursed to death, (though probably the Masai who told me this story only wished Olonana had died an accursed death.) Simel told me that Olonana had died at a place called Keputie and that as far as he knew he died of natural causes.

As Simel said this I saw the wizened elder, Ole Seronei, rolling his eyes and looking very doubtful. Simel went on to say that Olonana was still young when he died.

We had drunk a lot of beer by now and we were all rather high and cheerful. Simel called the drinking pace, and he was thirsty.

There is a place in Kenya called the Kinangop by Europeans, but its real Masai name is Kinopop. This place, where they had always held their circumcision ceremonies, was sacred to the Masai. In the first agreement made with the British they were promised that Kinopop should remain to them forever. But that too was soon taken from them, and many Masai told me that they now want it back, if the British are going to 'give it to the Kikuyu'.

'When was the last circumcision ceremony held at Kinopop by the Masai?' I asked Simel, 'and what was the name of the age- group'?

'The elders will give you the answer to that question,' Simel said, reaching for more beer. Then he made way for the old men, Ole Seronei and Ole Kaiyet.

We had finished the beer and Simel had worked up an even deeper thirst. He went down to Entisekera village in the forest for more beer, but would probably finish up on the new Masai novelty, Bristol Cream sherry.

CHAPTER FORTY-TWO

Ole Seronei and Ole Kaiyet, the two elders, were of the Iltareto age group, the last age group to go through the ceremony called *Emouwo Olkiteng* near Naivasha before the Masai began their migration to south of the railway.

Ole Seronei, grizzled, thin, halting, gentle, and sharp witted, leaned on his staff and listened to all my questions, sieved them, thought, and then replied. A real elder.

Ole Kaiyet, bald, with the face of an Ancient Egyptian priest, had the same grave manner as Ole Seronei. They would consult each other, count years, go through age groups, nod, make way for each other when one thought the other more able than himself to expound on a point. When one spoke well the other would nod with pleasure.

'In the matter of the position of Laibon between Olonana and Senteu,' they said, 'we will first tell you how a Laibon is selected by the Masai.

'The son who takes over from the Laibon, is given the original calabash of medicine handed down from Kidongoi, by his father. After that the Laibon calls all the elders and says to them, "I call you all to show you the son I have chosen to take over from me the duties of Laibon."

'Usually the elders accept the son appointed by the Laibon, and the calabash is handed to him by the father, and after that the elders will send out to every corner of the country to collect cattle, which are then given to the new Laibon. The elders themselves then give cattle, drinks, and respects to the new Laibon. From then on he is recognized by all as the Laibon of the Masai, and later on the people organize a ceremony for him, when the elders and the young men go to the Manyatta of the Laibon. The elders bless the new Laibon and give him the right to use the original calabash given to him by his father. Then the Masai will present him with a new, specially made calabash. The Masai will only recognize one Laibon, the one who has been given the original calabash.

'The oldest age group listen to the Laibon, and the chief, and

256

the Government, as we elders do now of the oldest age group called the Iltareto. For instance the chief sent a message yesterday that he wants the elders to come and be interviewed, and that is why we are here, because we respect the chief.'

I asked the old men what changes in their lifetime had impressed them most.

'We have seen many changes,' they said, 'but the biggest was the removal of the Masai from their lands. That is the most important change. And another change is that previously the Moran (warriors) were very important, and the Laibon's influence outstanding in the country. The Laibon had nothing to do with petty politics or petty cases. All such cases were dealt with by the elders. At present the Laibons can be chosen as chiefs at the same time as they are Laibons. That is another change.

'Once upon a time if the elders decided on something no one could contradict them, and young age-groups never held an important meeting without consulting the elders first.

'Things have changed greatly in that now it is the young who shout about this and that.'

'What change for the good have you noticed?' I asked.

'The most important good thing we have seen is that since the coming of the white man we have enjoyed peace, law and order. The terrible tribal fights have been stopped completely, and that is a very great thing.'

Later on I asked one of these old men, when he was alone, whether the two sons of Mbatian, Senteu and Olonana, were on good terms in their lifetime or not.

'They were not on good terms,' he said, 'because they split the Masai between them, Senteu leading the Iloita and Damat clans, and Olonana the rest of the clans.' This and the smallpox—the wars of annihilation—weakened their power.

'Who did take over the real leadership from Mbatian?' I asked.

'Senteu was a son of the favourite wife,' the old man replied. 'Olonana's mother was not the favourite wife. It was Senteu who was called by Mbatian and told to come early the next morning (when Mbatian knew he was dying). Olonana had hidden in the hut and overheard what his brother was told. He left the hut unseen and on the following morning he came earlier than his brother, and his father blessed him.

'Later, Mbatian called both of them and he removed *Eseenga* from his neck (a decoration round his neck) and gave one piece of it

257

to Senteu and the other piece to Olonana, and he told Senteu to go to one section of the Masai and Olonana to another. He warned them not to fight each other, saying that the one who started to attack the other will be defeated by the other.' But war was inevitable.

'Later Olonana defeated Senteu and he surrendered.'

Ole Kipoin said, 'I have heard that Senteu went to Olonana's manyatta and entered a hut where there was a small child sleeping, and he picked it up. Is that true?'

'That is true,' the old man said. 'We used to do that as a sign for mercy. Yes. Senteu went to his brother and they became on good terms for some time, and oxen were killed for establishing a permanent peace.

'The peace did not last for long. They became enemies again. Then Olonana died and all the Masai clans except the Loita said that Olonana had been bewitched by Senteu. Then Senteu was driven out and chased into the Kipsigis country, but it was the youths of my age group who rescued him and brought him back to the Loita hills. And since then his family have been here.'

The old man sighed and looked hard into my eyes and told me it was the first time he had ever sat down and talked with a white man, and that he could tell me the story of every hill and rock, and of the generations that were gone.

'Did you ever know Ole Gilisho?' we asked him. 'The one who lived and spoke at the time of the meetings with the British before the Masai were moved?'

'Yes, I knew him well. He died at Narok, and it was in the house of Ole Leparakwo that he was taken ill. He was among the Moran who moved the Loita clan at Naivasha. Yes, there were many wars between the Masai who supported Senteu and those who supported Olonana, and at the end it was Senteu's people who were defeated.

'Ole Gilisho was a slim man and of the Ilmirisho age group, and he was a very good orator. When he grew sick at Narok we took him to his home to die.

'He, and Ole Masikonde of the Purko clan, protested when the special place at Kinopop where the Masai held their ceremonies was taken from them by the Government. They had been promised that they could keep that place. They protested because by losing that place of ceremonies the Masai were to be cut off from the past. My age group, the Iltareto, was the last there to undergo the ceremony of *Emouwo Olkiteng*, which took place near Naivasha.

The boys were from the Purko, Kekonyokie and Loita clans. That was after the first agreement with the British (1904) and before the First World War, and it was before the second agreement (1911).'

The old man was tired now. He saw me lighting a cigarette and he asked could he try one, as he had never smoked one. I gave him one and he puffed at it thoughtfully, shook his head, threw it away, thanking me for it, and took a small buckhorn from under his red blanket and tapped snuff on to his wrist, sniffed it up and smiled at us.

'Once upon a time,' I said, 'the Masai were said to have very broad-bladed spears, and were known for them. And now the spears are all long and slender-bladed. Can you tell me anything about that, father?'

'Yes,' he said. 'I have heard about those very broad-bladed spears in old times, and they were carried by the age groups of Laimer, Ilnyangnei and Iltuati. The narrow spears came from the Olokutu side but I don't know why this change in the shape came about.'

'Father, what would be your advice to the young generation of today?'

'I will ask them to obey the law of the country, and to keep away from mischievous activities, and not to oppress the weak.'

'Is there anything else you would like to say, father?'

He shook his head, and courteously in the Masai way said, 'And is there anything else *you* would like to say?'

We said no, and we stood up and the old man shook hands with us and went off on the arm of the young Samburu man who had brought him.

CHAPTER FORTY-THREE

I was so impressed by that old man, Ole Seronei, who had never talked to a white man before, never smoked a cigarette, and now leaned on the arm of a young Samburu—very strange that, a Samburu this far south of Mount Kenya—that I went out of the hut to have a last look at them as they made their way along the sandy track.

Would there ever be a time when people would be allowed to be what they wanted to be, themselves, even to rot, if that was what they wanted, when nobody with power to do so would tell other people how they should, could, or more usual, *must* live? For me, who knew where that Samburu came from, how very far from here his tribe lived, a 'lost' part of the Masai people, it was strange to see him helping this old man who was young when the Masai had lost all the territory between here and where that Samburu came from. Now the Samburu wanted to be part of the Masai people again, and the Masai, who had rather despised them as 'lost', wanted them too, now.

What problems Jomo Kenyatta, *Bwana Mzee*, was going to have to deal with, all these tribes, all these separate cultures coming up again through that thin alien governmental cement which had not even had time to set and harden in seventy years of safari and world war.

Watching Ole Seronei on the arm of the young Samburu, one in language and custom, but separated by history, history, so swift but made great in distance, territory, made me think of the very old European I had gone to meet a few weeks before, away up on the slopes of Mount Kenya. He had known Kenya in its very early days before the Masai were moved from that country to south of the Kenya-Uganda railway line. I drove up to his *shamba* and he came out of the house to meet me, leaning on the arm of his oldest friend, a man as old as himself, a Masai. They were both cattlemen, and perhaps the Masai are the oldest cattle people anywhere on earth today. We sat on the verandah steps in the sun and talked, and it touched me to see how the two of them became wistful, nodding to each other as they recalled the migration of the Masai with their enormous herds, sixty years ago.

'Did they want to go? Were they willing?' I asked.

The old men shook their heads and the European said, 'No. Would you?' he said. He waved at the hills and plains.

No, I wouldn't. Just over there, a few miles across the *donga*, as a red sun rose and burned away white mists, thirty-four years ago, I had waited for flights of impala, you could only call them that, flights, those long slow graceful enormous bounds peculiar to that beautiful antelope, waited for them to pass me by, so that I could kill a Thomson's gazelle for the pot. And then the swarms of game were on the move as I went through the wet grass, hungry, to pick up the Tommy; eland, kongoni, wildebeest, zebra, by the thousand, moving as the sun rose over them and flashed golden on their coats.

Silent for a time, we sat there, the three of us, loving the country, staring out across it to where it becomes shapeless in bluish haze.

'We grazed next to each other then, didn't we?' the European said to the Masai, '*Mzungu* and Masai, their cattle next to each other. It could have worked. It could have worked.'

Yes, some of the early British officials had not wanted the Masai moved out of the highlands, had believed it would be a happier country if those Europeans who wanted to pioneer there among the Masai and the rhinoceros, the buffalo, the lion and the antelope, had made their deals with the Masai, as many did.

The two old men remembered aloud for me, fondly, many long safaris they had made, to buy cattle from Masai clans, so as to breed 'grades', as we used to call crossbreeds from native and European cattle.

Kenya was a tough country to ranch in, what with the free-loading lion with a taste for easy steak, and the diseases like rinderpest, Texas redwater, quarter evil, bacilliary necrosis (a ghastly one, that), and anthrax. And if you were stupid enough to grow crops, there were the locusts, unbelievable darkness as the endless and voracious waves hid the sun, before falling on a crop, desert makers so deadly that 1932 in Kikuyu is called *Kyangige*, The Year Of The Locusts, and 1927 as well, and they are so remembered for their devastation that 1891 is called *Kyangige* too.

'Did you know Olonana?' I asked the two old men, and the European's aged blue eyes, and the Masai's, dark but bluing too with great age, brightened with another memory of that far off time.

Olonana, always called Lenana by the Europeans, the one who tricked his father, Mbatian, and usurped his brother, Senteu's position as laibon of the Masai, had had to give the orders for the move of the Masai, once the decision had been made.

Even though he had this painful task he comes out well in the memory of those who knew him, Masai and European.

Sir Frederick Jackson, Lieutenant Governor for East Africa from 1907 to 1911, was in Kenya when Mbatian was still alive, and he knew the Masai well, and a lot of other tribes too. Of Olonana, he wrote, 'Lenana, though unprepossessing in appearance, struck me then and always as very quiet, not to say gentle in his manner, considering his position as ruler over so war-like a race; but he was in every sense a chief, and his principal *elmoru* (elders) showed that they regarded him as such. In fact, he was the only real chief in British East Africa.'

In 1895, when Kenya still belonged to the tribes, with the Masai as the overlords, Olonana was on a ceremonial visit to Fort Smith, a British outpost in the Kikuyu country. The British had just officially taken over the territory and the construction of the Kenya-Uganda railway had begun at Mombasa. It was Olonana's first meeting with a European official at a Government outpost, and he must have felt some trepidation, some uneasiness, and even more when a few terrified survivors rushed in to tell of what became known as the Kedong Massacre. His people, the Masai, had just wiped out a food caravan which was returning to Fort Smith from Eldama Ravine. The Masai warriors had speared hundreds of Kikuyu to death, and here was Olonana with his elders, in the middle of the Kikuyu country, while the District Officer, a man named Gilkison, added up the numbers of the dead as the news came in. The total of the slain came to:

540 Kikuyu porters
85 Coast porters (Swahili from the Mombasa area)
13 Askaris
6 Kikuyu headmen
2 Coast headmen
1 white man.

The Kikuyu tribe was well organized for war, and though they never went out to look for trouble they had shown the Masai, and others in the past, that they could deal with it when it was brought to them. Gilkison's fear was that the Kikuyu would break into the small outpost and seize Olonana and the elders, and that the food which the Kikuyu supplied for stations further up country would never again be made available to the Government. It was a very dangerous situation and Gilkison could easily have lost his head. A weaker man might have arrested Olonana and his elders, if only to placate the Kikuyu, and the fact that his warriors had killed a white man was an extra burden for Olonana. Ainsworth, Gilkison's chief, was notified of the massacre by runner and he came up from Machakos in the Wakamba country. Ainsworth was a remarkable man, and if all white men in Africa had been like him the writings Fanon left us might have been even more interesting.

With Olonana and the Kikuyu chiefs Ainsworth sorted out the last hours of the food caravan.

There was no European in charge of the caravan, which was under the command of a Swahili headman. A mixture of nearly a hundred Swahili askaris and porters were armed with Snider carbines, and there were over seven hundred Kikuyu porters.

Coming back through the Kedong Valley the caravan camped near some Masai *manyattas*, and some of the armed Swahili, who must have been quite new boys in the Masai country to do what they did, entered the *manyattas* and tried to seize some of the Masai women.

Some of the porters and askaris had, the day before, stolen milk from a Masai manyatta and had tried to get women to go with them to their camp. A senior Masai warrior had gone to the caravan headman and warned him to control his men.

When the Swahili, on this second occasion, were dragging the Masai women away, Masai warriors appeared, and the Swahili opened fire. The Masai went in to them with the spear and started to kill. It became a fight to a finish as the Swahili riflemen in their camp were attacked by the Masai, and they killed many of the Masai warriors. As soon as they had finished their ammunition the Masai speared all the Swahili, having lost nearly a hundred warriors themselves. Then they began on the Kikuyu, pursuing them down the Valley until they had killed all they could find.

An English trader called Andrew Dick happened to be passing through the Kedong on his way to Baringo for a shooting expedition. He came across some survivors of the massacre and then went on and began to round up Masai cattle, as a reprisal on the Masai.

The Masai followed Dick, who opened fire on them. He shot one Masai warrior who carried a particularly fine spear, which he

263

went out to get, but another Masai came out of the bush and speared Dick to death. When Ainsworth had taken all the evidence, he told Olonana that the Masai were not to blame for the affair, that the warriors, maddened by this behaviour of the caravan, had lost all control of themselves, and that the blame must be laid on the caravan. All firearms seized by the Masai were to be returned, and the seized Masai cattle would be shared out among the relatives of the slain Kikuyu as compensation.

Many Kikuyu elders were present when this meeting took place.

Olonana was very moved by this handling of the trouble, and he thanked the white men, saying he had heard of their justice and now he had seen it for himself. He said too, that he remembered his father's (Mbatian) advice not to have war with the white man, and it was his resolve to keep the peace always with them. When he later had to stand by that resolve and move his tribe he knew there were officials who resented and opposed the business.

Ainsworth wrote later,'This incident was practically the beginning of Lenana's friendship and loyalty to the Government. From that day onwards all roads in Masailand which had been doubtful before, were safe for small parties to traverse.'

Olonana, and Ole Gilisho, were both parties to the British decision that the Masai should leave their old grazing grounds, though it seems certain that Ole Gilisho was not as willing to agree to this as was Olonana.

Sir Frederick Jackson did not like the way the Masai were pushed out of Kenya to make way for white settlers. Ole Gilisho, (known always in English documents as Laigalishu) was a leader of the Masai warriors, a most important man, and here is how Sir Frederick Jackson saw him.

'Laigalishu was a spare and very little man with a long and rather sulky looking face, and with very prominent teeth, but of undeniably strong character.

'As a *Laigunan* he controlled his men in a manner I never saw equalled off a parade ground. On one occasion, when in charge of over four hundred of them, during the second Nandi expedition, it was part of my duty to issue, through that little man, the orders for the next day, and I can assert that no one but a negrophobe could have stood by him, as he issued his orders regarding advance guards, flankers, cattle guards, etc. and deny or belittle his grip on them. There was not a murmur.

'It was, however, as a patriot, delegate, obstructionist, call him what you like—probably the latter if from hearsay, and not personal experience—that Laigalishu excelled as much as he did as *Laigunan*.

'Up to that time when I ceased to have anything to do with the Masai I probably had more dealings with him than any other Government official except Collyer, and I always regarded him as a very remarkable and reliable man.'

Jackson seemed to foresee that a time would come when the white settlers, who had been encouraged to settle in Kenya as though forever, would be deserted when the British Government had to dismantle its empire.

In 1904 the government decided to move the Masai out of the great Rift Valley up into Laikipia in Northern Kenya.

Writing further on Ole Gilisho and the new government's treatment of the Masai, Sir Frederick Jackson had this to say:

'Up to the time of Sir Donald Stewart's treaty, or agreement, whereby the Masai were to evacuate the Rift Valley and move on to Laikipia, he (Laigalishu) was more or less kept in the background, but he came forward and began to make himself felt, when he saw the once spendid, close-cropped grazing grounds round about Naivasha going to ruin and becoming overgrown and sour; and with scarcely a head of stock on them. Can it be wondered at that he and his fellow tribesmen felt bitter? The result was that a certain number went back, in some cases on to land already allotted to settlers, but not occupied, and although the Masai herds and flocks were really doing more good than harm in keeping the grass well grazed, there was such an outcry that I was eventually deputed by Sir James to traverse and delimit the western boundary. My fellow delegates were Hobley, the P.C. Naivasha, and Collyer, the D.C. Rumurute, while Laigalishu, with a few others, represented the Masai.

'From the start it was quite clear that Laigalishu was taking nothing for granted. On our line of march he was here, there and everywhere, climbing hills either to get a better view all round, or to satisfy himself that they would make good boundary marks. All this "making sure" was very irritating, but we had a very pleasant little trip, and we all agreed on a boundary.'

Ole Gilisho was wasting his time, anyway, for as Sir Frederick Jackson goes on to explain, the Masai were eventually to be removed from all Kenya north of the railway line.

'A little later on, however, another agitation began, this time for the complete removal of the Masai from Laikipia on the Northern Reserve, to Loita and the Southern Reserve.

'At first I, for one, was strongly opposed to it, until it became evident that trouble was bound to arise, that there were grave risks of a *casus belli* being created, and there was no knowing what it might lead to. I then, in the interests of the Masai themselves, changed my view, and was in favour of the move. I am, however, thankful that I had nothing whatsoever to do with the negotiations that led to it, or to the move itself. I should certainly not have interpreted Laigalishu's last sentence when he wound up the debate: "If you wish us to go, we will go, but we do not want to go" into "quite willing" as was cabled home. Nor would the only two officials, Collyer and Maclure, who could speak and understand Masai, have been unemployed during the move. The former was sent to the Amala River to receive the immigrants, and when they never arrived, he was transferred to Nyeri, presumably to make quite certain that he would be completely out of touch with them. It was indeed a sorry show.'

The Masai knew well that it would be better to 'show willing' than not. The old men of the Masai living today all say they knew that force lay waiting, should they refuse to move out of their old grazing areas. Yet Mbatian had prophesied all of it.

CHAPTER FORTY-FOUR

IN the thirties when I lived on the Maranya river near the Meru border I noticed how many of the Meru tribe used Masai customs and were proud of the Masai blood they claimed. I began to understand that the plains of Timau at the foot of Mount Kenya, across which we hunted lion and cheetah, and on which the game swarmed, had been part of the Masai grazing grounds. The old Meru used to tell me that the Masai herds lived right up beside them on the Maranya river before the Masai had been moved by the British government.

Now, years later, old Masai, far down in the Loita hills on the Tanganyika border, confirmed this for me. They had lived there in their youth, before the great move south. In fact the senior chief of the Masai, Ole Senkale, had lived with the Meru as a boy, north east of Isiolo, and his mother had been a Meru woman. An old Masai told me this, and advised me to speak with Ole Senkale.

I found Ole Senkale sitting over an Indian *sigri*, a charcoal stove, in a hut outside Narok. It had been raining and he was trying to get warm.

Ole Senkale, warm and kind and straight, was extremely pre-occupied in trying to understand why the British were 'suddenly' leaving Kenya and, as he said, leaving the Masai, as well as the whites he had known there all his life, having 'broken their agreements with both peoples'. Yes, the Masai gave Kenya to the whites, on the agreements that the whites could have it for as long as the Masai remained a people, and on condition that they never give it up to any other people. The Europeans could have stayed there forever with the agreement of the Masai.

'I know Europeans much older than you, who were born here,' the senior chief said to me. 'Now why must they leave Kenya? We are friends who have lived side by side. I cannot understand it.' He shook his head and stared down into the pan of glowing charcoal.

'I hear you were one of the Masai who once lived in the far north of Kenya, at Laikipia, when you were young,' I said. 'And

267

that you were a warrior on the great move south of the railway. Tell me about that, please, father.'

He looked up at me with glowing eyes, remembering his youth. He nodded, remembering.

'Yes,' he said. 'That is true. I will tell you about it.'

He was a burly, powerfully built old man with a short thick neck and piercing, humorous dark eyes. He looked like a real chief, one whom warriors would obey and follow, and he had a spellbinding voice, firm and husky, making all his statements like one used to being listened to, short, crisp and to the point, pausing to let the listener absorb each statement.

He reeled out the beautiful Masai place-names of Northern Kenya as he began by telling me he was of the Purko clan, and that when small he had lived at Naivasha (Naiposha when properly pronounced in Masai.)

'We left Naivasha with our cattle and then we went beyond Ol Bolossat to Ongata Pus, and then we came to a river crossing called Elangata Enchata and that in Masai is called Enaiuruur, which today is called Thomson's Falls. We crossed there and went to Eluai Enkitashot, and then on to Olomuruti (called Rumuruti today). And then we went on to Inkushu e Korei which is near Ilariak le Misisi. And from there on to Enaipiriyiki which is beyond Engare Nyiro (the river called Wuaso Nyiro today.) There are two Engare Nyiro, one in Narok district and the one I mean which is in the Northern Frontier of Kenya. And we went on to Nanyuki, called by the Masai Engare Nanyokie, and from there we went to Iltaikan, and from there we roamed about until we came to Poré, and from there we grazed and settled right up to a place called Lenterit. And then on to Olorien le Naunere.'

He described how they went on up on to Lorroki (Loroghi).

'All that country is what the Masai used to call Entorror, and the Laikipiak Masai used to live there. Other people call that place Laikipia.'

'How did you come here to Narok in the south?'

'There was a great meeting . . . Masai came from many places to that meeting. For instance from Keputiei there was a chief called Leoposo, and there was Ole Kodonyo from Ilkeekonyokie, an old man from the same age-group as Leproso Ole Ngomeya. He was a chief. And he was a brother of the father of the present living one. Also at the meeting was another elder called Lesingo. Also there was Olegilisho (known in British documents as Legalishu) of the

Purko clan. And there was Lemooke Ole Kotikash from Lemek. And there was Suakei Ole Kishoyan, the elder in his family, and there was Olonana. At the end of the meeting with the British the Masai agreed to move south to where they are now.

'It was the British Government, with Olonana, the Laibon, who told us we must move to south of the railway up to the Mara river. But since that time the Government has been pushing us away farther south from the railway. After the move our northern boundary was the railway running eastwards to a point where Olonana placed an iron boundary mark at a place called Kerarapon, the course of the Athi river (now called Embakase).'

Beautiful women came into the little hut where the old chief sat dreaming aloud about the past. One of them, the most beautiful, with red-brown, glistening skin, stood in the doorway and examined us all, the men, minutely, unblinking, with her flat, black eyes. She smiled snowily whenever one of us looked at her. And the chief's husky voice went on to tell us of the great migration made by the famous fighting clan, his own, the Purko. Right down from the northern frontier they came, from the Loroghi plateau to Naivasha, across the great Rift Valley, with their thousands of cattle and goats.

'The whole of the Purko clan were moving slowly southwards, from Likia up to Mau, and from Mau on to Orgos le Kipoor, and during the movement we spread right across the country, so that in the west the Purko passed through the country of the Kipsingis to a point called Inshipiship. And so it was we came to settle in all this area up to the Mara river. And that was how we moved so that our territory was between the railway and the Mara river, but the Government has not kept to the agreement and has gradually moved us farther south from the railway.'

The old man shook his head sadly and spat into the fire, the black and white beads round his neck clinking, and the long steel tweezers, for plucking his beard, hanging at the back of his neck from his beads glittering in the watery sunlight now filtering into the hut.

I told the chief that as a youth I had lived beside the Meru above Isiolo on the northern slope of Mount Kenya, and that many of the place-names there were Masai, and that the Meru had told me that the Masai had lived beside them there. Could he confirm that the Masai and Meru were neighbours?

The old man looked at me, his eyes delighted as he remembered that marvellous country with its splendid grazing, its vastness, the lions, the teeming game and the buffalo herds.

'Indeed they were,' he said warmly. 'Indeed they were neighbours, the Meru on one side of Mount Kenya and we Masai on the other. We lived together at Poré in that country. We had our mutual agreements. We were friendly after we had had one or two fights, and we came to peaceful agreements.'

I never knew that the Masai, the Meru, and the Masai-speaking brethren of the Masai race, the Samburu, had watered their cattle together, by agreement at Isiolo, that sweltering group of tin huts where we used to buy onions and cigarettes before heading across the wastes to Abyssinia, to El Wak and Mandera and Somalia.

'Isiolo?' old Chief Ole Senkale said, smiling. 'Why, yes, the water of Isiolo was used only by the Masai, the Meru, and the Samburu used to come down there too.'

These memories of when he was young had stirred the old man, and the women, joined now by some young warriors, stood in silence and listened to him as he spoke of his youth, when the Masai, unknowingly, had made way for the Kikuyu by obeying their Laibon, who obeyed the British.

The Kikuyu have always been on the side of progress, new crops, change, cash, civilization (despite the anthropological explosion of Mau Mau), and the Masai love the past, and Ole Senkale represented that past as he sat over the coals and talked. He represented all the cattle and camel worshippers, the nomads who prized the gesture of contempt for death more highly than a diploma, and their time seems to be gone now.

When I had ridden the plains and the dongas of North Kenya I used to sit down sometimes for snuff with the old tribesmen who guarded the sheep and cattle against lions, and we would talk of when they were young. There were many signs of old Masai *manyattas* in the ground, and the old men always told me the Masai had grazed all along Timau to Meru. I asked Chief Ole Senkale if he could give me placenames.

Near Maranya there was a crater which the old men used to call Bugi Ngai, in which I once got a big, splendid, almost black leopard who had slain so many sheep in his bloodlust. Had Ole Senkale ever heard of Bugi Ngai? There had been a *manyatta* in it in old times.

'No.' He shook his head.

'I will tell you the place-names I remember of that country when

270

we grazed it,' he said. 'Right up to the Meru boundary. Now, the Europeans have confused many placenames and have changed some of them. For instance Engare Nanyokie (now called by Europeans, Nanyuki). We were grazing from there right up to Iltaikan and to Poré where we lived beside the Meru.'

Iltaikan! They must have grazed right up to the edge of Mount Kenya's forest, ten and eleven thousand feet up, right round towards the Sacred Lake called Gunga in the Meru country.

We had an old Kikuyu herdsman who had grazed sheep up there once, alone on a great plateau at the edge of the forest, and he had been sitting in a small movable corrugated iron hut, and had seen a rhino coming straight for him across the plain, and he had survived charge after charge, escaping when the rhino finally drove its horn through the metal. The rhino had then mangled the hut. The grazing up there is fine, and the mornings piercingly cold until the rising equatorial sun burns it away.

Iltaikan is the Masai name for the warrior's pigtail, and also describes the lianas hanging from forest trees. Perhaps that placename has died out, for I never came across it in African speech, or on a map.

To write the real story of the Masai one would have to travel with an old man like Chief Ole Senkale across the wide territory they vacated on the orders of their Laibon, Olonana, for it is only in human memory that the real story of a people survives, not in Government documents. And when the men of the generation of Ole Senkale are dead the story of the Masai will have gone with them.

I suggested to Jomo Kenyatta that all the legends, folk stories, and all the history contained in the place-names of the Kikuyu people should be written down now, for soon the knowledge of them will be gone with the generation who cherished them. He agreed, but he has so much other more urgent business to deal with that it is unlikely the material will ever be collected. Africans, in fifty years' time, will wish they knew half of what is now vanishing of their ancient tradition. And some of the white men now leaving East Africa know more of it than most of the young Africans who watch them go, just as the elders of the tribes, so often laughed at now, contain in their heads the wisdom of many generations of extremely hard-earned knowledge.

It was said a Masai once picked a mosquito off a roof beam, when malaria was still a mystery, and told a white doctor that this was what gave them malaria. The Masai, an old man once told me, used

271

to leave children with infantile paralysis out in malarial swamps, finding, they claimed, that the malaria killed the other sickness. Folk tales? Why don't we find out? Earlier in this book I described the making of arrow poison by the Midgan of the Mijertein in Somalia. They must have come by such precious knowledge the very hard way, like all of Africa which has made its struggle in climates which kill casually. And there is plenty of such knowledge vanishing today all over Africa.

'Why are you going already?' Chief Ole Senkale protested when we got up to go. 'I would like to talk for hours.' He was in the mood for reminiscence, had forgotten that we are all now ensnared in time and its passage. I had to go to Narok, and various arrangements had been made. I would have liked nothing better than to talk with Ole Senkale for a whole week. But it could not be.

We shook hands and said goodbye. I told Ole Kipoin as we went away that were I a Masai warrior I would follow Ole Senkale anywhere. They are the only people I know who are deprived because they deprive themselves, and don't feel deprived.

CHAPTER FORTY-FIVE

THERE was one old Masai character we hunted up and down Masailand. He was about ninety but he moved about like a twenty-year-old, and always on foot, passing over mountains and marshes that I could not negotiate with the Land Rover. This was Marieni Ole Kertella and every Masai, when they heard of my interest in Masai history and tradition, said, 'You've got to meet Ole Kertella. He knows more about the past than any Masai alive.' He had been an interpreter at the early meetings between the British and the Masai before the First World War. He had been a warrior and had fought in many battles, and it was still his pleasure to walk up and down the territory still left to the Masai, and twice we nearly found him.

It was time to leave Masailand now and as we were packing our gear a message came from the District Commissioner at Narok to say that Ole Kertella was at a place called Nairagè Engare. Should we have this one last try to find the old man? These old men were the last link with the pre-European past, in a society which has no public records, no filing systems, but which relies on the human memory of old intelligent men like Ole Kertella, and as a lover of tradition I could not leave East Africa without meeting him and recording what he had to say.

On the long dusty trail to Nairage Engare an old bent man was trudging about five hundred yards in front of our truck. A Masai who was standing in the bush ran out to him and tenderly put his arms about the old man and ushered him into the thorns off the trail, smiling at us as we passed. That was very Masai, that tenderness. Earlier on the road we had come on two Masai warriors. One was kneeling beside the other, an arm round his shoulder supporting him. Their two long spears were stuck in the soil beside them. The kneeling Masai waved to us and we stopped.

They had walked for days, from the Mara River, and one was grey faced, weak with malaria. We put the sick Masai into the back of the truck, but the fit one refused the trip, saying he would walk. I asked him for the sick man's spear and said I would hand it to the doctor for safekeeping, but smiling, he refused, saying he would keep both spears. He feared that someone would steal the sick man's spear. He said he would arrive at the dispensary the next day and would stay there until his friend was well again. He did not like to ride in trucks, they made him feel sick.

The Indian doctor at the dispensary near Narok took a look at the sick Masai and confirmed that he had bad malaria. He treated the Masai with that mixture of pity and admiration which most of us feel for this people who will not recognize civilization except in extremity like illness, who will not conform to the facts of this century. There *is* something rather fine and pitiful about this Masai wish to stay as they were, while knowing that their world is finished.

The next day while I was wandering around in the open market held under the thorn trees, looking for fresh maize to buy, someone tapped me on the arm. It was the Masai we had left behind on the road. He was grinning, his own spear and his friend's gripped in his left hand. He shook hands with me Masai style, and told me that his friend had had plenty of medicine and would soon be well. We shook hands again and said goodbye and I watched him saunter off and then squat down with some women who were selling snuff. He held out his hand and one of them sprinkled fresh snuff on to the back of it, which he sniffed up. They all smiled at each other, strangers to each other in our terms, but members of a big and scattered family in reality. The women began to tell this man from the far bush about the prices of things spread out in the market about him, about the weather and the doings in this tiny village so far from the Mara river. They would tell each other their tribes, their sections, their problems. There were no strangers for long in Masailand.

At the end of the track low grey hills rose above Nairage Engare which was about twelve tiny wooden, tin roofed stores, many lean, mangy dogs loping about nearby and waiting for scraps. The usual small groups of Masai stood about chatting, or gazing at coloured beads for sale. They love colours, especially colours to hang on their necks and ears.

Ole Kertella? He had just gone. Well, about two hours ago, that way, over the hills. The Masai who told me this was an elder and already knew that I was the curious white man who went about stopping old men and asking questions about times so long ago that only a few could remember. Ole Kertella was looking for us too, and had gone over the hills to find us near Narok. We all laughed.

Could I follow him in the Land Rover? Impossible. There was no track, and it was marshland for miles. This was the end of the road.

'Never mind,' a tall Masai with a short beard and clipped moustache said to us. 'If you love history that is a good thing. So come into my store and let us drink some beer.' It had been a long, dry journey and we followed him into his little cool store. While he set up a row of bottled beers on the tiny bar the Masai, whose name was Leshinga Ole Nagoyek, said to me, 'I'll find Ole Kertella for you. Don't worry about it. I'll send for him and find him. You're right to want to see him if it's history you love, for Ole Kertella knows more than any of us, about the old days when the Masai owned it all—' He grinned and swept his arm to indicate Masailand, and beyond it, Kenya and the rest. 'Yes, we owned it all, and now it's politics and votes.' He laughed, shaking his head as he prized the metal caps of the bottles of Tusker. He filled the glasses and raised his own. 'To you all and your journey and your work,' he said, and we drank to that. Then we drank to Leshinga Ole Nagoyek and to his luck and his warrior age group, which was of 1940, and after that we drank to the old times, and then to the times to come— may they be prosperous etcetera, and then we just drank because the talk was flowing well and Leshinga lined the bottles up again and again. Several times he called to a man with a Kikuyu face sitting nearby to come and have a beer with us, but he refused each time, and I could see Leshinga's eyes flashing. The man sitting down on the bench by the wall was wearing a battered slouch hat and a khaki bush shirt and shorts, a Public Works Department badge on his breast. He was about fifty, good looking, with dark brown skin and the unmistakable Kikuyu eyes which have quite a different expression in them from that of the Masai, or from most other tribes in East Africa. The very secrecy of the real Kikuyu shows in their eyes in a sort of watchful and inscrutable stillness.

This Kikuyu came up to me when I was alone for a minute and said in a low, angry, puzzled voice, 'Why do you drink with these Masai? Why do Masai drink with white men like this? What is it about? It is not right that white men and Masai drink together like this.' I looked into his face and was interested to see how urgent this question was for him. I was annoyed and let him know it, adding, 'And why don't *you* have the beer which Leshinga has offered you three times? Because there is a white man present? Or because you do not like the Masai? Or because you behave like an old time Kikuyu, shut up like a lock with your secrets? And what have you to be afraid about, or to be secretive about? You are in Masailand—you should follow Masai custom. Or is it politics? Why don't you go to Leshinga and complain about his drinking with white men? Why come to me?'

Some Masai who had been listening came up and they made the Kikuyu accept a bottle of beer, laughing at him as he took it. Leshinga lectured him, and addressed the bar, 'No. He does not like the Masai and the white men to drink beer together. That is not good politics, he thinks. Well, he is among the Masai now and will do as we do, and when he goes back to Kikuyuland he can do as they do there.'

This Kikuyu had courage to do what he did, for he had revealed a feeling of superiority to the Masai which Leshinga had not missed and had picked on as the basis of his lecture to the angry Kikuyu. The Kikuyu had revealed that he, the Kikuyu, belonged to what he considered to be the superior race in East Africa, the one which would rule the Masai when the white government had gone. And he did not like the Masai and the white men to mix socially, any more than he would have approved of Kikuyu and white men drinking beer together in some Kikuyu backwater village. Behind his attitude, though, was a deeper reason for his bad manners. He felt certain that any white man drinking beer with Masai in Nairage Engare just now, when Kenya was about to become independent, must be some sort of agent anxious to entice the Masai away into some political gesture of their own against the Kikuyu who were going to rule Kenya.

'We do not want politics dragged in here while we are drinking beer and talking about things we enjoy,' Leshinga told the Kikuyu. 'We are men talking here, not politicians.' The Kikuyu, whose anger had caused him to be overheard while talking to me in the first place, was silent. He sat there with lowered head, and then drank his beer, and in a way it was exactly as it had been in the beginning when the first white men arrived in Kenya.

The Masai had come forward, to fight or to talk with the white men, to buy, to seel, while the Kikuyu had hung back, suspicious, and concerned with maintaining a dignity in unwillingness to be surprised or amazed. Nothing would have convinced that Kikuyu bent over his beer while the Masai chided him for his bad manners, that I or Maurice Brown of the B.B.C. who stood at the bar with the Masai, were not agents working among the Masai against the Kikuyu. He had overheard all our talk about the Masai past, and it was this that had awakened resentment and suspicion in him. How could a white man be interested in the Masai past for its own sake? There must be some deeper reason, some anti-Kikuyu plan.

Maybe he should have spoken out, even in that tiny bar far down in Masailand, a lone Kikuyu among many armed Masai, what he really felt in his heart when he saw the white men and the Masai laughing together and talking about age groups, and marriage customs and dead ceremonies. The Masai would have respected him had he said what he really felt, which would have gone like this—'Who resisted the white men when they first came? We did, the Kikuyu. Who were suspected for it, and were told by the white men that they had no military tradition? The Kikuyu. Who were lauded and romanticised by the white men for their warriorhood and their bravery and their colourful tradition? The Masai. But who, once they saw that the white men could not be resisted, came out and started to learn from them, went to school, worked for a few shillings a month on isolated ranches and sent their children to mission school so as to better themselves? The Kikuyu. Who realized first that the white men had a colour bar when it came time for the rare educated Kikuyu to enter the white man's world? The Kikuyu. And what were the Masai doing all this time? Leaning on their spears in the sun and thinking about the past. And who finally went out and fought, so as to smash things as they were—the colour bar, low wages, lack of schools and opportunity, lack of the proper political rights of freedom? The Kikuyu. And who lost nine thousand dead in the fighting? The Kikuyu. And who is it still think they are superior to the Kikuyu and to everybody else by some natural right? The Masai. Who were always preferred by the white man, and praised for their charm, their courage, their good looks, their friendliness? The Masai. Who never did anything except stand in the sun and look like warriors of the old times, never sent their children to school, never tried to get freedom for Kenya from the white men, never did anything constructive as we the Kikuyu, and all people who have ambition see it? The Masai. And who is it now who suddenly complain that they have no education, and that the Kikuyu are taking over the government of Kenya? The Masai. And who got angry and was unable to contain it, when he heard the white men getting you to describe your past as a tribe, the white men who always have a good reason of their own for making such conversation? I, a Kikuyu. *Natererei*—I tell you you do not understand the white men or the past or the future. *Moigwa*—

it is we, the Kikuyu, who will lead you all to the good life, if only you will follow us and listen to our advice, for it is we who have learned the hard way and know the new rules, not you. That is why it burns my heart to see you all laughing and talking with the white men in this way. You seem to have no suspicion, no guile, no understanding that all that past you talk about is gone and finished, and that you have no schools, no doctors, no politicians, only your spears and your thorn trees after seventy years of the white man in this land—' But he said none of this, his eyes glittering as he watched Leshinga Ole Nagoyek bring out a treasured possession which he wanted to give me as a farewell present, now we had finished the beer, and the talk and the good-natured and enjoyable *shauri* was ending as darkness came.

'I want you to have this as a remembrance of this happy talk we have had with the beer,' Leshinga said, handing me the ostrich feather ball, the *susel*, which warriors carry on their spear points when visiting peaceful fellow tribesmen far afield; the symbol of his warrior age group. I did not wish to take this from him but he insisted I have it, and we shook hands when I took it and we all went out to the Land Rover in the darkness. 'It is good that you have come this far down to us at Nairage Engare to find out about our vanished past,' Leshinga told me. 'For it is being forgotten, and if you write it down men will be able to read it in times to come. And I will find Ole Kertella for you and send him to you before you leave Kenya. I promise you that.' We said goodbye with much handshaking and then drove off down the thick yellow dust of the track towards the Rift Valley.

No matter how right that Kikuyu could be had he summed up aloud what he felt in his angry heart, for whatever reasons, I had enjoyed hours of a kind of talk with the Masai which I could never have with the Kikuyu, and yet one had to respect that effort the Kikuyu made to keep a wall between the white men and the Africans, pointless though it was. But when it came to the good qualities of courage and dignity there was not much to choose between the Masai and the Kikuyu, but the Kikuyu cannot open his heart yet, as the Masai can, not even to his fellow Africans. When he can he will be surprised how much more he will enjoy life, and how much more people will enjoy him too. I suppose one likes the Masai for what he is, and respects the Kikuyu for what he promises to be, the most progressive people in East Africa. They strive for a dignity which they do not seem to know they have always had, and the

278

Masai are quite contented with the dignity they know they have, for it is only now the Masai have begun to feel that they look primitive with their spears and their red ochre on their nakedness, because the Kikuyu have won. And there is no doubt about it at all, that the Kikuyu have won.

We drove up into the hills to a hotel by the road and while we waited for dinner we listened to a Madagascan African head barman snobbishly tell us how much he suffered now that rude and un-lettered Africans were allowed to come into his bar for drinks, like white men. The country was going to the dogs. He did not know how long he could put up with things as they were now, and there was no way of getting Africans out of the bar. They had the right to be there now. If only they would agree to a separate bar for them-selves, somewhere else, even on the hotel property. But no, they wanted to drink alongside the white men. It was strange how things were going. The white man had lost his grip and was giving in to everything right and left. Forty years he had been a barman and he had never thought to see things come to this—and so on.

There is no one so snobbish as the gentleman's gentleman. I felt sorry for him, much sorrier than I felt for the Masai.

CHAPTER FORTY-SIX

WHEN it came time to leave East Africa, after dragging it out as long as possible with friends in Nairobi, writing notes and drafting a book as an excuse, I felt depressed. I had come for a 'last visit', to get the country out of my system forever, but now I knew I was never going to recover from the place, and I did not want to leave at all. I was even beginning to like Nairobi.

A message came all the way up from Masailand, from Leshinga Ole Nagoyek—do not leave yet, old Marieni Ole Kertella has been traced. No wonder my old friend, Jim, had decided to spend his last years down among the Masai. What better life could a man live, drifting through sunlit days among the Masai? With friends like Leshinga Ole Nagoyek.

Down River Road I had a few drinks with some old retired Sudanese soldiers, black shining burly men who brewed their own Nubian gin, which you could blow a safe with.

One of my last jobs as a soldier, while waiting for my number to come up, was to look after the affairs of these old Sudanese. It was the first staff job I had ever had and consisted of long happy hours talking with these old sweats. One day, as we blessed each other on their leaving my office, (they were all Muslims) one of them stayed behind the others. He said he had something to ask me. He was old but I did not realize just how old he was.

'It's about medals, Effendi,' he said.

'Well, you've done all right,' I told him, nodding at his row of unknown ribbons. He plucked the silver bristles on his black chin and studied my face. He was well over six feet, but beginning to stoop with age.

He jerked his head at the others outside in the sun.

'You see that two of them have the medal of the Sudan campaign, Effendi?' He looked at me hard, eyebrows raised.

'The Sudan campaign?' I said.

'Yes, Effendi. I was in that campaign too. But I never got the medal. *They* got it, though.' He indicated the others outside again.

'The Sudan campaign? Which Sudan campaign are you talking about?'

'The Mahdi's war, Effendi,' he said, patient, respectful.

'*Wallahi!* Were you in that war? Then why didn't you get the medal for it?'

He looked at the floor for a time, considering, and then, worried, looked at me. It was 1947 and a good few years since the Mahdi failed to convince God he was the long awaited Messenger, late in the day to claim a medal, if his claim was genuine.

'There *is* a difficulty, Effendi,' he said, sombre now. 'And yet I cannot see why I cannot have the medal, as I fought, and fought hard.'

I took up a pencil. 'All right, give me the details,' I said. 'Unit and so on.'

He sighed. It was a long resigned sigh. 'I was a soldier of the Mahdi, Effendi,' he said, and then, seeing my expression, went on hurriedly. 'What's the difference, Effendi? I fought there, didn't I? A battle's a battle. But I have no medal to show for it. Couldn't you—'

One of the Mahdi's warriors. I tried to see him as he must have been then, a youth with the huge fuzz of hair and the long spear, charging across those sands at Omdurman.

'My advice to you,' I said, 'is, get yourself a medal ribbon and put it up at night, and then take it down again in the morning. They'll never give you the medal, you must know that.'

Frowning, he nodded. 'And *they* wear it, those two,' he said, nodding at his friends outside. 'It doesn't seem right, Effendi.'

I put my arm round his shoulder, laughing, for I could not hold it any longer, and went with him to the door, and he smiled as he shook my hand. 'Just mention it to the General, Effendi. You never know,' he said gently.

'Has he been talking about his medal again, Effendi?' one of his grizzled friends called. They all laughed when I nodded. Then they dressed off, the Mahdi's warrior with them, and saluted, still laughing.

'He's dead,' one of the Sudanese told me as we drank the Nubian gin in River Road. 'He tried all the officers but he never got the medal.'

With two old friends I drove to Mombasa to catch a ship sailing for Aden.

Elephant herds were on the move and we had to wait while a cow

281

gently pushed a new tiny grey-pink calf on to the road, groups of the herd ambling up behind. A big bull swung up towards us looming, his ears rising, and when we saw that we backed out of there fast. He stood guard till the whole herd had crossed the road. How long would they last, I wondered, but there were thousands of them on the move, and in Mombasa hunters told me they thought there were about twenty-five thousand elephant in the coast area.

The Portuguese bastion, Fort Jesus, looked the same and I wondered again if it was true that Camoëns had sat on its ramparts and written some of his Lusiad, looking out at the palms and over Mvita, Mombasa's real name, the island of war.

In the old Arab port the sight of the dhows at anchor made me wish I had never returned to Europe from this marvellous country, for I had once made a hard decision there. I had twenty-four hours in which to decide whether to go partners with an Italian in a shark fishing venture or not. That would have meant ranging the whole Somali coast, from Kismayu round the Horn to the Gulf of Aden. We had sailed down to Mombasa from Mogadishu in a converted dhow. While I pondered it that night in Mombasa I felt the first familiar oily taste in the throat, and the nausea of oncoming malaria. I counted back the days to the last mosquitoes. Yes, accursed Belet Wen where the strip of tarmac began south of the Mudugh, and I had slept without a net, too tired to bother after the last day's drive in the battered truck across the last of the rocks and sand, obsessed to reach that black sweltering strip of tarmac.

When the shakes hit me and the massive iron depression after the spasm followed, I made the wrong decision. I should have remembered Lamu and Malindi, gone there and got well, and stayed on. I had been years away from Europe, but Europe is really no use to you again after Africa. When the cold rain gets into your guts and you feel surrounded by too much furniture, and you can't tear your mail up without reading it, you realize that you've lost three quarters of yourself years ago where the rain, when it comes, is warm and alive, and where ninety per cent of what seems to matter, in Europe, doesn't matter at all.

At Nyali I saw a fat black Swahili lying under a palm tree, exhausted with contentment, stretching and yawning. Then he closed his eyes and dozed off. Behind the times, he should have been slaving his guts out in order to pay some bills he'd run up because he wasn't earning enough money.

As the freighter pulled slowly out into the stream I shouted good-bye to the Swahili dock labourers, '*Kwaheri*'.

They grinned, waved, shouted '*Kwaheri*'. And one of them yelled 'Are you going for good, or are you coming back?'

'*Sijui*,' I called back. 'I don't know.'

Next to me at the ship's rail was a small dumpy woman with a sad face.

Her tale was tragic. She had had a lovely little business going for three years, and then 'when things began to change, *you know*,' she said significantly, an African had come into the shop for a pair of shoes. 'Got out of a big car, had a chauffeur too. A politician. He sat down and expected me to fit him for shoes. I could *see* it. You'd never have had anything like that a couple of years ago. Never.' She had not been able to bring herself to do it. Sent him packing. That was the red light. She had sold up. Her head was shaking slightly with pride and indignation as she spoke.

That such great strength of character was returning could only be a gain for Europe.

Feeling despair I went into the bar for a cold beer and watched Africa slide slowly past the open window.

APPENDIX I

It was late at night when Marieni Ole Kertella arrived at the broadcasting studios in Nairobi. Ole Kipoin and I got up to greet him and he shook hands with us. He was a fine looking and dignified old man, over ninety, yet he looked sixty, his healthy red brown skin shining in the electric light as he smiled at us and waited to be asked to sit down. He sat down and looked round at the machinery and then at the microphone on the table before him.

'That's the thing I'll talk into?' he said.

'That's it.'

'And it keeps what I say for ever?'

'Yes.'

He laughed. 'I will tell you anything I know,' he said, 'and if I don't know it I will tell you I don't know it.'

He wore the Masai blanket about his shoulders, and plenty of beads and copper ornaments. Sometimes he spoke Masai, sometimes Swahili, sometimes English, but when a fine point came up he would explain it in Masai to Ole Kipoin until all was clear. The talk went like this—

Q. Father, do you remember where you were born?

A. As far as I can recall I only know what my parents told me. And I can remember the place where they told me I was born. It was in Naivasha at a place called Empirish naji Enololdia. In the Masai custom whenever a family goes back to a place where a child was born they take a piece of Kikuyu grass and tie it on the ankle of the child. My parents did this to me whenever we went back to that place, until I realized the importance of the practice and started doing it myself. So I was born at Empirish naji Enololdia.

Q. Where were you circumcised?

A. In Kinopop. (Now known as Kinangop).

Q. What is your age group?

A. Iltareto.

284

Q. Do you remember the catastrophes which befell the Masai long ago?

A. Yes, I do. I remember when the rinderpest epidemic broke out and finished the Masai cattle.

Q. What happened?

A. Rinderpest was the first catastrophe, and it started like this. First of all there was an eclipse of the sun and it took place at about five o'clock in the afternoon. At the time I was grazing sheep and goats and the people were singing and praying for the eclipse of the sun to pass. It was then that the rinderpest attacked the cattle. The epidemic finished the Masai cattle.

Q. When you were looking after the sheep and goats at that time were you a Moran (warrior) or a boy?

A. When the epidemic attacked the cattle I was a boy, but quite a grown up boy with good sense.

Q. Do you remember the outbreak of smallpox?

A. Yes. I remember the smallpox epidemic. Rinderpest came first and the smallpox followed when the cattle were finished. The Purko section of the Masai had a man whom I supposed came from the Rendille tribe, and he vaccinated the legs of people and applied the pus from the affected part of the face.'

I thought this was so interesting that I asked the old man to tell us more about it.

A. This man came from or was sent by God from somewhere. I think he came from the Rendille country.

Q. Was he a Masai?

A. He looked like a Masai, and I think he had Samburu blood, but whoever he was he was sent by God from somewhere and he vaccinated the people. What he actually did was this. He scratched the thighs of the sick and applied pus from the affected part of the face. The vaccinated part grew into a wound as big as that ash tray you are using there. People flocked to him for vaccination and he saved very many lives in the Purko section. The Ildamat section were greatly reduced in number because they got no vaccination at all. All this I remember very well.

Q. Did the smallpox epidemic affect the whole of Masailand?

A. What I know is that it affected the whole country. It would be hard to find a people who did not suffer from that epidemic. However I cannot speak for the Kisongo people in the south, but all the people in the north got it.

Q. By that time were you a *Moran* (warrior), a *laiyoni* (a boy) or a child?

A. During those two catastrophes I was a boy. First came the rinderpest and then the smallpox and in both cases I was a boy, and a very intelligent boy too.

Q. When did the Masai start to recover from these catastrophes?

A. The Masai recovered about the time they began fighting among themselves. The Ildamat section attacked the Ilkeekonyokie, and the Purko attacked the Ildamat to stop the fighting. Then the Ildalal Lekutuk were attacked and the Loita attacked the Ilkaputiei and the Ilmatapato at Ngong. Then the Loita went further and attacked the Ileekonyokie, and after that there was no peace and the sections fought one another. The fighting was among the age group called Iltalala. Then the age group of Imirisho was circumcised and they are the ones who attacked and conquered the Loita. They captured cattle called Inkishu Olmoti (the prey from Olmoti), cattle called Inkishu naji Nosero (the prey from Nosero) and cattle called Norgosua (the prey from Norgosua). The Purko section led in that attack, with the *Morans* of the Kaputiei, Ileekonyokie, Ilmatapato, and Ilwasinkishu. The Masai had by then recovered in strength and cattle. It was during that period that the railway reached Nairobi. The railway reached Nairobi with a number of Indians who were building it, and the Masai, who were in Kikuyuland, came out and found the Government in power.

Q. Do you know which lands the Masai occupied in those days?

A. Yes. The rear of the Purko section was at Ongata Pus, and the head was right up at Loroki (now called Loroghi of the Northern Frontier district) and Kisima. Kisima is in the Samburu country. Yes, they were right up to Loroki and on the other side they could see Ogata Olbarta (The Plains of the Horses).

Q. And what about the Samburu. Where were they?

A. The Samburu were in the dry country called Olpurkel which extends from Oldoiyo le Ngiro and spreads north to Marsabit hill. They occupied all that land right down to a point near Kisima.

Q. What about the other sections? Where were they?

A. The Ilkeekonyokie were at Kinopop until the Masai were forced to leave that area. They were at Kinopop, Sision, Imunyi, and as a matter of fact that section (the Ilkeekonyokie) had the biggest area of Kinopop. They stretched from Kijabe

286

hills right up to a place called Enkushuai, and to Enkume where the oxen used for Masai ceremonies used to be kept. That was the land they had. And the Purko occupied the other side called Enkutoto e Kamja where there is a road today to Nyeri.

Q. And where were the Ildamat section?

A. That section was at a place called Enaigusungus and they extended right up to Kinopop. They lived side by side with the Purko, and the Ildalal le Kutuk lived side by side with the Ilkeekonyokie, occupying a place called Karat.

Q. And the Iloital section?

A. The Iloitai were to be found as soon as you cross the bridge of Engare Ngiro today in Narok district, and they extended on that side and took in Ogata e Loita (Loita plains) right down to the Ongata e Siringet (Serengeti plains) in Tanganyika. All that was their land.

Q. And the lands between Engare Ngiro in Narok district and Kinopop (modern Kinangop). Who had those?

A. All land on this side of Engare Ngiro including Engare Narok (Narok river), Syapei river, all that belonged to the Ildamat section. And although they occupied all the land right up to Naivasha some of the Purko section, and some of the Ildalal le Kutuk and Ilkeekonyokie were living among them there, even though the area belonged to the Ildamat you found a number of other sections living there too.

Q. Tell us where the Lodokilani section lived.

A. The Lodokilani were living in Mosiro and took in Kimoren and Enkopiri. All Mosiro as we know it now belonged to the Lodokilani.

Q. And the Kaputie section, where were they?

A. The Kaputie area was as follows—they had the whole of Ngong, Ololaiser (the Ngong hills) including Rura, Kukuya, Narok Omon (where the army camp is today). All those areas including Nairobi, Ilkejek Onyokie, Olmanie Loo Nokopen, and also the present Kabete, Enteijia (Ndeiya), Imorog (Limuru), all that belonged to the Kaputie section.

Q. What about the Isikirari section?

A. They had Oldoiyo Oibor (Mount Kilimanjaro)—I mean this side of the mountain, and they had Oloitokitok, Osilalei, Lolpenyet, Ongata e Kinyawa (The plains of Simba railway station today) right up to a place called Oloitilai le Mosonik and

287

Ildoiyo Lolkirosion, and that is the end of the Loitokitok Masai area.

We had a cigarette after that long description of Masai geography as it had been in Ole Kertella's boyhood. His description of the territory gives an idea of how far the Masai stretched before they were moved south of the Mombasa-Uganda railway, which move Ole Kertella wanted to describe for us. But first I wanted to ask him about the Laibon Olonana.

Q. Do you remember, or did you ever see Olonana in the flesh?
A. I remember him very well.
Q. Did you see him?
A. Yes, I did.
Q. Will you describe him for us? Was he tall or was he thin, or would you say he was heavily built physically?
A. He was slim, and his pigmentation is what I would call *mungie*, that is midway between black and brown. He was tall, with a bald head, but you could not see his bald head because he covered it with a headgear of leather called *Enkaranda*. His teeth were white and one of his front upper teeth protruded. Yes, and he was very slim. I knew him well. He had long ear-lobes which reached down near to his chest. (Stretched artificially in the Masai way).
Q. Was he a good orator?
A. He was not a good orator, but he was an expert Laibon.
Q. Socially was he good company, or did he lose his temper quickly?
A. Socially he was good company. He spoke very quietly and was very reserved, and not many people could speak with him. He introduced a strange system by appointing an interpreter to speak to the Masai. I knew the man. He was called Saboye Ole Ntaanipenyo of the Kekonyokie section. When people went to consult Olonana the interpreter would go to him and say 'The people want your opinion about such and such a thing.' Then Olonana would call them to him and ask the interpreter to tell him what they wanted. After hearing them through the interpreter he would answer through the interpreter who would say 'The Laibon says so and so in answer to your question.' He always spoke very quietly.
Q. And do you remember Senteu, the other Laibon?

288

A. Yes. I remember him too. He came to a place called Kileleshwan. He came there with a group of about seven or eight warriors who were escorting him. Yes. The day he arrived at Olonana's *boma* I was there. That was the *boma* at Kileleshwan.

Q. Were you a *moran* (warrior) by then?

A. I was Olaiyoni. (A big boy).

Q. Tell us how he came, father.

A. Senteu left the fertile hills of Loita where he lived and walked all the day and arrived at night. When he arrived the whole area was covered by mist, and it was dark too. He arrived at Olonana's *boma* in the early hours. There he entered a hut and it was too dark to take the calves out and milk the cattle. Inside the hut he found a woman and he asked her to light a fire, and she lit one. Then he told her to tell the people that *Olamal* had arrived (Olamal is usually a group of *morans*, women or elders, who go about praying and singing and praising God for a certain purpose, and must be treated well wherever they go), and that the *Olamal* is headed by the Laibon called Senteu. The woman was taken aback and said 'Did you say you are Senteu?' and he said 'yes', and the woman left and reported the presence of Senteu in the *boma*. The news was taken to Olonana who said 'So he has come, and he is leading *Olamal*' (a mission of peace).

It was then that the mist cleared away and the calves were led out and the milking of cows began, and the time was about nine o'clock in the morning. Then Olonana said 'Take them to the *boma* of Sananga's sons,' which was at a place called Mapenae near Kukuya. Kukuya is near what is now called Dagureti, but it is on this side of Dagureti. You don't know Kukuya? On the small plain called Kabati (modern Karen near Karen von Blixen's old house) there is a white building (Mr. Rodney Chilton's present house) on the edge of the plain and that is the real place of Kukuya, and when you stand there you can see red buildings on the plain at the place we used to call Rora. That area belonged to the Ilkaputiei section and that is why the girls of the Kaputiei section praise themselves when they say 'We are Rora girls.' Yes, Olonana said that Senteu and his *Olamal* were to be taken to the *boma* of Sangata's sons near a place the Masai called Nolchoro and which is now called Dagureti.

After that Olonana called together the warriors of the

Kaputiei and Purko Sections, because all these warriors were in the Kaputiei country at that time. And the chiefs were called. For instance there was the Chief Leposo, and Ole Melua, Ole Manei, Ole Sereka (the father of Lekimani and the grandfather of the present Doctor Lekimani). Yes, all these chiefs were summoned to come and discuss the arrival of the Laibon Senteu. It was a long discussion and at the end they came to the conclusion that he was genuinely heading *Olamal* (a mission of peace) and they decided to call him and hear what he had to say.

When Senteu arrived before them he said he had come to surrender, and that he wanted to be let live among them because he had been defeated by them. And it was agreed, and he left the *Olamal* which had escorted him and he went to live at Ngong. Do you know where the present market is at Ngong? And if you happen to know where Mr. Nonkimojik's *shamba* was, then that is near where Senteu established his home on the plain at the foot of the hill. After that the Loita and Damat sections, who had come together by then, were sent to the Naivasha area and they lived there with the Purko section. And it was not long after that the Government forced the Masai to leave Naivasha and Kinopop.

Q. There is a story that when Senteu entered that hut in Olonana's *boma* he picked up a child that was lying on a bed there. Is that true?

A. I never heard of that.

Q. Where did Olonana die?

A. He died at Enomatasiani (about three or four miles East of modern Ngong township), and he died of illness. It seems as if he was bewitched, and he became sick and started roaming all over the country. Sometimes he climbed trees and he became somewhat insane until he died, at Enomatasiani.

Q. Can you remember the earlier Laibon, Mbatian? (the one who forecast the coming of the white men and the railway).

A. Yes, I remember Mbatian's death, but I never saw him. He died at a distant place, at Oldoiyo Orok (Black Mountain— modern Namanga Hill).

Q. Did you ever hear what Mbatian looked like?

A. I always heard it said that he was a small man physically, and many said that his son Nanunuaki resembled him. But Nanun- uaki is dead.

Q. Now when Mbatian died who truly inherited his position (as chief Laibon of the Masai), Senteu or Olonana?

A. Both Senteu and Olonana were Mbatian's sons, but it was Senteu whom he wished to be his legal heir. Then I heard that before he died Mbatian called both of them to him to give them his last words. Then, when the two sons were leaving the hut he called Senteu back and told him to come again early the following day, before his brother Olonana. Apparently Olonana had been suspicious and he hid and heard what was said to Senteu by Mbatian and the next morning he rose before his brother and went straight to his father's hut. When he entered his father's hut Mbatian said 'My son, Senteu, have you come?' And Olonana pretended to be Senteu and said, 'Yes, father, I have come.' And then Mbatian blessed him and made him his successor. Later on Senteu arrived, after Olonana had gone, and he said to Mbatian, 'Father, I have come.' When Mbatian realized that it was Senteu speaking he asked who it was that had come before him and Senteu said that it might have been Olonana. Then Mbatian said to Senteu, 'I am afraid he has beaten you, because I have already blessed him and made him my successor.' It was after that Olonana became the chief Laibon of the Masai, although Mbatian had not wanted it.

Q. Is it true that it was Mbatian who forecast the coming of the white man?

A. Yes, he was the first one to predict the coming of the white man.

Q. What did he tell the Masai about that?

A. When he told them of the white men who were coming he said 'You will be ruled by uncircumcised people, and they will have a piece of wood with water and fire in it, and it will shout and cry as it moves, and it will carry people.' (The steam engine.) And Mbatian went about picking up war clubs and saying 'Let me strike the head of this snake,' but he was asked not to strike it, though he repeated this demand many times without success. At the end of it he said 'I have left it, but a long snake will cross the country from East to West, with no tail and no head, and as soon as it arrives you will be ruled. There it is. I have left it.' So you see he was the first one to predict the coming of the white man.' (and the Kenya-Uganda railway).

Q. Did the white men find Mbatian alive?

A. No. He was dead when they arrived.'

As the Masai always held their circumcision ceremonies in what is now called the Kinangop in Kenya, but was Kinopop to the Masai, I wanted Ole Kertella to tell me, for the historical record, who were the last age group to go through the ceremony there before the British took over that land for white settlement.

Q. Do you remember the last age groups which had their *Eunoto* ceremonies at Entoror?

A. The last age group who were supposed to undergo that ceremony there were the age group of Ilemek of the Kekonyokie section, but when they and the same age group of the Purko section were ready for their ceremony Olonana refused and told them they were to move south, and he would tell them where they would have the ceremony, and that was that. And he moved them across the Kekonyokie country right down to Enomatasiani and the ceremony was held there. And it was after that that the Masai were moved down into the present land units held by the Masai. (This was the old man's way of telling me that the Olonana was obeying the new British government.)

Q. Do you remember the first Treaty between the Masai and the British government, when Olonana was chief Laibon?

A. Do you mean the Treaty after which we vacated the Naivasha area? Yes. I was there.

Q. Do you mean you were present at the first Treaty or at the second one?

A. I was present at the first one.

Q. Were you a warrior then? Tell us about it, father.

A. I was a big boy then. The British government and Olonana had a private meeting and reached a certain conclusion or decision, and no one else knew about it. This is a secret I am telling you. After that a meeting was called and it was at that meeting that the British government told Olonana that they wanted Kinopop and Naivasha, and that the Masai should move to Ngatat—their present land unit. Olonana agreed to this demand. When the meeting was summoned Ole Masikonde and Ole Gilisho were instructed to ask all the elders to attend, the Iltalala age group and the Ilnyangusi, and any of the Ilpeles group if they were alive. They were told that Olonana and the Governor would be at the meeting. The meeting was advertised for a week. When it was held the crowd was so big that it was held under a big tree outside the town called Olamaloti.

Q. Can you remember who were the Europeans present at that meeting?

I looked at the old man when this question was asked, wondering if he could possibly remember the names of the Europeans there after fifty-eight years, and I was amazed by his reply which included even native nicknames. (See the actual Treaty further on for how good a memory Ole Kertella proved to have).

A. The ones who were there numbered eight. One of them was called Mr. Ainsworth, and the Masai called him Njuaini. There was Mr. Hopline, called by the Masai Kobilo. There was Mr. Lane from Fort Hall, Mr. Macmillan, Mr. Back, and His Majesty's Government representative, the Governor, whose name I cannot remember, and there was Mr. Gibson whom the Masai called Gibrisen, and there was one who had had an arm amputated called Mr. Smith and whom the Masai called Smith Kikono. How many is that now?

We told him that he had given eight names.

A. Well, I think they were the only white men present at that meeting when I attended.

Q. Can you tell us what happened before and after the meeting?

A. Well, as I have already told you, elders were there in hundreds, most of them from the Purko section. The Iltuati age group called Ilmirisho were there and headed by Ole Gilisho and Ole Patiak, because by then the Ilmirisho age group were warriors. Yes, Ole Gilisho and Ole Yiaile were there, and there was another man who was the last to pass away of that age group but I have forgotten his name.

Q. Who opened the meeting?

A. It was opened by Mr. Hopline.

Q. Was there an interpreter?

A. Yes, a man of my age group called Moyei Ole Tuukwo. Mr. Hopline, addressing Ole Gilisho and Ole Masikonde, said, 'In this meeting we are here to tell you all that the Government want you to leave Naivasha and Kinopop, because the Government have built a railway from Mombasa across the country to Kisumu. The Government are going to bring many things on that railway. We shall bring cattle which are descendants of of buffaloes, and these cattle will beat and defeat your cattle if

293

they fight. Our bulls are stronger than yours, and our cattle likewise. And we shall bring sheep which are so different from yours that you will not like them and will want to kill them, thinking they are wild animals, like hyenas. But they are sheep, just like yours. For instance yesterday Koresh Ole Tanyiny and Kosion Ole Karia killed two of our pigs which they found feeding on the salty earth at a place called Embolio Emuny. When they saw those pigs they thought they were hippopotamus calves, and they speared those pigs. That was a great mistake they made, because those were not hippopotamus calves but our pigs which we keep as you keep cattle. They were lucky, because during the hearing of the case we realized that they did not do it deliberately, otherwise they could have been heavily fined and sent to gaol. It costs us a lot of money to bring these pigs into the country, and you people must not continue to kill them, because they are real pigs. In this case we ask you to leave this area and to move to Ngatet.

'The new boundary,' Mr. Hopline went on to say, 'will start at Eusso Empakasi (modern Athi River) and will follow the river to the East to a point where there is a railway bridge, and from there the railway will be the boundary, right down to where the boundary of the British Government and Germany (Tanganyika—old 'German East') meet at a place called Ildoiyo Lolkirosion (The Hills of Ilkorosion). On the West the boundary will start from the same point at the source of Empakasi (Athi River) and will run northward to Engilai e Nengosie.

Q. Where is that place?
A. It is on the upper side of Kerarapon and passes Inkoiropij, and Inkoiropij is on the upper part of Enteijia (modern Ndeiya) and goes down to Kisekekwan which is near Euaso Ongkidongi (Uaso Kidong) where the tarmac road is now. From there the boundary drops into Kitilikine, which is a river. Right in the place where the red house of Mr. Williams used to be, where you drop into the Rift Valley, that is the place called Kitilikine. The boundary goes on to the West and passes Morijo Hills on the left side of the present tarmac road, where there is a settler's farm who possesses many white cattle, near the Narok road diversion from the main Nairobi-Nakuru road. The boundary passes between a place called Ogerai (between Longonot and

Kijabe hills) where the present main road passes, then the boundary runs straight into an island in Lake Naivasha called Olamangalei. The lake is divided in two, and then passes where I was born at Olgilai Otua on to Oldoiyo Opuru (Smoky Mountain) and beyond that to a place called Olorok Oshoke to Nakuru. 'The area on the left,' Mr. Hopline said, 'is to be left to the Masai, and the government will take the land on the North side of the railway, and will include Naivasha, Ongata Nairoua, and Kinopop.' The Masai were asked to move to Ngatet. The Government speaker finished his speech by telling us that that was all the Government had to say.

Q. And that was at the first meeting?

A. Yes. The government also said that they were going to move the Kaputiei section from their land to Empakasi, Ongata Rongai and Nomatasiani, and that they could occupy the land right down to Kinyawa (modern Simba railway station) and that their boundary would be the railway. But the Purko section refused to leave Naivasha and Kinopop and go to Ngatet. If they were asked to move up into Endoror they might reconsider the matter. They protested and said that Ngatet was too far and at last the Governor asked Olonana for his opinion, saying, 'As you have seen, the people don't want to move to the land we agreed on. What have you to say?

Then Olonana said, 'If they want to go to Endoror (in Northern Kenya) let them go there.' The white men present then had a conversation and they then agreed to what the Laibon said. Anyway the Government wanted the Masai to move to Ngatet and the Laibon, Olonana, wished them to follow the government's instructions. The Kekonyokie too were very adamant and refused to be moved either to Ngatet or to Endoror. The Purko, the Damat, the Iloitai, and the Ildalal le Kutuk, all agreed to move to Endoror.

Q. And what part of Endoror did the Masai occupy after that?

A. They reached Ongata Pus, to a place called Lesirko right up to Loroki (modern Loroghi where the Samburu live.) We occupied all that land up to a place called Taun. Yes, we all moved up to that part and it was I who became an interpreter at Olomuruti (modern Rumuruti). European settlers started occupying the land the Masai refused. Olonana moved all the Masai who were at Ololaiser (Ngong Hills) and Kisaju, to Endoror, together with the others on the other side of the hill called Olosho Oibor, but these people were not many. The Europeans started to farm, for instance, in Naivasha as soon as the Masai had left. They occupied the land right up to Mau. Gradually they filled the land as they believed that the Masai would never go to that country again.

Some years passed and it was said that the Lamek age group were to undergo their Eunoto ceremony at Kinopop. I think that it was after seven years. It was agreed and an area was set aside at Kinopop for all ceremonies to be held according to Masai custom. The Government agreed to this arrangement and an area was set apart for that purpose. Then, when the Lamek age group of the Purko section were ready to hold their ceremony there Olonana refused and said 'I know where the ceremony will take place. And the warriors left for the unknown destination and passed a place called Olgos Lolpironito, and came to Ngatet. The *Moran* came to Enomatasiani, (where Olonana died), and that was where the ceremony took place. It was after that ceremony that the Government ordered the Masai to leave Kinopop and the Kekonyokie were also forced to leave Endoror.

Q. And was there any other meeting between Government and the Masai?

A. There was an insignificant meeting.

Q. Where?

A. The first meeting was at Olomuruti (Rumuruti) and then there was another at Ngong. I would rather say there was no proper meeting. At these meetings the Masai were merely told 'You will now have to move down to Ngatet.' They were called on and given orders. The Masai refused, saying that they had agreed to move from Naivasha and Ongata Nairouwa and they were not prepared to move again. Ongata Nairouwa is now called Nakuru. But the Government insisted that the Masai must move from the areas mentioned. Soldiers were brought to force the Masai to move, and they moved the people from early in the morning until late at night.

Q. Soldiers were in charge of this move?

A. Yes, and they had two officers with them, one called Brown, and another who died later at Ngong.

(How often I had heard in the past of this officer, Brown, who had moved the Masai. I was told by old men, Kikuyu and Meru as well, that he had heaped up the Masai shields and spears and burned them before their eyes, and that the Masai warriors, broken by this terrible sight, knelt down and wept. And an old European told me before the war that all Brown had carried during this dangerous operation was a swagger stick. He must have been a courageous man.)

Q. Was Olonana alive when the second Treaty was made?

A. Olonana died when the Masai were being moved to their present area. I remember that very well because I was *Oloi-bartani*, (just circumcised). (Oliobartani is the stage between circumcision and warriorhood.)

Q. What did Olonana tell the people to do at that time?

A. Olonana wanted the Masai to move to Ngatet. He wanted the Masai to give the land for European settlement. And as far as that second Treaty is concerned don't be told that there was a proper meeting which drafted it. The Masai were merely called to be given orders, and when they protested no one listened to them. The Government insisted that they must move and that was that.

Q. Where were you in Endoror then?

A. I was at Olomuruti (Rumuruti). The Masai were forced to move out of that part of the country—and, the name of the European I had forgotten is Mr. Armstill. This European and Mr. Brown were the ones who forced us to move. In other words they were in charge of the move.

Q. During the move did the Masai break back?

A. When we reached Mau quite a big number turned and went back to Endoror. Afterwards they were brought back by force, and it was then that Ole Gilisho hired a lawyer called Mr. Morrison with the intention of fighting the Masai case so that we could go back to Endoror. The case lasted for quite a time and they went down to Mombasa at one time where was the head of the Government. Anyway the Advocate had quite a big fee. During the case I was summoned to give evidence. We lost the case and did not raise it again. Yes, the breakback took place at Mau because the Masai did not want to move to Ngatet, but being forced to they demonstrated in that way against the move. That move was quite different from the first one, because in the first move an agreement was reached between the Masai and the British Government, but in the second one there was no agreement, and it was a show of strength and we were moved by force.

Masai had complained to me that even after the second move when the Masai went south of the railway the Government went on nibbling away at their agreed land boundary. I asked Ole Kertella about this.

Q. What are the facts about pieces of land said to have been taken from the Masai after the settlement?

A. The Europeans took the land gradually. Olonana had said that only one European would be allowed to remain within the Masai land unit, and he lived at a place called Eor Enkitok. This European was a friend of Olonana. If you leave Ngong for Nairobi and cross the river, then turn to the left, not far from there you will find a small clearance, and that is Eor Enkitok. That is the place where Mr. Arnuer (Arnwell?), Olonana's friend, used to live, and the Masai used to call him Kagethua. He had cattle which had white spots round their mouths.

Q. Is that the place where the army camp used to be? (There was a training camp there during World War II called Karen Signal Camp.

A. Do you know where Captain Ridge's house used to be? That house has been turned into a hotel (modern West Wood Park Hotel) and on the left there is a small plain, and that is Eor Enkitok. And that was what Olonana said, that only one European would remain inside the Masai boundary, and he stayed there. That European was given that land by the warriors of the Kekonyokie section because they had worked for him at Euaso Kidong. Later the boundary was altered, and I think that if Olonana had been alive they could not have altered it. Since the death of Olonana the Europeans have gradually penetrated into Masai land and occupied the land they have there now.

It was getting late now and I said to the old man, 'Are you tired of talking yet, father?' He smiled and said he would answer any question we asked him and would not get tired. I thanked him and said I was glad, for I was leaving the country soon and probably would never see him again to ask these questions which only he knew the answers to now, of all alive. I asked him if he would tell

298

me what he knew of the wars in the old times. Yes, he said, he would tell me what he knew of that forgotten history.

A. I was born near the Ilpeles age group. I was born during their last fight, which was called Enyore Enkojongani (The War of Malaria or The Mosquitoes), and after that fight they ceased to be warriors and they laid down their shields. It was those age groups, the Ilpeles and the Ilnyangusi who fought the Ilaikipia. And they fought the Uasing Inkishu. At that time the Masai were strong and brave and no one could face them. They fought the Kitoshi, the Ilkamogori, Ilkamuriongo, Ilkoony, Ilumbwa, Iltiangual, Ilmutende, Ilmaru, Isunguma, and they fought the Iltatua. They fought all the tribes they could reach. After that age group we had the age group called Iltalala, and it was this age group which started the fighting among the sections of the Masai. It started when the Damat and the Kekonyokie sections fought, and then the Purko section attacked the Ildamat because they did not want them to fight the Kekonyokie. The Damat were defeated and then the Ildalal e Kutuk were attacked and they fled to the Meru after they were defeated. Yes, they went and lived with the Meru and that is why they are called Ilkangere, because they ran to the Meru. Later they were brought back and they lived again with the other Masai . . . Masai fights and wars were so many that it is impossible to recall them all. The Government arrived and governed the country and stopped all the fighting. I tell you that if the Government had not arrived in time we could have swept away quite a number of tribes—' He turned and looked at Ole Kipoin—and you, especially your age group could have done wonders in the same line. You would be circumcised and your duty would have been nothing but fighting. My son, the Masai adventures and wars with these other tribes are so numerous that it is impossible to count them. We fought all the Kamba and the others, let alone the Kikuyu—they were women. The reason why we did not finish the Kikuyu is due to the fact that they had no cattle to take. It is interesting to see them being proud now. Yes, war was our main pastime. If a tribe defeated the Masai in a fight the Masai would never rest until they destroyed that tribe completely.

Q. What preparation did the Masai make when they went to war?

A. The warriors would first fill themselves up with meat at a place called Ilpuli, and they would drink medicines made from special herbs, and then they would meet and discuss the attack. They would then go to the Laibon who would choose which tribe was to be attacked. That was the procedure. The warriors were fierce then and some of the very brave ones called *Intorosi* would charge about, mad, tearing their dress and crying for war morning and evening. They would pray for war and death. They would lose many people in their wars. Once the Kekonyokie warriors, for instance, came up from Euaso Kidong and they started killing the Kikuyu from a place called Rarin (modern Uplands) and they went right into the Kikuyu land somewhere near Fort Hall, where most of them were killed by a European the Kikuyu used to call *Nyahoro*, whom I think is the father of Kangani, and he was a Mr. Horne. He killed them with bombs, and he killed a lot of them, and the Kikuyu chopped the dead in pieces. By that time I was a boy and looking after calves, and it was the time of the rinderpest epidemic.

Q. Do you remember the last time the Masai went to war?

A. Mine was the last age group to go to war.

Q. Where did you fight?

A. It was a big fight involving many warriors and that attack was on a place called Ooloile and Goroine. We passed the Serengeti plains and attacked a tribe living in a place called Goroine. On the first day we lost 127 warriors, Purko and Kekonyokie warriors among them, and we captured very many people, and we killed many of the enemy. Then we attacked the Watende and brought many cattle home. The cattle were brought to Oldoiyo Oyokie, and the Government made the warriors pay for that. The warriors had seven guns they got from the European who lived at Eor Enkitok, the one I said was a friend of Olonana. The Government took half of the loot and the warriors kept the other half . . . yes, those were the last fights the Masai engaged in . . . forget the petty thefts of the junior age groups.

Q. Is it true that Masai power reached down below Isiolo, and that if any tribes wanted to use the water holes there they had to have permission from the Masai? (I still could not believe that the Masai power had extended that far down to the desert below the Meru country.)

The old man saw my readiness to doubt and he smiled.

A. Yes, it is true. Those are the Kombe waterholes. I know Isiolo. Those waterholes called Kombe are on the side of the Meru country we call Ilmero le Our (The Meru of the desert). My dear son, most of Kenya belonged to the Masai, and as you can see all these other tribes are not few, and they used to live in small parts of the land, like plots.

Q. What can you remember of the white men coming to Kenya?

A. I will tell you what I know. I know the British came to Mombasa first, but I think it was a long time ago, and they stayed there for some time before they came up country. They came up after the Masai cattle were finished by the rinderpest. The first white man to be seen in the Masai country came from the North. I don't know whether he came from the Rendille or the Boran country. He passed down through the Samburu country from the Rendille side. When he reached the foot of Oldoiyo Keri (Mount Kenya) on the plains we call Poré (near Timau) he came on the Masai who were living there then, the Kangere. (These were the Masai who had fled to the Wa'meru, and whom the Meru had been so proud to claim blood relationship with when they talked to me of them before the war.) I don't know what misunderstanding they had, the white man and the Masai there, but I understand that it was the white man who started the quarrel or did something bad. During the fight the white man was killed, and he was killed by a man called—' Here the old man hesitated—'I cannot recall his name. The following day there was an eclipse of the sun, the one I have mentioned already. The people said that the eclipse of the sun had come because yesterday a white son of God came and was killed, and it was said that milk poured from his wounds. Many believed that to be true. Later on it was said that the white man killed was a European (Olmusungi), and that it was blood that poured from his wounds. The scene of the fight was described. The white man wounded very many people during the fight, for instance he wounded Ole Kapusia, Ole Tinka, and others, but he was killed.

Later on there was another white man killed. That was at Kitilikine, near Morijo Hill where there was a *manyatta* of warriors. The white man's name was Dick and he came with a big caravan, and no one knew where he had come from. In his safari he had Kikuyu and Kamba and Swahili. When he reached the *manyatta* he left the caravan and rode up on a horse. The Swahili stayed behind him beating drums and singing and dancing. The Masai warriors came out with the mothers and children and the Elders to watch. When the white man saw the crowd coming he fired a shot from his rifle, aiming at the entrance of the *manyatta*, and bullet hit and killed a calf inside the *manyatta*. The Masai rushed for their weapons and the men in the caravan picked up their guns and tried to stop the Masai by shooting at them, but it was in vain. The warriors attacked the caravan and killed, or rather lynched, the porters and the gun bearers, but most of them dropped their guns and ran. They were chased right up to the place I named, Kitilikine, and it was there that the warriors caught up with the white man. He stopped and faced them and he killed quite a number of them. Some of the warriors were sent round behind him and they killed him. The name of the warrior who killed him was Ole Lekutit. But then the railway had reached Nairobi, and during the hearing of the case it was found that the Masai warriors were in the right, because they had been attacked first. Olonana was arrested and with him a very famous chief of the Iltalala section called Terere. He was both chief and *Olotumo*. Then, after finding out the truth the Government said we had all better forget the whole thing and live in peace. The Government went on to say that both sides should forget those they lost in that fight. And oaths were taken on both sides swearing that neither side would look for revenge and that they would live peacefully. And I heard that that oath was taken in the following manner. The finger between the nail and flesh was pricked by a needle and the blood of the Masai was sucked by a white man, and then the blood of the white man was sucked by a Masai. After that we lived peace-fully.*

* As to the second 'Agreement' as Ole Kertella might put it, Ainsworth says, 'However, early in 1910, I learnt that Lenana had made a request to the Government that the 1904 Agreement should be altered to the extent that the whole of the Masai tribe should come together in one Reserve, and that the Southern Reserve should be that area. At the time I was somewhat surprised to hear of this request and was inclined to suspect that outside pressure had been brought to bear on the Laibon.

'It occurred to me later, however, that there was a possibility that Lenana was finding that the existence of two separate reserves, with restricted communication between them, was tending to undermine his authority as the principal Laibon of the whole tribe.'

Q. What are the bad things you have seen from the time of your childhood until now, Father?

A. The first thing is the rinderpest epidemic which finished our cattle. Every section suffered during that time. We lost so many people from the smallpox after that that I cannot compare them with the numbers lost in fights and wars. The good thing I have noticed is that since the coming of the white man the tribal wars have been stopped, and justice has been brought into the country. One can move in the country without fear, and no one can deprive you of your property.

Q. And what are other good things you have seen in your life?

A. That is the main good thing I have seen, that since the British Government came law and order has been maintained and the tribal wars have stopped. When we were young we used to say that the Government had done a bad thing by stopping us from attacking other tribes to get cattle, as our fathers did, but later on we realized that they had done a good thing. I have noticed that our numbers have increased, because if an old man has ten sons he can bring them all up without losing them all as used to happen during the tribal wars. And we say thanks for that. And if it was not for the droughts and famine like the recent one in the Kajiado district we had lost few cattle for a long period of time. Yet, at the same time, we feel very bitter about our land which was taken from us by force—the place of our birth—and that we see as a very bad thing. When the white man came here first they lived side by side with the Masai, for instance here in Nairobi and at Pangani and at Eastleigh and in many other places there were Masai *manyattas*, but later they were moved away. The other thing is the taxes. We started paying three rupees, and since then it has increased tremendously. The water we are using is not artificial, and the firewood we use we get from the forest. In all I feel we are paying more than necessary because we get less than we deserve. A good thing is that there are jobs, or the chances of getting jobs, for as soon as you work you can earn money.

Q. When you see the world changing the way it is what do you think would help the Masai?

Old Kertella was silent for a few moments while he thought about this question. He scratched the white bristles on his chin. I wondered what he would say. Schools? He looked at me with serious eyes.

A.   To help me as a Masai when the British Government has gone from this country—we, the Masai, say that we shall have to prove to these other tribes that we are still as brave as we used to be. And we shall hold our shields as we did in the past. I know that some tribes, like the Kikuyu, despise me as a Masai simply because I am not educated. But they do not understand that the reason we did not respond to the idea of education is because we love cattle more. Anyway, as the British Government is leaving the country they had better return all the lands they have taken from each tribe to their former owners, and let each tribe rule itself in its own area. I feel that if the white men leave and we start to fight as we used to, we shall stand where we used to stand.

Old Kertella shook his head slowly and looked at us with his sombre old eyes, and went on to finish.

There is only one way for the tribes to live in peace, and that is for each tribe to rule itself.

Was there anything else we wished to ask or to say to each other? We decided no. We got up and thanked each other for the conversation we had had, and I thanked the old man for telling us his memories. He said he had enjoyed it and we went out into the bright moonlight where a car was waiting for Ole Kertella.

I felt sad as I watched him go, that relic of another Africa.

APPENDIX 2

AGREEMENT, dated 10th August, 1904, between His Majesty's Commissioner for the East Africa Protectorate and the Chiefs of the Masai Tribe.

We, the undersigned, being the Lybons and Chiefs (represent-atives) of the existing clans and sections of the Masai tribes in East Africa Protectorate, having, this 9th day of August, 1904, met Sir Donald Stewart, His Majesty's Commissioner for the East Africa Protectorate and discussed fully the question of a land settlement scheme for the Masai, have, of our own free will, decided that it is for our best interests to remove our people, flocks, and herds into definite reservations away from the railway line, and away from any land that may be thrown open to European settlement.

We have, after having already discussed the matter with Mr. Hobley at Naivasha and Mr. Ainsworth at Nairobi, given this matter every consideration and we recognize that the Government, in taking up this question, are taking into consideration our best interests.

Now we, being fully satisfied that the proposals for our removal to definite and final reserves are for the undoubted good of our race, have agreed as follows:—

That the Elburgu, Gekunuki, Loita, Damat, and Laitutok sections shall remove absolutely to Laikipia, and the boundaries of the Settlement shall be, approximately, as follows:—

> On the north, by the Loroghi Mountains.
> On the west, by the Laikipia (Ndoror) Escarpment.
> On the south, by the Lesuswa or Nyam and Guaso Narok Rivers.
> On the east, by Kisima (approximate).

And by the removal of the foregoing sections to the reserve we undertake to vacate the whole of the Rift Valley, to be used by the Government for the purposes of European settlement. Further, that the Kaptei, Matapatu, Ndogalani, and Sigarari sections shall remove into the territory originally occupied by them to the south of Donyo Lamuyu (Ngongo), and the Kisearian stream, and to comprise within the area the Donyo Lamuyu, Ndogalani, and Matapatu Mountains, and the Donyo Narok, and to extend to Sosian on the west.

In addition to the foregoing, Lenana, as chief Lybon, and his successors, to be allowed to occupy the land lying in between the Mbagathi and Kisearian streams from Donyo Lamuyu to the point where both streams meet, with the exception of land already occupied by Mr. Oulton, Mr. McQueen, and Mr. Paterson.

In addition to the foregoing, we asked that a right of road to include certain access to water be granted to us to allow of our keeping up communications between the two reserved areas, and further, that we be allowed to retain control of at least five square miles of land (at a point on the slopes of Kinangop to be pointed out by Legalishu and Masakondi), whereat we can carry out our circumcision rites and ceremonies, in accordance with the custom of our ancestors.

We ask, as a most important point in this arrangement, that the Government will establish and maintain a station on Laikipia, and that officers whom we know and trust may be appointed to look after us there.

Also that the Government will pay reasonable compensation for any Masai cultivation at present existing near Nairobi.

In conclusion, we wish to state that we are quite satisfied with the foregoing arrangement, and we bind ourselves and our successors, as well as our people, to observe them.

We would, however, ask that the settlement now arrived at shall be enduring so long as the Masai as a race shall exist, and that European or other settlers shall not be allowed to take up land in the settlements.

In confirmation of this Agreement, which has been read and fully explained to us, we hereby set our marks against our names, as under:—

> LANANA, Son of Mbatian, Lybon of all the Masai.
> MASAKONDI, Son of Arariu, Lybon at Naivasha.

Signed at Nairobi, August 15, 1904:—
> LEMANI, Elmura of Matapatu.
> LETEREGI, Elmura of Matapatu.
> LELMURUA, Leganan of Kapte.
> LAKOMBE, Elmura of Ndogalani.

LISIARI, Elmura of Ndogalani.

MEPAKU, Head Elmoran of Matapatu.

LAMBARI, Leganon of Ndogalani.

Naivasha, representing Elburgu, Gekunuku, Loita, Damat, and Laitutok:—

LEGALISHU, Leganan of Elburgu.

OLMUGEZA, Leganan of Elburgu.

OLAINOMODO, Leganan of Elburgu.

OLOTOGIA, Leganan of Elburgu.

OLIETI, Leganan of Elburgu.

LANAIRUGU, Leganan of Elburgu.

LINGALDU, Leganan of Elburgu.

GINOMUN, Leganan of Elburgu.

LIWALA, Leganan of Gekunuki.

LEMBOGI, Leganan of Laitutok.

Signed at Nairobi, August 15, 1904:—

SABORI, Elmura of Elburgu.

We, the undersigned, were Interpreters in this Agreement:—

C. W. HOBLEY, (Swahili).

MWE s/O LITHIGU (Masai).

LYBISH s/O KERETU (Masai).

WAZIRI-BIN-MWYNBEGO (Masai).

I, Donald Stewart, K.C.M.G., His Majesty's Commissioner for the East Africa Protectorate, hereby agree to the foregoing, provided the Secretary of State approves of the Agreement, and in witness thereof I have this 10th day of August, 1904, set my hand and seal.

D. STEWART.

We, the undersigned officers of the East Africa Protectorate Administration, hereby certify that we were present at the meeting between His Majesty's Commissioner and the Masai at Naivasha on the 9th August, 1904, and we further heard this document fully explained to them, and witnessed their marks affixed to same:—

C. W. HOBLEY, Acting Deputy Commissioner.

JOHN AINSWORTH, His Majesty's Sub-Commissioner, Ukamba.

S. S. BAGGE, His Majesty's Sub-Commissioner, Kisumu.

J. W. T. McCLELLAN, Acting Sub-Commissioner,
Naivasha.
W. J. MONSON, Acting Secretary to the Administration.

I, Donald Stewart, K.C.M.G., His Majesty's Commissioner for
the East Africa Protectorate, hereby further agree to the foregoing
parts of this Agreement concerning Kapte, Matapatu, Ndogalani,
and Sigarari Masai, provided the Secretary of State approves of
the Agreement, and in witness thereof I have this 15th day of
August, 1904, set my hand and seal.

We, the undersigned officers of the East Africa Protectorate,
hereby certify that we were present at the meeting between His
Majesty's Commissioner and the Masai at Nairobi on the 15th
August, 1904, and we further heard this document explained to
them, and witnessed their marks affixed to same:—

C. W. HOBLEY, Acting Deputy Commissioner.
JOHN AINSWORTH, His Majesty's Sub-Commissioner.
Ukamba.
T. T. GILKISON, Acting Land Officer.
W. J. MONSON, Acting Secretary to the Administration.

I, the undersigned, hereby certify that I translated the contents
of this document to the Masai Lybish, who, I believe, interpreted
it correctly to the Masai assembled at both Naivasha and Nairobi.
JOHN AINSWORTH, His Majesty's Sub-Commissioner.

APPENDIX 3

AGREEMENT OF 1911

We, the undersigned, being the Paramount Chief of all the Masai and his regents and the representatives of that portion of the Masai tribe living in the Northern Masai Reserve, as defined in the agreement entered into with the late Sir Donald William Stewart, Knight Commander of the Most Distinguished Order of Saint Michael and Saint George, His Majesty's Commissioner for the East Africa Protectorate, on the ninth day of August, One thousand and nine hundred and four, and more particularly set out in the Proclamation of May thirtieth One thousand nine hundred and six and published in the Official Gazette of June first One thousand nine hundred and six, do hereby on our own behalf and on behalf of our people, whose representatives we are, being satisfied that it is to the best interest of their tribe that the Masai people should inhabit one area and should not be divided into two sections as must arise under the agreement aforesaid whereby they were reserved to the Masai tribe two separate and distinct areas of land, enter of our own free will into the following agreement with Sir Edouard Percy Cranwill Girouard, Knight Commander of the Most Distinguished Order of Saint Michael and Saint George, Member of the Distinguished Service Order, Governor and Commander in Chief of the East Africa Protectorate, hereinafter referred to as the Governor.

We agree to vacate at such time as the Governor may direct the Northern Masai Reserve which we have hitherto inhabited and occupied and to remove by such routes as the Governor may notify to us our people, herds and flocks to such area on the south side of the Uganda railway as the Governor may locate to us the said area being bounded approximately as follows and as shown on the attached map.

On the south by the Anglo-German frontier.

On the west by the Ol-orukuti Range, by the Amala River, otherwise called Ang-are-dabash or Eng-are-e-'n-gipai, by the eastern and northern boundaries of the Sotik Native Reserve, and by a line drawn from the most northerly point of the northern boundary of the Sotik Native Reserve to the south-western boundary of the land set aside for Mr. E. Powys Cobb on Mau;

On the north by the southern and eastern boundaries of the said land set aside for Mr. E. Powys Cobb, and by a straight line drawn from the north-eastern boundary of the said land to the highest point of Mount Suswas otherwise called Ol-doinyo Onyoke;

On the east by the southern Masai Native Reserve as defined in the Proclamation dated June eighteenth One thousand nine hundred and six, and published in the Official Gazette of July first One thousand nine hundred and six.

Providing that nothing in this agreement contained shall be deemed to deprive the Masai tribe of the rights reserved to it under the agreement of August ninth One thousand nine hundred and four aforesaid to the land on the slopes of Kinopop whereon the circumcision rights and ceremonies may be held.

In witness whereof and in confirmation of this agreement which has been fully explained to us we hereby set our marks against our names as under:—

> Mark of SEGI, son of Ol-onana (Lenana), Paramount Chief of all the Masai.
>
> Mark of OL-LE-GELESHO (Legalishu), Regent during the minority of Segi, head of the Molelyan Clan, and chief spokesman (Olsigwenani) of the Il-Kitoip (Il-Merisho) age-grade of the Purko Masai.
>
> Mark of NGAROYA, Regent during the minority of Segi, of the Aiser Clan.
>
> Mark of OL-LE-YELI, head of the Mokosen Clan of the Purko Masai, and one of the spokesmen (Ol-sigwenani) of the Il-Kitoip (Il-Merisho) age-grade of the Purko Masai.
>
> Mark of OL-LE-TURERE, head of the Mokesen Clan of the Purko Masai.
>
> Mark of OLE-LE-MALIT, one of Masikondi's representatives, of the Lughumae branch of the Aiser Clan of the Purko Masai.
>
> Mark of OL-LE-NAKOLA, head of the Tarosero Clan of the Purko Masai.

Mark of OL-LE-NAIGISA, head of the Aiser Clan of the Purko Masai.

Mark of MARMAROI, uncle and personal attendant of Segi.

Mark of SABURI. The Prime Minister of the late Chief Ol-onana (Lenana) and principal elder of the Southern Masai Reserve.

Mark of AGALI, uncle of Segi, representing the Loita Masai.

Mark of OL-LE-TANYAI of the Tarosero Clan, chief spokesman (Ol-sigwenani) of the Lamek (Meitaroni) age-grade of the Purko Masai.

The above set their marks to this agreement at Nairobi on the fourth day of April nineteen hundred and seven.

A. C. HOLLIS,
Secretary, Native Affairs.

OL-LE-MASIKONDI, head of the Lughumas section of the Aiser Clan: chief elder of the Purko Masai, called in the former treaty of Ol Oiboni of the Purko Masai.

OL-LE-BATIET, head of the Aiser Clan of the Purko Masai on Laikipia, Ol aigwenani of the age known as Il Merisho.

The above set their marks to this agreement at Rumuruti on the 13th day of April nineteen hundred and eleven.

E. D. BROWNE,
Assistant District Commissioner,
Laikipia.

Witnesses:

A. J. M. COLLYER,
D.C. Laikipia.

His mark: OL-LE-LENGIRI, of the Aiser Clan Purko Masai.

His mark: OL-LE-GESHEEN, head of Tarosero Clan of Purko Masai.

His mark: OL-LE-SALON, brother of Ol-le-Kotikosh, as a deputy for Ol-le-Kotikosh.

The witnesses mentioned on the previous page set their marks to this agreement at Rumuruti on 19th day of April 1911.

E. D. BROWNE,
Assistant District Commissioner
i/c Laikipia.

We, the undersigned, certify that we correctly interpreted this document to the Chief, Regents, and Representatives of the Masai who were present at the meeting at Nairobi.

A. C. HOLLIS,
OL-LE-TINKA, of the Il-Aiser
Clan.

We the undersigned certify that we have correctly interpreted this document to the Representatives of the Masai at Rumuruti.

A. J. M. COLLYER,
District Commissioner.

OL-LE-TINKA. His mark.

In consideration of the above, I, Edouard Percy Cranwill Girouard, Knight Commander of the Most Distinguished Order of Saint Michael and Saint George, Member of the Distinguished Service Order, Governor and Commander in Chief of the East Africa Protectorate, agree on behalf of His Majesty's Government but subject to the approval of His Majesty's Principal Secretary of State for the Colonies to reserve for the exclusive use of the Masai tribe the area on the south side of the Uganda Railway as defined above and as shown on the attached map, which area is coadunate with the Southern Masai Native Reserve and to further extend the existing Southern Masai Native Reserve by an addition of an area of approximately three thousand and one hundred square miles, such area as shown on the accompanying map the approximate boundaries being on the south the Anglo-German frontier, on the west the eastern boundary of the aforesaid Southern Masai Reserve, on the north and east by the Uganda Railway zone from the Athi River to Sultan Hamud Railway Station thence in a line drawn from the said station to the north-west point of the Chiulu Range thence along the Chiulu Range to the south-eastern extremity thereof thence by a straight line to the meeting point of the Eng-are-Rongai River to the Anglo-German frontier and to undertake on behalf of His Majesty's Government to endeavour to remove all

European settlers from the said areas and not to lease or grant any land within the said areas (except such land as may be required for mining purposes or for any public purpose) without the sanction of the Paramount Chief and the representatives of the Masai tribe.

In witness whereof I have hereunto set my hand and official seal this twenty-sixth day of April One thousand nine hundred and eleven.

(L. S.)

Signed sealed and delivered by the within named Sir Edouard Percy Cranwill Girouard in the presence of A. C. HOLLIS.

} E. P. C. GIROUARD.

We, the undersigned were present at a meeting between His Excellency the Governor and the Masai at Nairobi on the fourth day of April One thousand nine hundred and eleven, and we heard this document explained to the Chief and the representatives of the Masai who entered into this agreement of their own free will and with full knowledge of the contents thereof:—

R. M. COMBE
Crown Advocate.

C. W. HOBLEY,
Provincial Commissioner, Ukamba.

JOHN AINSWORTH,
Provincial Commissioner, Nyanza.

C. R. W. LANE,
Provincial Commissioner, Naivasha.

S. L. HINDE,
Provincial Commissioner, Naivasha.

J. W. T. McLELLAN,
Provincial Commissioner, Kenya.

A. C. HOLLIS,
Secretary for Native Affairs.

C. C. BOWRING,
Treasurer and M.L.C.

INDEX

HAMISH HAMILTON PAPERBACKS

'Among the most collectable of paperback imprints . . .'
Christopher Hudson, *The Standard*

All books in the Hamish Hamilton Paperback Series are available at your
local bookshop or can be ordered by post. A full list of titles and an order
form can be found at the end of this book.

THE YEARS WITH ROSS

James Thurber

Harold Ross was *The New Yorker*'s brilliant and often eccentric editor from its founding in 1925 until his death in 1951. When James Thurber joined its staff in 1927, he discovered Ross to be a prickly, unpredictable individualist with a rasping voice, unerring taste and a searing passion for facts. He was a disastrous administrator, and his relations with the staff and contributors tended to be stormy, but all admitted that he was an editor of genius. As one reads Thurber's wildly funny account of what went on, one is not so much surprised at the magazine's success as that it ever appeared at all.

'The classic tribute by Ross's most devoted colleague, to the magazine, the eccentrics who gathered round it and above all to its wayward, sometimes monstrous proprietor.' *Sunday Times*

PETER HALL'S DIARIES

ed. John Goodwin

Peter Hall's diaries, a top bestseller in hardback, cover the hectic eight years from 1972 to 1980 during which he fought to create the three-auditorium 'palace', the National Theatre, on London's South Bank. He reveals what it is like to be head of a great artistic enterprise under burning public scrutiny. He illuminates how he develops his own productions. And he tells the story of the personality clashes, the constant delays to the opening of the building, the press attacks, strikes, and resignations which had repercussions throughout the entire theatre world.

'This is a stupendous book. It is the most absorbing book on the theatre I have ever read.' Harold Hobson

A LATE BEGINNER

Priscilla Napier

In 1921, Priscilla Napier, aged twelve, left Egypt where her father worked in the colonial administration. In this funny and perceptive memoir she brilliantly recreates a child's view of the exotic surroundings of those early years. It was a world of comfort and security, of calm routine and Cadbury's Tropical Chocolates, with the excitements of scorpions in the nursery cupboard and black beetles in the garden, and long sea voyages to England, a country of endless green lawns inhabited by endless relations. But the impact of war was far-reaching and the world changed.

'She is a born writer. Mrs Napier displays the most professional skill in modulation between her childhood feelings and adult commentary.' Raymond Mortimer, *Sunday Times*

MRS PAT
The Life of Mrs Patrick Campbell

Margot Peters

Beautiful, witty, talented, Mrs Patrick Campbell became a legend in her own lifetime. Her theatrical career encompassed tremendous triumphs and unmitigated failures. Her private life was controversial and tragic. In this superb biography Margot Peters captures the magnetism of an outstanding actress and extraordinary woman, who remains today as intriguing as ever.

'The book has been researched with exemplary care and accuracy. The famous bons mots – nearly always witty, sometimes cruel and personal, but usually devastatingly apt – are quoted with appropriate relish. There is a wealth of material, never before made public, to enthrall the reader.' John Gielgud, *Observer*